GOING SOUTH

DEBRA L. SCHULTZ

GOING SOUTH

Jewish Women in the Civil Rights Movement

Foreword by Blanche Wiesen Cook

New York University Press • *New York and London*

NEW YORK UNIVERSITY PRESS
New York and London

© 2001 by New York University
All rights reserved

Library of Congress Cataloging-in-Publication Data
Schultz, Debra L.
Going South : Jewish women in the civil rights movement /
Debra L. Schultz.
p.   cm.
Includes bibliographical references and index.
ISBN 0-8147-9774-1 (acid-free paper)
1. Afro-Americans—Civil rights—Southern States—History—
20th century. 2. Jewish women—United States—Political activity—
History—20th century. 3. Jewish women—United States—Biography.
4. Women civil rights workers—Southern States—Biography.
5. Afro-Americans—Relations with Jews. 6. Southern States—Race
relations. 7. Civil rights movement—Southern States—History—
20th century. 8. Oral history. I. Title.
E185.61 .S364 2001
323.1'196073'0923924—dc21   00-012211

New York University Press books are printed on acid-free paper,
and their binding materials are chosen for strength and durability.

Manufactured in the United States of America

10 9 8 7 6 5 4 3 2 1

Bob Fletcher, Liz Aaronsohn, Mary Ellen Capek, Jan Sherman, Miriam Molnar, Ann Snitow, Deborah Gray White, and Yael Zerubavel. I would like to thank Lawrence Pero and Barbara Harris for encouraging my early interest in women's history.

Contents

All illustrations appear as a group following p. 106.

Foreword

Blanche Wiesen Cook

For activists, the history of the twentieth century is the struggle for peace and freedom; the quest for a politics of justice and decency. Born female before or during the 1930s and 1940s, a significant number of Jewish women gravitated toward the civil rights movement during the 1960s. Debra Schultz's study of Jewish women who went south explores the important and often surprising ways in which the past is prologue, in which traditions of learning and resistance matter. Antiracists who fought against violence and segregation in the United States understood that European fascism, built on dehumanization and brutality, connected the continents and linked the centuries by bloodshed and terror. A sense of responsibility and an active dedication to justice and dignity forged pathways to a better life.

Who were these activists? How did they come to be? Where did they find support? Why did they choose to move, when others stood still? Why did they choose to speak, while others remained silent? How did they find allies, join the movement, rebuild the house of courage and commitment, enlarge their own hearts, save their own souls?

Debra Schultz gives us their stories in their own voices. More than that, she provides context and legacy: Activism, Power, Hope. For the twenty-first century to be less treacherous and wicked than the past, we need to revisit these proud moments of action, of protest, of community. The legacy of these brave and steadfast women working beside their many partners, white and Black, Christian, Muslim, Jewish, male and female, tells us much about where we might go today, and tomorrow, as we confront the residue of a century of dishonor, broken promises, unfulfilled dreams.

For women, for Jews, for dignity, the fight is ongoing; the struggle evermore intense, evermore global. In this mean moment of greed and selfishness, when millions of homeless, hungry, and devastated people are ignored by politicians of both major parties, this high-spirited work is timely and essential. With this lyrical, passionately written book, Debra Schultz has given us a galvanizing, encouraging gift for history and reflection, for action and the future.

Acknowledgments

I had many allies along the journey that resulted in the publication of this book. Lloyd Wilder's love, support, and faith in my work sustained me. Similarly, my parents, Mae and Harold Schultz, were always there with the perfect blend of humor, sympathy, and willingness to help.

I thank the many extraordinary teachers who have expanded my ways of thinking and being over the years, yet Elizabeth Kamarck Minnich stands out as the most generous and generative intellectual ally I have ever had. Only by striving to emulate her unique example of engaged scholarship and authentic friendship can I ever give back all that she has given me.

Mariam K. Chamberlain, the visionary founding president of the National Council for Research on Women, where I spent six formative years, serves as both a mentor and a friend. Blanche Wiesen Cook's groundbreaking essay, "Female Support Networks and Political Activism," helped catalyze my commitment to writing activist women's history. I remain inspired by her skill and tenacity in writing works of significant historical scholarship.

Without the generous, committed, self-reflective, warm, and funny women you will soon meet, this book would not exist. I thank the following women for their trust in me, for sharing their stories and for understanding my aims: Elaine DeLott Baker, June Finer, Roberta Galler, Miriam Cohen Glickman, Jan Goodman, Barbara Jacobs Haber, Elizabeth Slade Hirschfeld, Faith Holsaert, Florence Howe, Jacqueline Levine, Trudy Weissman Orris, Vivian Leburg Rothstein, Carol Ruth Silver, Harriet Tanzman, and Dottie Miller Zellner.

Several scholar/friends deserve special thanks for their holistic approach to supporting me and this project: Leslie Hill, Riv-Ellen Prell, Dorothy Helly, Mayra Bloom, and Timothy Diamond.

I thank Anastasia Posadskaya-Vanderbeck for being such a constant and dear friend and for inviting me to share the challenges of starting the Network Women's Program of the Open Society Institute. My gratitude and respect go to my colleagues in the Network Women's

Program, especially the staff in New York and Budapest, for their commitment, vision, and generosity.

Several very important friends helped me keep things in perspective: Deborah Meyers, Jan Paris, Teresa Cortes, Leslie Wiltshire, and Denise P. Levine. Thanks go to my cousins, aunts, and uncles for their encouragement. In addition to being a beloved family friend, Alvin Lidsky shared his extensive knowledge of Yiddishkeit, and Rita Lidsky and the Schwartz clan always made me feel welcome.

Thanks to those who provided refuge: Cynthia Lubow and Osha Hibbard in Berkeley during my California interviews; Pearl and Ralph Babin in New Orleans throughout my entire life; and Cynthia Secor in Taos, New Mexico, whenever I needed a spiritual/writing retreat. I would like to express my appreciation for the ways in which Elizabeth Sackler and Kat Duff live their lives with a unity of spirit, intellect, and politics.

I am grateful to Alida Brill-Scheuer and Steven Scheuer for the research grant the Brill-Scheuer Foundation awarded me, as well as for their personal encouragement and enthusiasm for my project. Special thanks to Barbara Emerson for helping me reach SNCC veterans.

In addition to being a great editor, Cecelia Cancellaro is extraordinarily gifted in the art of friendship. She cared about this manuscript in its earliest form, thus paving the way for future publication. My original publisher at NYU Press, Niko Pfund, has been an excellent editor, a wickedly humorous email correspondent, and a genuine ally in the work of completing this book. I'd also like to thank Eric Zinner, Cecilia Feilla, Despina Gimbel, and everyone at NYU Press for their warmth and professionalism.

Joyce Antler, Deborah Dash Moore, and Kim Lacy Rogers were generous and extremely helpful outside readers; thank you for your encouragement and your own work. Thanks to Susan Weidman Schneider and the staff at *Lilith* for publishing an excerpt from my book. For their friendship, as well as editorial and/or typing support, I'd like to thank Deborah Siegel, Erika Katske, Katie Sanders, Martha Heller, and Roger K. Smith.

My appreciation goes to the many scholars and activists who shared illuminating thoughts with me. Among them are Hasia Diner, Carol Stack, Minnie Bruce Pratt, Sara Evans, Colin Greer, Si Kahn, Joseph Jordan, Candace Falk, Doug McAdam, Heather Tobis Booth, Temma Kaplan, Melanie Kaye/Kantrowitz, Lise Vogel, Joanne Grant, Martha Prescod Norman, Chuck McDew, Charlie and Carol Horowitz,

Bob Fletcher, Liz Aaronsohn, Mary Ellen Capek, Jan Sherman, Miriam Molnar, Ann Snitow, Deborah Gray White, and Yael Zerubavel. I would like to thank Lawrence Pero and Barbara Harris for encouraging my early interest in women's history.

Preface

It was a time when southern Black men dared not lift their eyes to look a white woman directly in the face; when white women were seen and not heard; and when Jews tried to blend unobtrusively into the social fabric. On a hot May night in 1951, a young New York Jewish woman lawyer, Bella Abzug, returned to Jackson, Mississippi, after five years of defending her client, Willie McGee, a Black man wrongly accused of raping a white woman with whom he was having a relationship.

After McGee lost his first trial, twenty-five-year-old Abzug became his chief counsel. Successfully appealing the case before the Mississippi Supreme Court, she had won two stays of execution by arguing that the death penalty for rape was applied only to Blacks and that Black people were systematically prevented from serving on juries.

Abzug was back yet again to appeal McGee's conviction and to plead for a third stay of execution. But the hotel at which she had booked a room refused to house her and no other room could be found. In this menacing environment, the pregnant young advocate chose the Jackson bus station benches as her safest option. An anxious night there did not keep her from arguing for racial justice for six hours in front of the justices the next day. The court upheld the original decision and on May 7, 1951, Willie McGee was executed with a crowd of seven hundred whites cheering outside.

Bella Abzug subsequently had a miscarriage, but the earlier traumatic experience only emboldened her in her quest for social justice, nurtured in the Jewish culture in which she grew up. Abzug's roots in antiracist activism would inform her career as the first Jewish woman elected to the U.S. House of Representatives. She also founded many women's organizations, including the Women's Environmental and Development Organization (WEDO), through which her inclusive vision grew to embrace concerns for global peace and survival.[1]

Bella Abzug established a standard of integrity and chutzpah (nerve, courage) that challenges us all to tell the truth and to fight back. There was and there will only be one Bella. But what about other Jewish women, who were not so prominent, not so fearless, not so vocal (who could be?), but who nevertheless took the same risks and fought for the same ideals?

These are the women you will meet in *Going South*. I hope you will laugh with them, be inspired by them, ponder their contradictions, and feel connected to the many traditions they represent. Above all, I hope their journeys spark new or renewed appreciation for the southern civil rights movement, the crucible in which racism was contested and second wave feminism forged in the United States.

This book was inspired by my desire for an intergenerational dialogue about women's antiracism and Jewish identity. It took form through oral history, which has transmitted knowledge and values across generations for many cultures throughout time. Yet, in contemporary culture, as Jonathan Boyarin writes, the efforts of Jewish ethnographers, folklorists, poets, and others can "do little to change the conditions blocking face-to-face intergenerational transmission of memory."[2] This is a particularly vexing problem for progressive, unaffiliated Jews. Unlike synagogue members, secular Jews do not have ongoing social contexts within which to tell and retell our collective history.[3] Seeking an entry point to address such dilemmas, I set out to create conversations with Jewish women activists that would transmit memories and lessons learned, as well as generate insights for historical scholarship. Taken together, this material would, I hoped, also contribute to Jewish political legacies, the kind for which I had yearned.

Born in Brooklyn, New York, in 1961, the same year that mobs were attacking buses filled with Freedom Riders, I grew up in a household with a tenuous connection to both Jewishness and progressive politics. As did the families of the women profiled in this book, my family instilled in me the conviction that being Jewish created an obligation to discern and fight for "what is right." Still, the force of assimilation left a vacuum when it came to locating myself in a tradition. When I discovered women's history in high school, I embraced it. Feminism, not Judaism, became my tradition. Women's history became my practice.

However, my identification with women's historical struggles left a number of questions unanswered. During the heyday of identity politics and multiculturalism, why had I spent years in women's studies examining the history of so many groups that had been "othered," while paying scant attention to my "own"—Jewish women? In this same multicultural environment, why couldn't feminists break the impasse over white women's racism? While taking responsibility for examining my own internalized racism, there was a part of me that did not fully inhabit the category, "white woman," and it had something to do with being Jewish. Yet, how could I be so fiercely proud of being Jewish without knowing exactly why? This led to a proactive question, the most generative one: "What kind of Jew do I want to be?"

Answers to such questions required finding predecessors, people who shared my values and who had weathered such controversies. Antiracist Jewish women were an obvious choice and the civil rights movement the most logical place to find them. However, despite the presence of many Jews in the civil rights movement, Jewish women are barely visible in movement histories. As a Jew and as a feminist historian of women's activism, I wanted their stories to be told.

This book is an oral history, reflecting on the experiences of fifteen Jewish women who went south for civil rights.[4] They worked primarily with the Student Nonviolent Coordinating Committee (SNCC—pronounced "snick"), a radical, spirited southern civil rights group led by young Black organizers. Between October 1993 and December 1994, I interviewed these women who had been south for civil rights during the years 1960 to 1967. Among numerous potential interviewees, I chose them because their experiences span a broad range of roles and locations in the southern civil rights movement. They were also willing to share their stories in ways that required them to reflect on the meanings of Jewishness *to them*.[5]

With the exception of one woman born in 1946, the women were all born before the baby boom generation. The majority of them were born between 1935 and 1943, a period spanning the Great Depression and World War II. The stories of three women born earlier are included because they are "foremothers" who represent different life trajectories for antiracist Jewish women activists. They moved from the Old Left to civil rights; from Jewish communal liberalism to antiracism; and from working-class Jewishness through civil rights to feminism.

The book does not claim to represent all the experiences of Jewish women in the southern civil rights movement, nor in the national movement.[6] Clearly, hundreds and perhaps thousands of Jewish women made significant contributions to the civil rights movement nationally, whether through their campus activism, their work in major civil rights organizations, or their roles in Jewish organizations.[7] *Going South* focuses on a group of boundary-crossing, northern Jewish women who had the opportunity, means, and will to put their bodies on the line to challenge the entrenched system of southern racism in the 1960s.

To get a sense of these women in their movement context, I flew to Jackson, Mississippi, on June 24, 1994, to attend the 30th Anniversary Reunion of the Mississippi Freedom Summer Project volunteers at Tougaloo, a historically Black college and movement center. In the surprisingly spartan auditorium, with plastic folding chairs and a modest podium, movement veterans reconnected with one another, laughing and hugging. Michael Thelwell, former director of the Mississippi Freedom Democratic Party's Washington, D.C., office, joked about "the graying of hair and the gaining of pounds." There was the joy of reunion and a bit of shyness in the air, as if the power of the past made it hard to know how to be in the seemingly less urgent present.

During one workshop, Freedom Summer Project organizer Bob Moses asked all participants under thirty to come to the center of a circle gathered around him. Raising simple questions in the gentlest of voices, Moses encouraged the young people "to see what you want to say to each other." As they planned a young people's meeting for that afternoon, eventually raising $2,000 to run future projects, the Mississippi organizing tradition was passed on. Bob Moses had challenged and empowered another generation to take its own leadership. In that moment, the lure of SNCC's group-centered activism became palpable.

To make real the promise of the reunion's theme, "Mississippi Homecoming 1994," organizers planned bus tours to movement sites where the volunteers had served; they would be hosted by "local freedom fighters," their former coworkers. The destinations read like an honor roll of Civil War battlefields: McComb, Lexington, Canton, Greenwood, Ruleville, Hattiesburg, Philadelphia, and Meridian (where an eternal flame was lit at the graveside of James Earl Chaney, who had been killed with Mickey Schwerner and Andrew Goodman).

As the Greenwood-bound bus rolled through the Delta, I noted how little the landscape had changed from the 1960s images I had internalized from history books and documentaries. The bright sun highlighted stark contrasts between fields of lush green grass and the weary-looking gray wooden shacks planted haphazardly within them. A sense of sorrow and disbelief at the persistence of poverty dissipated as we were met warmly by local people from several modest, proud churches, many of whom eagerly shared their stories of what had happened when the movement came to town.

June Johnson spoke in what was once called the "First Christian

Church for Colored." In 1963, local police arrested the fifteen-year-old Johnson in Winona, Mississippi, with Annelle Ponder and Sunflower County organizer Fannie Lou Hamer, a riveting speaker who would later "question America" about the contradiction between racism and democracy at the 1964 Democratic National Convention. Beaten with nightsticks and a leather strap, Johnson lost consciousness twice. Hamer recalled hearing Johnson screaming and seeing blood running down her face as guards carried her back to another cell.[8]

Standing in front of the ten-pew church thirty-one years later, June Johnson spoke through her tears, "Our children are literally dying. This is not what Mrs. Hamer fought for. We've gotten so selfish and bitter. Freedom ain't free; we've got to get recommitted. We have to teach the truth; we have to tell the story." Later during the weekend, former SNCC chairman Chuck McDew (a Black northerner who had converted to Judaism) linked the civil rights movement to the struggle against fascism during World War II. He, too, said to the reunion participants, "The only way this movement will survive is if you tell the story."

Like Johnson and McDew, I believe that memory is essential to progressive political movements. Like most Jewish people born after the Holocaust, I have also internalized the injunction "Never forget." Writing at the end of the twentieth century, a number of American Jewish scholars have critiqued the ways in which American Jewish identity often seems based primarily on memory of the Holocaust, perpetuating a feeling of victimization inappropriate to contemporary Jewish life in the United States.[9]

What does, however, seem appropriate is to honor the memory of those who died in the Holocaust by continuing the fight against racism (including anti-Semitism). In the U.S. context, this requires remembering the genocide of Native Americans, the horror of slavery, and the resilience of racism in myriad forms. Although this may seem obvious to some, it is challenging to remain aware of our own implication in this history. As the grandchild of Russian Jewish immigrants who fled persecution and found security here, I wanted to contribute to ongoing efforts of memory and action by making visible an antiracist Jewish women's tradition.

Encouragement came from the work of Judith Plaskow, a pioneer among audacious Jewish feminist theologians, who urges Jewish women to "reshape Jewish memory to let women speak."[10] Similarly, Jonathan Boyarin notes that "Jews have always used narrative to recreate their shared identities across time."[11] Thus, even as it might be defiant for Jewish women to speak in traditional religious contexts, it is also customary for Jewish women to tell stories that create identity and clarify values for the community. This book enables antiracist Jewish women activists to speak to many communities, to be in dialogue with several historical narratives.

The women's stories presented here provide sources for new interpretations of Jewish history and memory. They may serve to empower progressive Jews, to demystify political activism, and to encourage multiple generations to reflect on the meaning of the civil rights movement. They provide material to fill gaps in several fields, including American Jewish women's history, civil rights history, and the history of Jewish radicalism. The stories establish historical continuity by invoking a passionate tradition of Jewish women's activism for social justice.

May these stories of "ordinary" women remind us that the capacity to take risks and to act upon ethical commitments is available to everyone. As we see follow these women south, it becomes clear that such paths are not as mythic or inaccessible as they might seem. They are open to those who decide to act.

NOTES

1. Amy Swerdlow, *Women Strike for Peace: Traditional Motherhood and Radical Politics in the 1960s* (Chicago: University of Chicago Press, 1993), 144–145; Blanche Wiesen Cook, "Bella Abzug," in Paula Hyman and Deborah Dash Moore, eds., *Jewish Women in America: An Historical Encyclopedia* (New York: Routledge, 1998), 5–10.

2. Jonathan Boyarin, *Storm from Paradise: The Politics of Jewish Memory* (Minneapolis: University of Minnesota Press, 1992), 50.

3. Based in New York, Jews for Racial and Economic Justice is one group that addresses this problem by conducting public teach-ins.

4. Literature in feminist methodology, standpoint theory, oral history, and postmodern ethnography informs this work. What these methods have in common is a commitment to self-reflexivity on the part of the researcher, a willingness to engage political questions, and a reliance (though not uncritical) on the subject's narrative as primary data.

As a feminist historian, I have been drawn particularly to oral history as an activist method of producing knowledge about women's experiences. I hope this study will contribute to an ongoing conversation about the relationship among feminism, antiracism, and anti-Semitism (initiated by such pioneers as

Adrienne Rich, Melanie Kaye/Kantrowitz, Letty Cottin Pogrebin, Elly Bulkin, Minnie Bruce Pratt, and Barbara Smith). To engage in this conversation more fully and authentically, I wanted to find an appropriate, historically grounded standpoint as a white, Jewish, antiracist feminist. I also wanted to acknowledge the vital contributions of Black feminist activists, scholars, and theorists, who raised the kinds of challenging questions about race and difference that have made studies like this one possible. A rich body of Jewish feminist writing, as well as ongoing public debate and burgeoning literature on Black-Jewish relations, also inform my thinking.

5. Primary interviews with the women will be referenced by date; subsequent quotations without reference note numbers appended are taken from the same interviews.

6. It is beyond the scope of this project to determine exactly how many Jewish women were active in the movement. As I discussed with scholars such as sociologist Doug McAdam, author of *Freedom Summer* (New York: Oxford University Press, 1988), the available documents (such as Freedom Summer applications) do not make it easy to identify religiously unaffiliated Jews. McAdam's survey, which asked the summer volunteers to note how they heard about the project, lists one of the choices as "through minister or rabbi." Thus, to quantify the number of Jews or Jewish women who contributed to the southern civil rights movement (even just from 1964 to 1965) would require acts of interpretation and intuition, as well as significant resources. One would have to identify the ethnicity of staff members, volunteers, and donors to SNCC, CORE, SCLC, NAACP, foundations active in the South, and Friends of SNCC groups, as well as to identify activists among local politicians, temple sisterhoods, Jewish organizations, and so on. Such research would be a worthwhile long-term collective endeavor.

This study also does not compare Jewish women civil rights activists with other civil rights activists or 1960s radicals, though similarities and differences with white female and Jewish male civil rights activists are noted where relevant.

7. As Melanie Kaye/Kantrowitz, a founder of Jews for Racial and Economic Justice, pointed out in conversation, not all Jews could afford to go south and/or to jeopardize their place in college.

8. Charles Payne, *I've Got the Light of Freedom: The Organizing Tradition and the Mississippi Freedom Struggle* (Berkeley: University of California Press, 1995), 227–228.

9. David Biale, Michael Galchinsky, and Susannah Heschel, eds., *Insider/ Outsider: American Jews and Multiculturalism* (Berkeley: University of California Press, 1998).

10. Judith Plaskow, *Standing Again At Sinai: Judaism from a Feminist Perspective* (New York: HarperCollins, 1991), 56.

11. Boyarin, xvii.

GOING SOUTH

Introduction

Making the Decision

FIGHTING BACK

As a child in California, Vivian Leburg Rothstein (b. 1946) saw blue numbers that had been tattooed onto adult arms and heard the mournful, bitter stories of concentration camp survivors. She contrasted the romantic life her artistic parents had led in Europe with her mother's struggle to raise two children as a single parent and woman refugee. For Leburg, "[T]he Holocaust was the defining fact of my childhood. I was raised totally in a community of refugees. That's what propelled me into oppositional politics. I was used to being outside the mainstream. That made it easier to be critical and to identify with the oppression of Blacks."[1] Tired of being "a follower and not a leader" in the Berkeley Free Speech Movement, sophomore Leburg signed up to register Black voters in Mississippi for the summer of 1965.

Gertrude "Trudy" Weissman Orris (b. 1916) joined her husband, a military doctor, in Germany, at the end of World War II. As Orris recounts, "Whenever I met anybody German, I would say to them, 'What did you do during the war?'" One evening, a German musician said to her, "If you're asking me if I was a coward, I was a coward. I knew what was happening, but I couldn't do anything about it. My best friend was taken away. Now let me ask you something—what are you going to do when your turn comes?" Stunned, Orris recalls, "I stopped. I couldn't answer him. I said I didn't know what I would do but I would hope that I would do the right thing." The man said, "What you hope and what you do are two different things."

"When I came back to the United States," notes Orris, "I was a different person. I felt that the most important thing that I could do is to work in the Black movement. If anything happened, then somebody didn't have to say to me, what did you do?"[2] In addition to going south several times for freedom rides and major demonstrations, Orris would help bring national attention and resources to the southern movement as one of the founders of New York Parents of the Student Nonviolent Coordinating Committee (SNCC).

At age six, racism became a personal issue for Faith Holsaert (b. 1943). When Holsaert's parents divorced, her mother and Charity Bailey, Holsaert's African-American music teacher who rented a room in her parents' Greenwich Village apartment, became a "couple," raising Holsaert and her sister. This family, highly unusual by 1950s standards, endured constant taunts on the street and more subtle forms of racism, sexism, and homophobia from their communities. Yet even this couple balked twelve years later when eighteen-year-old Holsaert announced in December 1961 that she was going south for the first time to get arrested at a sit-in in Christfield, Maryland. Despite the fact that Holsaert's decision was a product of her upbringing in their household, her mother and Charity Bailey expressed ambivalence and fear. When several churches were burned in southwest Georgia in the summer of 1962, Holsaert had to find the inner strength to take the next step on her own—to go south as one of the first white women to join the volatile Albany, Georgia, movement.

Whether they knew it or not at the time, the decision to go south for civil rights would ultimately transform the lives of the fifteen Jewish women whose stories comprise this narrative. As the women describe their various motivations, distinctive patterns and themes emerge. This book examines their decision and documents the experiences of these women as actors in the 1960s civil rights movement. The stories recounted here are primarily those of northern women connected to the Student Nonviolent Coordinating Committee because in the South, SNCC (founded in 1960 by Black students) was the most grassroots and democratic organization accessible to white volunteers. SNCC provided a home for white antiracist activists at a time when the very notion of white antiracism was all too rare to most Americans, despite the existence of a white antiracist tradition.[3]

What Vivian Leburg Rothstein, Trudy Weissman Orris, and Faith Holsaert had in common was personal experience with the effects of fascism and racism. The civil rights movement gave them the opportunity to fight back and they seized it. Jewish women had many motives for going south, but their primary impetus was clearly to be part of a democratic movement to combat racial injustice. Like many young people of their generation, they sought to hold the United States to its democratic ideals. Yet, they made their decision to join the movement from a more specific historical location: as women in mid-twentieth-century American Jewish life.

Rothstein, Holsaert, and most other northern Jewish women who went south were part of a transitional generation. Born between 1935 and 1946, the Great Depression and the end of World War II, the core group of women in this book grew up in families intimately familiar with struggle. They were the daughters and granddaughters of Jewish immigrants striving to succeed in the United States. They had direct experiences with working-class Jewishness even as the American Jewish community began its extraordinary socioeconomic climb. At formative ages, many had moved from the warmth and tumult of urban extended family life to the more affluent alienation of the suburbs. For many, family deviations from the 1950s cultural norm (such as divorce, the early death of a parent, physical disability, or parental radicalism) made them feel different and helped them identify with others who were different. Their "in-between-ness" facilitated the decision to go south and their ability to cross boundaries of various kinds.

The act of going south required them to traverse geographic, racial, gender, ethnic, class, and political boundaries. Risking their lives for democratic ideals, they had little time to reflect on what these aspects of their "identities" might mean to them. Yet, Jewish women civil rights activists present an interesting example of women with multiple and contradictory identities. They were relatively privileged, well-educated northern students who chose to go south to work in a social justice movement; still they often felt slightly outside the mainstream. They were Jewish women from families and a culture that both encouraged and limited their life choices. They were the children of Jews struggling to assimilate into American culture without losing their Jewish connection entirely. They were white women in a movement led most visibly by Black men. They were competent and experienced, willing to take action before the feminist movement made it legitimate to do so. They were secular Jews in a Black Christian movement working in the anti-Semitic and virulently racist South. As such, they began to see their own experiences and those of African Americans from a variety of perspectives. This raised many challenging questions that would inform their complex responses to future movements based on identity politics. These movements led many groups to organize politically around a single facet of identity, such as race, gender, or ethnicity.

What did being Jewish mean, if anything, for the women who went south? Though most of the women interviewed did not identify strongly as Jewish while in the movement, "Jewishness" nevertheless played an important role in the development of their political, antiracist consciousness. Despite varying degrees of alienation and/or identification with Judaism, Jewish backgrounds, traditions, politics, and values did shape their worldviews and commitments. Though less directly than Rothstein and Orris, almost all the women interviewed had absorbed a sense of World War II and the Holocaust at young ages. Nightmares about Nazis and fantasies of joining the Resistance haunted their dreams. The Holocaust permeated their consciousness before the Jewish community could talk about it openly. Many, asking themselves how they would have responded if they had been in Europe, welcomed the chance to answer that question for themselves, to "resist" in a fight that was less obviously about their own survival.

Though the struggle was not directly about Jewish survival, it was not unrelated to Jewish identity.[4] In a range of ways, these women were exposed to a liberal Jewish moral framework of social justice that made involvement in the civil rights movement almost irresistible. As a number comment, once they heard about the movement, "I just knew I had to be there." For many, involvement in the civil rights movement was a creative application of a primary message of their parents' generation: to embrace both American and Jewish identity.

Some but not all were children of Old Left families. For these women, activism was in keeping with family values. Not surprisingly, those with roots in Left politics (Trudy Weissman Orris, Harriet Tanzman, Dorothy "Dottie" Miller Zellner) articulated the strongest connection between a Jewish cultural identity and their politics. Others who came from liberal Democratic families retained a sense of *tikkun olam* (Hebrew for "repair of the world"). For those politically disinclined toward Zionism as a nationalist movement, the civil rights movement before 1966 provided an opportunity to fight for both "American" and "Jewish" social justice ideals.

The stories of Jewish women activists in the civil rights movement prompt us to think about the meanings of Jewishness for Jews (particularly Jewish women) in antiracist and other social justice movements. The forces of tradition, history, and Jewish politics legitimize religion as the ultimate expression of Jewishness. Yet, this focus often obscures other complex relationships to Jewishness that do not fit the mold.[5] Despite a Talmudic tradition that invites dissent and multiple perspectives on any given issue, organized Judaism historically has alienated a number of questioning people who were born Jewish. It is perhaps a tribute

every
religion
P

to the power and tenacity of the Jewish tradition that so many rebels have struggled so hard to relate to it. Hegemonic definitions of Judaism impoverish our collective culture by not including a fine tradition of radicals, dissenters, and visionaries.

Antiracist activism is one expression of a universalist concern with justice that has roots in Jewish history, ethics, and political radicalism. For the women in this book, one link between Jewishness and future activism came through lessons learned in their families. Most of the Jewish women activists grew up with a nonpolitical, culturally based Jewish social justice imperative to "do the right thing." Although their families did not identify as "political," the message they sent certainly was.

As the women matured and sought to shape lives that would have an impact, their diverse Jewish backgrounds informed their decisions to take action. Once in the southern movement, their Jewish identities would mean different things in different contexts.

STEPPING INTO HISTORY

While routes to movement involvement came in many forms, catalytic events in the South often propelled northern Jewish women into action. Some who came from political families or were already involved in local civil right protests recognized this as the moment to step into a fight that would change the course of American history.

On February 1, 1960, four Black college students in Greensboro, North Carolina, ignited the sit-in movement by taking seats at a whites-only Woolworth's lunch counter. Images of their quiet dignity as local racists screamed at them and poured flour over their heads rocked the world. Within two months, Black students were demanding the right to be served at segregated lunch counters in seventy southern cities.[6]

By the end of the spring of 1960, students at one hundred northern colleges had mobilized in support of the actions in the South. Among them was Barbara Jacobs Haber (b. 1938), a self-described "bohemian-politico" at Brandeis University. After hearing a firsthand account of the Greensboro sit-ins from Brandeis graduate Michael Walzer, Jacobs was "absolutely galvanized. I'll just never forget what it was like to hear Michael tell in his very low key way what was going on there and to feel that YES inside myself that I had to be part of this and not to think twice about it, just to do it."[7]

In 1960, this Black-initiated nonviolent but confrontational form of protest catalyzed the white-student movement's militant activism.[8] During the course of the next year, almost every campus across the country experienced some type of civil rights–related activity: support groups, freedom ride committees, local sit-ins and pickets, and travel to the South. At Brandeis, Haber says, "[W]e got a hundred students out picketing every week at different Woolworth's. I became totally involved in the civil rights movement." Later that year, she would go south to attend SNCC's founding convention.

After dropping out of graduate school (a class "sin" from a middle-class Jewish perspective), Jacobs took a job in Baltimore as a social worker, a helping profession deemed appropriate for women at that time, yet her increasing involvement with civil rights activism challenged gender stereotypes. Like many Jewish women who went south, she got her training with the Congress of Racial Equality (CORE), an interracial civil rights organization founded in 1942. A member of Baltimore CORE, she relished the challenge of desegregating bars or restaurants in mixed groups: "I was a very macho sort of young woman—and in some ways, stupid. I just liked to go into these restaurants and bars and to be at the front, you know, in their face."

Dottie Miller Zellner (b. 1938) was another passionate young woman for whom the Greensboro sit-ins signaled the start of a journey on which she was eager to embark. A Queens College senior, she edited the student newspaper, as had Jacobs. A red-diaper baby attuned to world events, Miller was looking for a way to connect with the emerging civil rights movement as she graduated from college. That summer of 1960, she seized an opportunity to go south with CORE for training in nonviolent resistance. Miller went to Miami with thirty-five community leaders and was arrested immediately in a demonstration. In the segregated jails, Miller (the only white woman civil rights worker in the project) did her time with twelve white women criminals.

Confronting the culture of segregation was one of many adaptations the southern movement required. Though southern Blacks interacted with whites in various contexts, especially those related to work, they had separate social worlds. Even northern activists with impeccable civil rights credentials had to learn a whole new way of being when they crossed into the South. As Zellner notes, "Even though I had come from the Left all my life, this was my first real exposure to the whole Black social environment. It was my first exposure to Black culture, and certainly my first exposure to ministers and religious people." Cross-cultural communication proved to be one of the basic challenges in building these boundary-crossing alliances. Recalls Zellner, invoking her New York Jewish accent, "[T]hey couldn't understand me!"[9]

Despite these differences, Miller felt she was finally in the right place. Pleading with CORE organizers, "[D]on't send me home yet," Miller "wangled my way" to New Orleans for further movement work. Though it "was very nerve-wracking and scary," Miller also participated in the sit-ins there. Facing with great reluctance the prospect of returning home, she vowed to find a way back south. Her CORE colleagues told her, "[I]f you want to come back, the group to contact is SNCC." Though she did not know what SNCC was at the time, the organization would become her lifelong political reference point.

University of Chicago graduate Carol Ruth Silver (b. 1938) knew what she wanted: a year working in New York before going to law school. With a passionate interest in international relations, she talked her way into a clerk/typist job at the United Nations. Eager to learn, she manufactured excuses to watch proceedings of the Security Council. There in January 1961, she saw Soviet premier Nikita Khrushchev bang his shoe on the table during his famous address declaring the Soviet Union's support for national liberation struggles in Cuba and Vietnam.

Witnessing Khrushchev's historic challenge to U.S. hegemony in international affairs broadened Silver's thinking. Thus, she became more receptive to critiques of domestic affairs, such as the persistence of racism. In May 1961, when Silver heard CORE's radio call for Freedom Riders, "I felt as if it was a call to me personally. I could not say no."[10] Within weeks, she was on one of the earlier buses heading south to challenge segregation in intrastate travel. In a letter to her mother from jail, Silver wrote, "Don't worry about me, please. This should be one of the most interesting experiences of my life bar none and certainly something which I will never again get a chance to do."

Sometimes the decision to go south needed to germinate. During the heyday of early '60s radicalism at the University of Wisconsin at Madison, history major Harriet Tanzman (b. 1940) was struggling over what to do with her life. A member of the W. E. B. DuBois Club, Tanzman was also working with the local CORE chapter (headed by future SNCC leader Silas Norman). She had considered going south after hearing some freedom riders speak in 1961: "I was too afraid to do it, but I was very affected by them." Early in 1963, Tanzman heard two powerful Black women leaders speak about the movement. Diane Nash of SNCC had pushed successfully for the continuation of the Freedom Rides despite the violence they encountered and the resistance of CORE leadership.[11] Gloria Richardson, a rare woman leader of the Cambridge, Maryland, movement, endured death threats and physical repression in a violent fight to end school segregation. Enormously moved by Richardson, Tanzman recalls, "She basically invited us. She said that there's this work to be done and you could participate." Throughout the summer and fall, Tanzman continued to study and organize locally, "trying to get myself to feeling like I could just go south, especially since I was studying something I didn't like—social work."[12]

Sitting in the lunchroom of her fieldwork placement at the State of Wisconsin's Youth Division of Probation, Tanzman looked up at a television screen and saw coverage of John F. Kennedy's November 1963 assassination. Her sense that "enormous things were happening out there, the assassination, the war, the strife in the South . . . just somehow gave me the oomph to quit the next day." Tanzman took her scholarship money and went directly to stay with friends in Atlanta. In the first of several "stints" in the southern movement, Tanzman "just showed up in the SNCC office." She helped do paperwork and participated in the revitalized Atlanta sit-in movement.

BREAKING FREE AND SEARCHING FOR MEANING

For some northern Jewish women, the decision to go south blended a search for meaning with a desperate desire to break free of the constraints of 1950s life, including American Jewish gender norms. From today's perspective, it is difficult to conceive of sending young women to college without any expectation of vocation except for marriage and motherhood.[13] As Wini Breines notes dryly in her study of growing up white and female in that decade, "[M]arriage, the only sanctioned goal for girls in the 1950s, does not lend itself to rational planning as does a career."[14] The college-educated, second- and third-generation Jewish women in this book ran right into the dilemma of what to do with their lives when they realized they wanted more than marriage and family. "The concept of getting married, living happily ever after, and not doing anything after that always bewildered me," Janice Goodman (b. 1935) recalls. "I did a lot of housecleaning as a child. I did not see cleaning the house as an occupation."[15]

The need to escape confinement to the home was a recurrent theme. For these primarily urban Jewish women, images of suburban life symbolized the trap they sought to avoid. When asked what enabled young

Jewish women like her to face the danger of going south, Rita Schwerner Bender replied firmly, "I did not see myself as saving anyone, but I did have a view of saving myself from a split-level house."[16]

During the postwar period when future civil rights activists were growing up, the development of Jewish suburbs epitomized rapid Jewish social and economic mobility (and its discontents). Jewish intellectuals criticized suburban Jewish life in general as bland, conformist, and materialistic, and looked upon suburban Jews' religious practice (building and attending synagogues primarily to make their socioeconomic success as Jews visible in the community) as anti-intellectual, spiritually shallow, and vulgar.[17] Radical Jews of the 1960s and 1970s were the most bitter critics of Jewish suburbia. Irving Howe contended that assimilation there had extinguished some of the most distinctive qualities of the Jewish spirit: "an eager restlessness, a moral anxiety, an openness to novelty, a hunger for dialectic, a refusal of contentment, an ironic criticism of all fixed opinion."[18] Certainly, these qualities describe the Jewish women activists in this book.

In Newark, New Jersey, housewife Jacqueline Levine (b. 1926) and her five-year-old daughter marched in an endless circle protesting Woolworth's segregated lunch counters. It was the late 1950s, before the Greensboro sit-ins galvanized a national civil rights movement. Not long before, Levine's husband had asked, "Are you just going to take care of the children and the house, or are you going to do something with your mind?"[19] Harkening back to her suffragist mother and grandmother, Levine stepped onto the picket line and into a forty-year career of volunteerism and leadership in the Jewish communal world.

Inspired by her mentor, Rabbi Joachim Prinz, she attended the 1963 March on Washington, which Prinz helped organize. Later, Levine flew in for the Montgomery rally at the end of the 1965 Selma to Montgomery march. Because there was a small contingent from the American Jewish Congress participating, she felt more comfortable going to Montgomery and proud to be there as a Jew. As a highly visible leader, Levine represents untold numbers of women in Jewish organizations who have pushed the Jewish community to live up to its social justice ideals in twentieth-century race relations.

Jewish women's hunger for meaningful action explains their tenacity in facing difficult movement experiences. After she describes a "horrible" 1963 jail experience in Albany, Georgia, that included a hunger strike, Miriam Cohen Glickman (b. 1942) explains why she stayed:

> I guess I need to be clear about my commitment. I had many horrible experiences. There wasn't anything else I could have been doing at the time that had anywhere near the pull that this did, of helping make the world a better place. I mean what were the alternatives? I could go back and get a 9-to-5 job somewhere. In those days, women were teachers, nurses, and psychologists/counselors. And Jewish women weren't nurses. So I had the other two to choose from. I would have stayed forever down there. I finally left because I was forced out. But all of us felt that what we were doing was the most important work that could be done. Nobody said this was a wonderful experience. If you find anybody that told you that, they've forgotten.[20]

Glickman's honesty demystifies the daily work of social-change movements. For Glickman as for other white women activists, including Jewish women, the work of the civil rights movement, while often very challenging, gave life a focus and a meaning beyond those expected for daughters of the rising white middle class at the time.

After Elizabeth Slade Hirschfeld (b. 1937) graduated from Cornell University in 1958, she worked in a genetics lab, at an Atomic Energy Commission lab located at Cornell, and at the Veterinary School. She also, in her words, "screwed around a lot." Although she didn't want to think about it, it was clear that "I wasn't getting married." Slade "was looking for a career or something compelling, something to commit to. The main career for women in the '50s was being a housewife and mother, and there were just no appropriate role models for me, certainly not in my family. I needed something to do that would be something for me. I didn't know what to do. So when the Freedom Rides came along, I felt it was a wonderful opportunity for me."[21]

Some Jewish women's decisions to go south seemed arbitrary on the surface but actually reflected an intuition that the movement experience would liberate them in unforeseen ways. Elaine DeLott Baker (b. 1942) exemplified this dynamic, crediting disgust with hypocrisy as her motivation.

A Radcliffe College junior, DeLott was staying at a friend's house in Cambridge over Christmas break, 1963. A group of friends came to visit, including "a guy who was part of our group and we ended up sleeping together. In that time, there was that kind of loose sexuality. In fact, we had never slept together before, and we never did again, but we slept together that night."[22] Breaking sexual taboos must have been both exciting and nerve-wracking for DeLott and her peers, who grew up in an era when even talking about sex publicly was taboo.[23] Despite the fact that the Pill liberated women of their generation to become more sexually active, young people's sexual expression was still subterranean and subject to social control in the early 1960s, as DeLott's story illustrates.

In the next room, also sleeping over, was a young girl who said she was a junior at M.I.T. When her uncle, a captain in the Cambridge police force, stormed in at five o'clock in the morning, they learned that she "was a townie, a junior in high school, a Catholic girl whose father was dead. Her mother sent the police to arrest her for being a willful child." The police arrested DeLott and her friends (only a few years older than the "willful child"), too, and charged them with fornication, lewd, and lascivious behavior, and corrupting the morals of a minor— one misdemeanor and two felonies.

Paroled into the custody of the college and her Harvard-based dean, DeLott endured a humiliating talk designed to uplift her morals. The dean told her the story of his own daughter, whom "you might call a little wild. But she married someone who was a little boring but who didn't care about her past. Someday you will find someone who doesn't care about your past." After this enlightening talk, the school first expelled DeLott and then readmitted her. "I had to have a police escort to my exams because the court hearing was the same morning as my exams."

As a working-class woman who struggled to find her place at an elite institution, DeLott was incensed. "I felt shame for my parents who had to come. I felt indignation as a woman of the world. As an intellectual, you knew that this was bullshit. So I finished the academic year and said, 'This place is fucked—I'm getting out of here.'" When two Harvard doctoral student friends invited her to join them to teach at the summer session at Tougaloo College, DeLott literally jumped on the SNCC bus heading toward Jackson. That was the beginning of her antiracist education.

DOING WHAT NEEDED TO BE DONE

Jewish women's ability and willingness to work—to handle a variety of necessary tasks—gave them access to the southern civil rights movement and legitimized their participation. Many Jewish women civil rights activists had direct proximity to Eastern European working-class

Jewishness and to working mothers. They were aware of the traditional Eastern European Jewish gender division of labor: women managed family and business; men studied Torah. They internalized a culturally derived, gendered work ethic of doing what needed to be done.

Embodying this Jewish women's work ethic, some northern Jewish women, often slightly older professionals, went south when they saw they had skills the movement needed. Florence Howe (b. 1929) was already a professor at Goucher College in Baltimore by the time she first went south. Having involved her students in local civil rights protests in 1963 and 1964, it was they who pushed her to deepen her commitment. She went to Mississippi in 1964, using her teaching and organizational skills to coordinate the Blair Street Freedom School in Jackson. In a much more dangerous assignment, she returned the following summer to work on school desegregation for a month in Natchez, a Klan stronghold.

During her internship at a Jewish hospital in Chicago, British-born physician June Finer (b. 1935) began to understand American racism. "I began to be really upset by the level of illness of the Black people who would come in at death's door. Their health would be neglected until they were really, really, really sick. It became increasingly clear that the differences in class and income were making a big difference in their health status."[24] Finer's relationship with Jewish activist and physician Quentin Young reinforced her perceptions and opened up a world of radical activism in Chicago. She became part of a long-standing interracial organization called the Committee to End Discrimination in Chicago Medical Institutions (CED). Finer headed south for the first time on a CED-chartered train to the 1963 March on Washington.

Providing care (a traditional women's role) in a nontraditional career for women at that time, Finer worked with the medical staff during the 1964 Mississippi Summer Project. She returned in the spring of 1965 to serve for five months as southern coordinator for the Medical Committee for Human Rights (MCHR). Finer managed and dispatched the many volunteer medical professionals who came south. MCHR literally bound up the wounds of SNCC activists on the front lines.

Not everyone who wanted to go south could do so at a moment's notice. Roberta Galler's priority was always to work where she was most needed and for a long time that meant the North. On leave from the University of Chicago, Galler (b. 1936) became manager of the journal *New University Thought,* an early northern-student chronicler of events in the southern civil rights movement. In 1961, *New University Thought* hosted a SNCC fund-raiser. As activists told their stories about the struggle in the South, Galler committed herself fully to the movement. She had planned to go back to school in the fall to finish her degree, but as she puts it, "I forgot to."[25] She helped found Chicago Friends of SNCC and became its first executive secretary.

From her fund-raising, organizing, and press outreach work in Chicago, Galler developed strong connections with many SNCC activists. Some would come to stay with her to recuperate from stress or injuries. Keeping in close touch with SNCC field offices on a daily basis, Galler made direct interventions that brought food, information, money, national attention, and personal support to SNCC centers across the South. Movements for radical social change (and organizations like SNCC) generally fight against great odds with limited resources. Women like Galler manage, protect, and preserve precious human and material resources. They function as connective tissue—taking care of people's needs. The work of revitalizing activist communities through authentic personal connections sustains individuals and their collective vision.

In the fall of 1964, Lawrence Guyot offered Galler just such a challenging assignment. He invited her to come to Mississippi to open the first statewide office of the Mississippi Freedom Democratic Party (MFDP) at a moment when the entire staff was demoralized and burnt out. After the high of Freedom Summer, SNCC had to face the failure to seat the MFDP delegation at the Atlantic City Democratic National Convention. The next wave of voter registration work that Galler helped organize in Mississippi would empower both staff and local people.

SNCC was small and worked in dangerous Klan territory in several southern states. Therefore, it required keenly aware coordinators who knew the location of each field organizer at any given moment. A number of the Jewish women profiled in this book played such roles for SNCC. This type of coordinating work called for the ability to deal with people across differences, to manage information, to run offices, to assess danger, and to handle multiple tasks amid chaos. These are also skills that women must develop to perform their traditional gender roles. The work performed by many of the women in this book illustrates the different ways they protected the network they cherished as SNCC's "beloved community."

PARENTAL REACTIONS

Once young Jewish women made up their minds to go south, they faced two hurdles: figuring out the organizational connections that would get them there and telling their parents. First, one had to be quite determined as a white woman to work for SNCC at any time other than the 1964 and 1965 Mississippi Summer Projects. Dottie Miller, Miriam Cohen, and Harriet Tanzman all wrote letters to the Atlanta office asking to work for SNCC. The letters went unanswered, probably because the office was understaffed and chaotic and there was no formal process for bringing white students into SNCC other than the Summer Projects.

Second, the women had to deal with a range of parental reactions when they announced their decision. Most Jewish women volunteers did not need parental permission to go south, but they certainly must have wanted their family's support.[26] Yet, those women who went, more often than not, confronted parental disapproval. Even women from progressive households had to face parental ambivalence.

The women's decision to put their bodies on the line to fight racism was a transgressive act on a number of levels. To begin with, it carried the potential to cross Jewish class boundaries. Throughout the twentieth century, American Jewish parents invested a great deal of energy and resources trying to protect their children and to ensure their children's future security. They saw higher education as leading almost inevitably to upward mobility and social safety. Activism threatened to disrupt this hard-won and privileged path.[27] Those who left college temporarily or permanently for the movement often widened the breach between generations.

For northern Jewish women, going south was also a transgression of Jewish gender norms. Women who had never rebelled before shattered their parents' perception of them as obedient daughters, nice Jewish girls. Jewish daughters were in training for marrying upward, building a family, maintaining Jewish continuity, and supporting a husband's and children's success. The primary injunction was not to make waves. Their job was to ensure that their family and the Jewish community would "make it" in the United States. Within twentieth-century American Jewish culture, the Jewish woman's body has been the medium for expressing the community's gender, race, and class issues. Specifically, Jewish women's bodies have symbolized Jewish ethnicity but as an affluent, acculturating presence.[28] Jewish women civil rights activists resisted this symbolic function.

Making waves in more ways than one, many Jewish daughters who went south knew that their parents would not be pleased. While trying to respect parental fears, daughters were mindful that they were enacting values learned at home. When Carol Ruth Silver told her mother she was going south on one of the early freedom rides, Silver recalls that her mother said, "'Oy, my heart, my heart.' My father said, 'Well, just be careful.' My mother said, 'You're going to kill me. You can't do this, it's dangerous.' I said, 'Mother, this is what you taught me to do and this is what you taught me to be. If I don't do it, then I will not be true to all that you have taught me.' She knew it was true and she was legitimately frightened for me. Now that I'm the mother of kids who take risks, I know that feeling, but it's in kids' nature to do that to their parents."

Even the most engaged parents found it hard to watch their children risking violence for an ideal. This hit home for longtime labor and peace activist Trudy Orris when her sixteen-year-old son Peter insisted on going with her on a Freedom Ride to Gwynne Oaks, Maryland, in 1963. "My son wanted to be arrested," she relates, "and I wanted him to go to school." As the bus rolled southward down the East Coast, the entire group passionately debated whether Peter should get arrested. "People took sides, and the majority decided that he should not. He was very young." Whenever she wanted to go south for the movement, Orris had to balance delicately her activist and mothering roles. This was a creative adaptation of Jewish gender roles.

Ambivalence was the best possible response Jewish daughters could expect when sharing their decision to go south. Because their daughters were usually acting in consonance with the values taught at home, parents had a hard time arguing against the morality of the impulse to take action. Still, naturally, they were frightened for their daughters' safety, and all the more so after the disappearance of activists Goodman, Schwerner, and Chaney in Mississippi in June 1964.

Ilene Strelitz, editor of the *Stanford Daily* and a protégée of former Stanford dean and liberal activist Allard Lowenstein, had a very stressful time with her mother during the training session for the 1964 Mississippi Summer Project at Oxford, Ohio:

Every night, in complete fear and anguish, I waited to see my mother on the [TV] screen. She had sent me a telegram signed with my brother's name saying that she had had a heart attack and I must come home immediately (none of which was true). Telephone calls, with her screaming, threatening, crying until I hung up, came every day. Long vituperative letters came from her for me. After the phone calls I would disappear into the ladies' room, and cry out the engulfing rage and accumulated frustration. When I recovered, I desperately threw cold water on my face as it was rather well advertised that there were psychiatrists around looking for people showing signs of breaking down and who thus should be weeded out before they got to Mississippi. *Mississippi had nothing over a Jewish mother.*[29]

A number of the women had more trouble with their fathers than with their mothers. This often required them to break explicitly with patriarchal authority and values, including overt racism. Janice Goodman had been out of school for seven years and involved in sit-ins and progressive New York politics by the time she announced that she was going to Mississippi in 1964. Goodman's mother reacted with "a mixture of fear and pride" that her daughter was "doing this very exciting, meaningful, and important thing." On the other hand, Goodman's father (from whom her mother had been divorced for some time) took her out to dinner to try to talk her out of going. Goodman recalls: "He said, 'God, it's dangerous, aren't you worried?' And then when he was getting no place with that, he finally said, 'Don't you realize, Jan, that those people down there, they rape and ravage?'"[30]

Although she was already a professor at the time she went south, Florence Howe's commitment also had repercussions for her relationship with her family. When Howe adopted Alice Jackson, a Black teenager she met in Mississippi, her family "was very angry with me. More than angry. They just refused to see me with her. Same thing. My brother was an incredible racist. I didn't see my brother for about fifteen years over Alice and a couple of other things."[31]

Elizabeth Slade Hirschfeld's mother "was very proud of me. Real, real proud of me. Yeah, she loved it." However, before she left on the sixth bus of the Freedom Rides, she had a huge fight over the phone with her Republican (assimilated Jewish) father. He was furious and screamed at her, "You're a damn fool." Later, Hirschfeld notes, "my dad came around. In fact, after I was married and he had been out here once, he said, 'The problem with you all was that you didn't stay with it.'"

Despite memories of her own flight from Berlin to Amsterdam to New York, Vivian Leburg's mother supported her daughter's decision to go south; her refugee father did not. Opposed to the idea of sending young people into such danger, he tried to bring other volunteers' parents around to his point of view at an emergency meeting of the local

Parents of SNCC group. In an August 8, 1965, letter responding to his daughter's youthfully militant letter from jail, Werner Leburg described this meeting, where, "I can assure you, I did not have an easy time when I talked against these professional speakers."[32] In the letter, Leburg's German-Jewish rationalism and moral intelligence warred with his emotions:

Dear Chicky:

As far as I can remember, I never could have tried to tell you that what you are doing is wrong. This would by no means be in line with my social conscience or ethical philosophy.

All what I tried to convey to you and as a matter of fact also to the parent committee was, that within my knowledge of so very many revolutionary movements in Europe and elsewhere I never came across a single fact where young girls have been sent into the front and fireline, except maybe for the so called "children's crusade" during the middle ages, which ended in a catastrophe.

However, whatever the opinions are for ways and means to achieve results, risks have to match possibilities of results and you should not construct your parents' concern about your safety as a disapproval of your present activities.

Chicky, do not take unnecessary risks and that is all we ask for, that is all we can ask for and if you even are able to do that we do not know and doubt it, but we hope so with all our heart. Keep well, Chicky, and good luck to you.

All my love, Daddy

Werner Leburg's poignant letter speaks for all the parents who balanced concern for their daughters' vulnerability with pride in their courage to make the decision to go south.

Exploring the significance of that decision and chronicling the actions that followed, this book acknowledges the ordinariness and extraordinariness of northern Jewish women who went south. Their stories reveal how "ordinary" Jewish women found ways to contribute to the extraordinary fight for civil rights led by Black people in the 1960s. As Dottie Miller Zellner puts it, "The primary lesson I learned is that ordinary people can do the most extraordinary things." Although Zellner was speaking primarily of local Black people, who were the heart and soul of the southern movement, her statement also applies to many northern Jewish women like herself, who moved out of a relatively comfortable existence into an unfamiliar and often dangerous context in order to take action on principles in which they believed.

JEWISH WOMEN'S INVISIBILITY IN
CIVIL RIGHTS HISTORY

The prominent Jewish role in the civil rights movement is well known. Jews provided a major portion of contributions made to such civil rights organizations as the National Association for the Advancement of Colored People (NAACP), which they helped found in 1911; the Congress of Racial Equality (CORE); the Southern Christian Leadership Conference (SCLC); the Student Nonviolent Coordinating Committee (SNCC); and the Council of Federated Organizations (COFO). One researcher has suggested that half of the white Freedom Riders were Jewish, as were half of the civil rights attorneys who went south. Approximately two-thirds of the white volunteers for the 1964 Mississippi Summer Project were Jewish.[33]

Although it is clear that Jews played a significant part in the Black civil rights movement of the 1960s, the documentary record and public perception of Jewish participation reflects the roles and experiences of men. In relation to the total U.S. population, Jewish women participated in the civil rights movement in disproportionate numbers. A few of their names appear in civil rights books and a few of their unlabeled faces peek out in photographic essays on the movement, but they remain, on the whole, anonymous. Even Rita Schwerner Bender, the most visible and historically remembered Jewish woman in the southern civil rights movement, receives short shrift as an activist in her own right. When Michael Schwerner, James Chaney, and Andrew Goodman disappeared in Mississippi in June 1964, they became symbols of Black-Jewish martyrdom for the civil rights cause. Andrew Goodman had been in Mississippi for one day when he was killed. Rita Schwerner had been working in Meridian for six months when her husband disappeared. History has seen Rita Schwerner as the widow of a martyr. Women's history demands that we see her fully embodied in time, a woman whose activism preceded and continued after the terrible summer of 1964. Rita Schwerner Bender is but one of many Jewish women activists whose less dramatic stories have yet to be told.

Jewish women's invisibility in civil rights history is not the result of an anti-Semitic, misogynist conspiracy. Their invisibility has more to do with the construction of academic disciplines, the complexities of Jewish identity, the development of identity politics since the 1960s, and the nature of the work Jewish women performed in the movement.

The contemporary disciplines most likely to discuss the experiences of Jewish women civil rights activists have ignored or missed them. For example, civil rights scholarship in the 1990s focused increasingly on making visible the integral organizing role played by grassroots southern Black people. The laudable move away from lavishing attention solely on charismatic leaders like Martin Luther King Jr. to giving credit to behind-the-scenes Black women catalysts like Ella Baker has created more space for examining the contributions of Black and white women on the ground. More community studies and biographies of Black women activists have emerged, but it is still true, as civil rights historian Steven Lawson has asserted, that "we need systematic studies of how ordinary women in their roles as mothers, wives, workers, churchgoers, and professors affected the nature of the movement."[34] Lawson does not mention synagogue-goers, Hadassah activists, and temple sisterhoods, but that research is necessary as well.[35]

Racial sensitivities of the past and present, however, still make such studies difficult, for there remains ambivalence about the role of white and Jewish participants in the movement. And white women, including Jewish women, generate even more controversy, due to the racialized sexual politics of the South in which they worked.[36]

The 300 white women who went to Mississippi in 1964 and the 350 who worked throughout the South in 1965 were "a relatively anonymous group who lived the daily lives of women's work in a social movement."[37] But, if women constituted one-third to one-half of the volunteers, of whom a majority were Jewish, it seems reasonable to assume that many of those anonymous white women volunteers were Jewish. And, as this book documents, Jewish women played diverse roles in the southern movement in addition to teaching and registering voters during the Mississippi Summer Projects.

Research that could inform analyses of Jewish women's participation in the civil rights movement does not address Jewish women directly. For example, although some Jewish philanthropists and activists used the early-twentieth-century phase of the Black civil rights movement as a medium for working out their own issues of American identity, as Hasia Diner has argued, Jewish men may have identified with

African Americans for different reasons than did Jewish women.[38] In a comparable way, in locating the roots of the women's liberation movement in the civil rights movement, Sara Evans discusses white women's experiences, highlighting the religious motivations of southern white Protestant women activists, without commenting on Jewish cultural and religious influences on Jewish women activists.[39]

Among scholars who do address white movement participation, ethnicity has not been a major factor in analyzing whites' reasons for going south. Religion, on the other hand, has been a central theme. Given the centrality of the Black church in the movement, the focus on Christian religion is almost inevitable. However, ethnicity, rather than religion, is a more useful framework for understanding progressive Jewish activists, many of whom did not identify as religious at the time. And to complicate matters further, ethnic definitions of Jewishness are diverse, as discussed in chapter 5, "Exploring Many Ways of Being Jewish."

While many civil rights scholars have had trouble seeing secular Jews as Jews,[40] Jewish historians have had trouble seeing Jews who are women. A growing number of American Jewish historians do integrate gender into their scholarship, but many tend not to include gender as a category of historical analysis in their research, writing, and teaching. Without gender analysis, it has been easy for historians to ignore the complex and painful racialized sexual dynamics that plagued relations among movement workers. Without this analysis, any attempt to understand the breakdown of the "golden era" of Black-Jewish civil rights collaboration remains incomplete.

Born of the identity politics of the 1960s, racial/ethnic studies seems a logical place to analyze intercultural collaborations for civil rights. Yet racial/ethnic studies has tended not to highlight the experiences of white ethnics. These academic fields started out as places where disenfranchised "minority" groups could recover their lost histories and cultures. More recently, racial/ethnic studies has influenced many disciplines with the central insight that race is socially constructed, its meanings changing over time. The historical complexity of Jewish racial identity seems appropriate to this line of analysis. However, the vexed relationship between the American Jewish community's self-perceptions and the frameworks of multiculturalism hinders reasoned discussion on the critical issue of American Jewish racial identity.

The majority of U.S. Jews are perceived as white and perceive themselves as white. Whiteness allows Jews to be invisible as Jews, enabling them to pass quietly into the dominant culture. This work questions the category of "whiteness"—particularly in the United States and particularly for Jews.[41] Given the "white skin privilege" accorded much of the American Jewish community, which enabled rapid and widespread economic success, it is difficult to characterize the nature of Jewish oppression in the United States. Thus, despite the existence of anti-Semitism, as well as working-class Jews and Jews of color, it has been difficult to locate Jews within discussions of multiculturalism. David Biale locates one source of this tension in American Jews' attachment to their "privileged" status as the model minority that would define America's relationship to minorities. In the post–World War II era, he argues, American Jews "found themselves for the first time in modern history as doubly marginal: marginal to the majority culture but also marginal among minorities. In the American histories of victims, Jews were no longer sociologically 'the chosen people.'"[42]

Similarly, despite the consciousness-raising efforts of such scholars as Evelyn Torton Beck, women's studies has neglected to fully integrate Jewish women's ethnic identity into its theoretical frameworks. This may be because Jewish women do not seem to fit well into the theoretical constructs that have energized the interdisciplinary field of women's studies as it has matured: the intersection of race/gender and postcolonial debates. A new generation of younger women and men, schooled in both Jewish studies and gender studies, is starting to create dialogue between the two disciplines.[43] Only cross-disciplinary conversations will provide frameworks for approaching Jewish women's experiences in the civil rights movement.

Jewish women activists were more comfortable fighting for Black rights than for specifically Jewish causes. One reason for this lies in the complex nature of Jewish "oppression" at that moment in United States history. Jews had religious freedom, but vestiges of social discrimination still existed, as did Jewish invisibility in a Christian culture. The wounds of historical anti-Semitism were very much alive, including awareness of historic persecution, pogroms, and the Holocaust.

Yet, in the past few decades, American Jews, including Jewish women, have achieved significant educational, occupational, and economic mobility. Most of the Jewish women in this study would classify themselves today as white, middle-class, relatively privileged Americans. The view of most sociologists of contemporary American Jewry is that Jews have "made it" in the United States; they are represented among the most economically secure and well educated of Americans, making their presence felt in academia, politics, and the professions. The majority are, if not completely assimilated, then mostly nonreligious and unaffiliated with synagogues or other Jewish institutions. The meaning of this lack of affiliation for Jewish group identity is a matter of debate among scholars and commentators.[44]

At the time they went south, most Jewish women did not identify themselves or their motivations primarily as Jewish. Jewish women, while participating in significant numbers in every social change movement from civil rights onward, have rarely examined their own identities within these movements—that is, from their own perspectives as women who are Jews. In the 1950s and 1960s, the category of secular Jewishness lacked both visibility and credibility. However, the ideology of universalism had tremendous appeal both within Jewish culture and progressive political circles. When asked about their Jewishness within the southern movement, many Jewish activists (men and women) said, "We didn't think in those terms then."[45] The universalist spirit is so strong in this generation of activist Jews that there seems to be a taboo against appearing ethnically chauvinist.

For those disinclined to announce their ethnicity, daily life in the southern movement provided little motivation to highlight their Jewishness. When they found their way south, Jewish women civil rights workers were grateful to be able to participate in a Black-led movement that was making history. They were anxious not to call any more attention to their white female Jewishness than racist southern culture already did. They were also working against at least two cultural stereotypes. To Black movement coworkers whom they revered, they did not want to appear as "pushy New York Jews." To the Klan, whom everyone feared, they were already marked as "nigger-loving, Jewish Bolshevik outside agitators."

There is still another reason that Jewish women have been invisible in civil rights history. The nature of some "back-office" work Jewish women performed for the movement reinforced their invisibility. Yet, Jewish women worked as campus organizers, fund-raisers, demonstrators, and desegregators; voter registration workers; fieldworkers and organizers; Freedom School teachers; strategists; communications coordinators; human resource managers; economic cooperative organizers; typists; cooks; sympathetic listeners; lawyers; doctors; and social workers. The kinds of roles Jewish women played specifically for SNCC helped build and sustain the infrastructure of a tiny, underfunded,

Black student–led organization that challenged and transformed the entire civil rights movement.

The narratives recorded here are part of the effort to chronicle the lives of Jewish women activists in what Melanie Kaye/Kantrowitz calls the Jewish "political diaspora."[46] The experiences of Jewish women civil rights activists are an integral part of a collective Jewish and activist heritage, one that must remain alive and accessible to future generations.

Going South is divided into two general parts, each comprising three chapters. Chapter 1, "Going South, 1960–1963," chronicles Jewish women's engagement with the southern movement prior to the 1964 Mississippi Summer Project, which first brought significant numbers of white northerners to the South. It follows the women as they witnessed the founding of SNCC, got on the bus for the Freedom Rides, faced firehoses in demonstrations, and endured days and nights in jail. Chapter 2, "Moving In On Mississippi, 1963–1965," profiles the roles Jewish women played as Freedom School teachers, voter registration workers, professionals, fund-raisers, strategists, and movement caretakers. Also profiled are Jewish women who came south independent of the institutional frameworks provided by the Mississippi Summer Projects. Chapter 3, "Crossing Boundaries: Jewishness in the South, 1960–1967," investigates the contexts in which Jewishness mattered for northern Jewish women civil rights workers in the South. Within the framework of twentieth-century southern Jewish history, it examines the stories of Jewish women's encounters with the Ku Klux Klan, southern Jews, and southern Black communities during the movement.

The second part examines the ways in which Jewish culture and contexts influenced the women's decision to go south for civil rights. Chapter 4, "Uncovering Family Legacies," examines the sources of activist Jewish women's developing consciousness by looking at family backgrounds. Family economic struggles, political culture, racial views, and gender dynamics fostered the women's receptivity to the radical call of the civil rights movement. Chapter 5, "Exploring Many Ways of Being Jewish," looks into the ways that the women see Jewishness shaping their worldviews and commitments. In addition to examining the women's early encounters with religious institutions, experiences of anti-Semitism, and knowledge of the Holocaust, the chapter locates these women in a broader tradition of Jewish women's radicalism. Chapter 6, "Creating a Living Legacy," looks at the women's efforts to find meaningful ways to live and contribute to social change after they had to leave the southern movement. One way of doing this has been to pass on their stories because the efforts of Jewish women antiracist activists provide lessons about the challenges and successes of multiethnic, multiracial collaborations for social change.

Going south gave northern Jewish women an opportunity to create existential meaning in their lives through moral action. Going south also provided adventure, "authentic" experience (in which theory and practice were linked), a sense of community, and escape from boring jobs, difficult families, and the prospect of marriage and life in suburbia. The movement offered these women the chance to learn from some of the most exciting activist/theorists in the country—people who worked with the Student Nonviolent Coordinating Committee (SNCC)—such as Ella Baker, Bob Moses, Fannie Lou Hamer, James Forman, Charles McDew, Stokely Carmichael, and a host of unsung local heroes. Working with SNCC provided an opportunity to explore one's "vocation," to experiment with different identities in a youth-led social environment. For some of the women, those experiments with identity included their first experiences with interracial collaboration, assuming leadership, becoming an activist, and exploring sexuality. Through it all, there was the intoxication of the "freedom high," of danger, and of putting one's full self on the line. Jewish women seized this opportunity to bring their skills, passion, and openness to the movement. Their stories deserve a place in history.

NOTES

1. Interview with Vivian Leburg Rothstein, June 26, 1994.
2. Interview with Gertrude Weissman Orris, January 21, 1994.
3. Herbert Aptheker argues that white antiracism, more common among the working classes, women, and those in direct contact with Blacks, has been underestimated in U.S. history. Herbert Aptheker, *Anti-Racism in United States History: The First Two Hundred Years* (Westport, Conn.: Greenwood Press, 1992).
4. As historian Hasia Diner has argued, the nature of twentieth-century Black-Jewish collaboration mixes altruism with self-interest. Identification with the plight of African Americans and efforts to "help" them enabled American Jews to explore and consolidate their own identities as Americans. Michael Rogin's linkage of Jewish civil rights workers with immigrant Jewish entertainers who wore blackface stretches the analogy too far. However, Naomi Seidman's analysis is more resonant with the experience of Jewish civil rights workers and contemporary Jewish progressives. She argues that "in the absence of a

particularist Jewish political affiliation that could also satisfy the progressive universalist agenda with which Jewish politics has been historically linked, adopting the particularist position of another group paradoxically becomes a distinctly Jewish act." Thus she "names" a "Jewish politics of vicarious identity," which, if conceptualized with respect for the real contributions of Jewish cross-cultural activists, helps illuminate the American Jewish progressive tradition. See Hasia Diner, *In the Almost Promised Land: American Jews and Blacks, 1915–1935* (Westport, Conn.: Greenwood Press, 1977); Michael Rogin, *Blackface, White Noise: Jewish Immigrants in the Hollywood Melting Pot* (Berkeley: University of California Press, 1996); and Naomi Seidman, "Fag-Hags and Bu-Jews: Toward a (Jewish) Politics of Vicarious Identity," in Biale et al., 261.

5. Jewish law defines any child of a Jewish mother as Jewish. Any group, particularly one as historically reviled as the Jews, must create boundaries to define who is a safe member of the community and who is a threatening outsider.

6. Aldon D. Morris, *The Origins of the Civil Rights Movement: Black Communities Organizing for Change* (New York: Free Press, 1984), 195.

7. Interview with Barbara Jacobs Haber, February 20, 1994. Michael Walzer went on to become a noted political philosopher and the author of many books, including *Exodus and Revolution* (New York: Basic Books, 1985), a meditation on the political meaning of the biblical Exodus story. Walzer has used his early civil rights experiences to reflect on contemporary Black-Jewish relations. See Walzer, "Blacks and Jews: A Personal Reflection," in Jack Salzman and Cornel West, eds., *Struggles in the Promised Land* (New York: Oxford University Press, 1997).

8. Morris, 222.

9. Quoted in Fred Powledge, *Free at Last? The Civil Rights Movement and the People Who Made It* (New York: HarperCollins, 1992), 222.

10. Interview with Carol Ruth Silver, February 9, 1994.

11. Clayborne Carson, *In Struggle: SNCC and the Black Awakening of the 1960s* (Cambridge: Harvard University Press, 1981), 34.

12. Interview with Harriet Tanzman, October 15, 1993.

13. By 1956, one-fourth of all urban white college women married while still in college. Elaine Tyler May, *Homeward Bound: American Families in the Cold War Era* (New York: Basic Books, 1988), 79.

14. Wini Breines, *Young, White, and Miserable: Growing Up Female in the 1950s* (Boston: Beacon Press, 1992), 107.

15. Interview with Janice Goodman, October 21, 1993. The rebellion of daughters of the aspiring white middle class against the idea of being "the wife of a house" helped inspire the early moments of second wave feminism. However, the failure to make visible the relationship between such aspirations and Black women's domestic work created tensions in the women's movement.

16. Telephone conversation with Rita Schwerner Bender, February 1994.

17. Edward S. Shapiro, *A Time for Healing: American Jewry since World War II* (Baltimore: Johns Hopkins University Press, 1992), 151.

18. Irving Howe, *World of Our Fathers*, cited in ibid., 152.

19. As recounted during interview with Jacqueline Levine, October 1993.

20. Interview with Miriam Cohen Glickman, February 11, 1994.

21. Interview with Elizabeth Slade Hirschfeld, February 10, 1994.

22. Interview with Elaine DeLott Baker, September 23, 1994.

23. John D'Emilio and Estelle Freedman, *Intimate Matters: A History of Sexuality in America* (New York: Harper & Row, 1988), 282.

24. Interview with June Finer, December 21, 1993.

25. Interview with Roberta Galler, December 10, 1994.

26. McAdam, *Freedom Summer*, 65.

27. Some Jewish women civil rights veterans became lifelong radicals, just getting by with modest wages from progressive organizations.

28. Riv-Ellen Prell, "Why Jewish Princesses Don't Sweat: Desire and Consumption in Postwar American Jewish Culture," in Howard Eilberg-Schwartz, ed., *The People of the Body: Jews and Judaism from an Embodied Perspective* (Albany: SUNY Press, 1993).

29. Excerpt from Strelitz's unpublished memoir, cited in Mary Aickin Rothschild, "White Women Volunteers in the Freedom Summers," *Feminist Studies* 5, no. 3 (fall 1979): 475, emphasis added. Also, see William Chafe, *Never Stop Running: Allard Lowenstein and the Struggle to Save American Liberalism* (New York: Basic Books, 1993), for discussion of Ilene Strelitz and other Allard Lowenstein civil rights protégées.

30. In recounting the story, Goodman said, "So hey, my father was a racist. You know, in his heart of hearts, he ended up being a racist. Not an active racist because he was a jolly person and he was a basically decent person. On a one-to-one [basis], he wouldn't hurt anybody and was good natured. But as a political matter, he was basically a racist." Goodman's distinction between "active racism" and her father's "political racism" is an honest attempt to grapple with the difficult question of Jewish racism. Adrienne Rich also distinguishes forms of racism, (1) active domination and (2) passive collusion; Jews may participate in both forms, as well as in resistance to racism. Jewish racism has its own dynamics. It often derives from a sense of victimization and consequent commitment to protecting oneself and one's family from harm, as with Goodman's father. See Adrienne Rich's classic essay, "Disloyal to Civilization: Feminism, Racism, and Gynephobia," in *On Lies, Secrets, and Silences: Selected Prose, 1966–1978* (New York: Norton, 1979).

31. Interview with Florence Howe, December 1, 1993.

32. I am very grateful to Vivian Leburg Rothstein for sharing her father's letter with me. She subsequently published parts of the letter in "Reunion," *Boston Review* (December/January 1994–95): 8–11, a piece reflecting on her ex-

perience at the 1994 Mississippi Freedom Summer Project 30th Anniversary Reunion.

33. Jonathan Kaufman, *Broken Alliance: The Turbulent Times between Blacks and Jews in America* (New York: Penguin Books, 1988), 93. Kaufman does not state the source of these figures, which are often repeated, as in Shapiro, 223.

34. Steven Lawson, "Freedom Then, Freedom Now: The Historiography of the Civil Rights Movement," *American Historical Review* 96 (April 1991): 456–471.

35. There is a modest literature on efforts by Jewish women's organizations to oppose racism. See Cheryl Greenberg on the National Council of Jewish Women in "Negotiating Coalition: Black and Jewish Civil Rights Agencies in the Twentieth Century," in Salzman and West. Joyce Antler contrasts the NCJW's cautious approach with the antiracist activism of the more working-class and radical Emma Lazarus Federation of Jewish Women's Clubs. Joyce Antler, *The Journey Home: Jewish Women and the American Century* (New York: Free Press, 1997).

36. Critiques of such white feminist historians of the civil rights movement as Sara Evans and Mary Aickin Rothschild, often center on the perception that they focus too much on white women's sexual experiences in the movement. Two forthcoming collections of essays by women veterans of SNCC—one by nine white women and one by an interracial group of fifty authors—will illuminate a broad range of women's experiences in SNCC.

37. Rothschild, "White Women Volunteers in the Freedom Summers," 475.

38. Building on Hasia Diner's insight that Black-Jewish collaboration mixes altruism with self-interest, *Going South* explores some of the "gendered" ways in which joining the civil rights movement helped Jewish American women expand their self-conceptions and life options.

39. Sara Evans, *Personal Politics: The Roots of Women's Liberation in the Civil Rights Movement and the New Left* (New York: Vintage Books, 1980).

40. Clayborne Carson has come the closest to explaining the Black-Jewish alliance in SNCC with his essentially accurate statement that "a number of Blacks and Jews became similarly alienated from prevailing white cultural values to the point that they became more like each other than like the most culturally distinctive members of their own groups." However, an undifferentiated interpretation of this "alienation" does not quite capture the ways in which Jewishness influenced Jewish civil rights activists—before, during, and after the movement—nor does it address issues of gender. See Clayborne Carson, "Blacks and Jews in the Civil Rights Movement: The Case of SNCC," in Jack Salzman et al., eds., *Bridges and Boundaries: African Americans and American Jews* (New York: Braziller, 1992), 38.

41. "Whiteness studies" has now become a multidisciplinary field that includes studies of Jewish "whiteness." Ruth Frankenberg's pioneering ethnography of women's whiteness also notes briefly the social construction of Jewish

whiteness. Karen Brodkin extends this analysis. See Ruth Frankenberg, *White Women, Race Matters: The Social Construction of Whiteness* (Minneapolis: University of Minnesota Press, 1993), 11, 275; and Karen Brodkin, *How Jews Became White Folks and What That Says about Race in America* (New Brunswick: Rutgers University Press, 1998).

42. For an analysis of American Jewish economic success, see Seymour Martin Lipset and Earl Raab, *Jews and the New American Scene* (Cambridge: Harvard University Press, 1997). For the challenges of placing Jews within discussions of multiculturalism, see Biale et al. and Marla Brettschneider, ed., *The Narrow Bridge: Jewish Views on Multiculturalism* (New Brunswick: Rutgers University Press, 1996). The quotation is from David Biale, "The Melting Pot and Beyond: Jews and the Politics of American Identity," in Biale et al., 27–28.

43. Evelyn Torton Beck, "The Politics of Jewish Invisibility," *NWSA Journal* (Autumn 1988); Peskowitz and Levitt; Laura Levitt, *Jews and Feminism: The Ambivalent Search for Home* (New York: Routledge, 1997); Rebecca Alpert, *Like Bread on a Seder Plate: Jewish Lesbians and the Transformation of Tradition* (New York: Columbia University Press, 1997); and Daniel Boyarin and Jonathan Boyarin, eds., *Jews and Other Differences: The New Jewish Cultural Studies* (Minneapolis: University of Minnesota Press, 1998).

44. More traditional scholars and commentators tend to focus anxiously on monitoring Jewish continuity (fear of assimilation). For a critique of dominant trends in discourses on Jewish identity, see Laurence Silberstein, ed., *Mapping Jewish Identities* (New York: New York University Press, 2000).

45. Debra Schultz, *We Didn't Think in Those Terms Then: Narratives of Jewish Women in the Southern Civil Rights Movement, 1960–1966* (diss.) (Ann Arbor: UMI Press, 1995).

46. Melanie Kaye/Kantrowitz issues a ringing call in her essay "To Be a Radical Jew in the Late 20th Century": "Everyone knows that Jews are all over progressive movements, what I've come to think of as the political diaspora. Maybe our task is to ingather the Jews, just a little, into a new civil and human rights coalition, in which we are present and visible as Jews. It means being proud of our collective strength, confident that we can use it right. Someone will always call us pushy. Isn't it time to really push?" Melanie Kaye/Kantrowitz, *The Issue Is Power: Essays on Women, Jews, Violence, and Resistance* (San Francisco: Aunt Lute Foundation Books, 1992), 149.

PART I

TAKING THE ACTION

I

Going South, 1960–1963

Part of the reason I went south so early was because I was romantic. But maybe that's not a bad thing. Maybe more people should be
romantic.   —Dorothy Miller Zellner

WITNESSING THE FOUNDING OF THE STUDENT
NONVIOLENT COORDINATING COMMITTEE (SNCC)

The Greensboro sit-ins signaled a sea change in the civil rights movement, one that veteran Black activist Ella Baker had been preparing for
since her civil rights activism began in the 1930s. Immediately recognizing the radical potential of the student-led sit-ins, Baker called a
meeting of those who had participated in them. Held at Shaw University in North Carolina, April 15–17, 1960, this became the founding convention of the Student Nonviolent Coordinating Committee (SNCC).
The practical and philosophical contribution of Ella Baker to SNCC, the
southern civil rights movement, and the entire student movement cannot be overestimated.[1] Baker asserted that what the movement needed
was "the development of people who are interested not in being leaders as much as in developing leadership among other people."[2]

Baker nurtured this potential in the Black southern student movement. SNCC was created as a coordinating body to bring together and
maximize the effectiveness of the local student movements.[3] Baker, then
fifty-six years old and increasingly frustrated with the hierarchical style
of the Southern Christian Leadership Conference (SCLC), which she
had helped develop, challenged the students to consider the strategic
question "[w]here do we go from here?"[4]

Among white observers from such groups as CORE, the YWCA,
the National Student Association, and nineteen northern colleges, Barbara Jacobs Haber was privileged to witness the birth of SNCC. She
found the convention "an absolutely mind-blowing experience, being

surrounded by people my own age, including Black students, and talking, talking, talking, and singing, singing, singing." More than two hundred student delegates, representing more than fifty colleges and high
schools in thirteen states, attended SNCC's founding conference.[5]
Through Baker's intervention, SNCC managed to stay separate from
more established civil rights groups like SCLC, CORE, and the National
Association for the Advancement of Colored People (NAACP). Rather
than enabling the students to evolve their own styles and strategies, the
larger groups simply wanted to harness students' energies toward the
groups' own goals. Characteristically staying out of the limelight, Baker
nevertheless imbued the students with her own ideals of grassroots
participatory democracy and group-centered leadership.

During the SNCC convention, Jacobs experienced the culture that
would come to characterize the southern movement and SNCC in particular. Staying in local Black homes where "people treated us so won-
derfully," she understood in a new way "the courage of the elders and
the students and the whole enterprise. I just wanted to be a part of it."

Returning to school, Jacobs was fired up to organize with CORE
and among the predominantly Jewish students at Brandeis. One day
she found a little ditty in her university mailbox:

> *There once was a coed in tights*
> *who went in for big racial fights.*
> *She said, I'm not a whore,*
> *I just do it for CORE,*
> *and color's the same without lights.*[6]

The ditty underscores a projection that Jewish women civil rights activists would have to face throughout their movement tenure, especially in the South: that they were promiscuous, seeking, in particular,
interracial sex.

Vowing to return south, Dottie Miller came home from the thrill of
the 1960 New Orleans sit-ins to "a series of awfully boring, horrible jobs
during that winter-spring." A job offer at the New York Department of
Welfare seemed a godsend because her weekly salary of $85 would
allow Miller to get her own apartment. "This was big time," she recalls,
until she got a call from her former professor James Moss. The Southern
Regional Council in Atlanta had just hired Moss and he offered Miller a
research job. In June 1961, "they hired me over the telephone" and she
went to Atlanta immediately. SRC was one of several movement "half-

way houses" that channeled young people into more direct involvement with the southern civil rights movement.[7]

From June until September, Miller worked at the SRC and "tried to work up the nerve to contact SNCC." Even though that was her main motive for going to Atlanta, she "was too awestruck to go over there." Meeting Atlanta activist Julian Bond's sister Jane at SRC gave her an excuse to show up at the SNCC office.

There she encountered the legendary "Miss Baker," as everyone respectfully called her. Baker had provided office space for SNCC in a corner of SCLC's office. Jane Stembridge, a white student from Virginia, became SNCC's first secretary. SNCC historian Clayborne Carson credits Baker and Stembridge with keeping the organization afloat during its first summer of 1960.[8]

In the fall of 1961, James Forman had recently become SNCC's executive secretary. Forman, a Chicago schoolteacher who had already participated in local antiracist activism in the South, had to be pressed into taking the job.[9] The one-room office was tiny, chaotic, and filthy. Forman recalled, "We opened the office at 8:30 a.m. and closed any time after midnight. At first, only Norma [Collins] and I were working there full-time. Occasionally field people would come in and Charles Jones would be there and sometimes then Dorothy Miller . . . and Julian Bond started coming in from time to time to help."[10]

From September to the end of 1961, Miller volunteered for SNCC at night, while working at SRC during the day. Fired by the SRC in early 1962, Miller believes it was because "the FBI came around [mentioning her leftist background]. And of course the SRC claimed it had nothing to do with that, but it did." Thus, Miller, like Jacobs (who had experienced red-baiting in CORE), had to cope with the consequences of her radicalism. The ever-present threat of red-baiting could keep them from doing the work they passionately believed in.

Fortunately for Miller, Forman had been biding his time, offering her (miserably paid) full-time work with SNCC after she left SRC. He had recognized her potential contributions immediately. According to Miller, "Forman was an organizational genius. He could find out in five minutes what you knew how to do, and in his mind he had a place for you to be. . . . He asked me the fateful question, which I teased him about many years later: 'Can you type?'" Like many young Jewish women of her generation admonished by parents to acquire a "marketable skill," Miller could type well. Forman put her to work typing affidavits from field secretaries returning from the front lines. "That was traumatic," she recalls, but she also reveled in the importance of chron-icling the early voter registration efforts of the small SNCC field staff.

"These unbelievable people were sitting next to me saying, 'I took Mrs. Smith to the courthouse in Liberty, Mississippi [to register to vote]' and I'm sitting there typing the whole thing up!'"[11] Such work docu-mented the scope of illegal attempts to deny African Americans the right to vote and helped legitimize SNCC's organizing efforts.

Miller, who soon felt comfortable enough to assert herself, told For-man, "'Not only can I type, I can write too.'" She recalls that instead of patronizing her by saying, "'Oh thank you, little girl,'" Forman imme-diately asked her to work with Julian Bond on SNCC's newspaper, *The Student Voice*. Working together in a small room ("[w]e had a desk right on top of each other"), she and Bond began a lifelong friendship. Across differences of race, religion, and gender, they created an enormously useful medium for communicating SNCC's needs, philosophy, and achievements. Bond, in fact, paid a poetic tribute to Dottie Miller Zell-ner's contributions for her sixtieth birthday in 1998:

> *Our story begins in Atlanta, G A,*
> *Where she first worked for S R C.*
> *But the SNCCers soon beckoned*
> *And Dottie soon reckoned,*
> *where the action was, she'd soon be.*
>
> *Without my being sexist, she whizzed as a typist,*
> *But as writer soon she made her mark.*
> *Composing, designing, refining, defining,*
> *To SNCC she made journalists hark.*
>
> *She gave us a presence, she broke through a blackout,*
> *that hid what we did from the world.*
> *She courted reporters, she told them the news,*
> *And the SNCC story slowly unfurled.*[12]

The Student Voice is one of the primary information sources on SNCC. In the early 1960s, it built community and morale among the movement's widely dispersed field workers and supporters. As SNCC activist Faith Holsaert writes, "*The Student Voice* strengthened my iden-tity as part of the Movement. I often knew about events before I read the *Voice*, but it gave me details and texture, knowledge which I shared with all SNCCs."[13]

At the time of its emergence, *The Student Voice* was one of the few publications reporting on the level of daily violence committed against southern Blacks, as well as movement workers. Forman recalls, "In the early days, our critical weakness was in the area of communications. . . . The mass media of the country printed very little news at that time of what was happening to Black people."[14] Miller helped bring the reality of southern violence to national attention.

Miller also began working on public relations outreach, an important task at that point in SNCC's development. She spent long hours putting out press releases, newsletters, and urgent telegrams to the U.S. Department of Justice, seeking protection for SNCC field workers.[15] When she and Bond were in the office together, they would share this work:

> We'd get a call that "so and so has been arrested." What happened? We would divide up and I would call some people and he would call other people. We'd write the press release, we'd crank it out, do the mimeographing. We would get the Atlanta press on the phone, and I used to call the radio stations and [arrange] hookups. Even then they could tape you on the telephone or do a live [report] on the phone.

Miller's public relations, publicity, and political appeals, like those of many other Jewish women who wrote about the movement and did fund-raising, played a significant though barely recognized role in shaping public perceptions of the movement.[16] With such effective representations of movement work, designed to elicit legal, moral, and financial support, SNCC was able to rise to national prominence quickly.

Miller adapted her skills and drive to this kind of behind-the-scenes role, typical of Jewish women in the movement. She was able to get along well with the early staff under trying conditions in SNCC's one-room quarters because "I had no illusions from the outset that I somehow was a leader of the organization, that I was in charge. I knew perfectly well who was in charge, and I was very honored and happy to be allowed to be there."

Ella Baker's quietly supportive modus operandi and her philosophy of group-centered leadership provided a political rationale that helped Jewish women accept such roles. SNCC's ethic of putting the community before the individual enabled them to create a place for themselves in the most groundbreaking organization of their time.

GETTING ON THE BUS FOR THE FREEDOM RIDES

Performing critical out-of-the-limelight tasks, such as typing affidavits and doing public relations, did not preclude Jewish women from engaging in direct nonviolent confrontational actions, such as the ongoing sit-ins. They also put their bodies on the line in the movement's next and even more confrontational campaign: the Freedom Rides. On May 4, 1961, the first group of thirteen Freedom Riders (three white females, three white males, seven Black male CORE members) left Washington, D.C., for New Orleans in two buses to test a 1960 Supreme Court ruling that banned segregated terminal facilities in intrastate travel.[17] They were met by hostile white crowds in the Deep South.

In Anniston, Alabama, Klan members stopped one of the buses, threw a bomb inside, and attacked the escaping riders as the bus burst into flames. The bus burned to the ground as state troopers took the injured riders to a local hospital. In Birmingham, a white mob met the second bus, attacking and seriously injuring several of the Freedom Riders. When CORE announced it was calling off the rides, Black student leader Diane Nash and a group of SNCC-affiliated students in Nashville, Tennessee, decided to continue them. The designated "riders" endured more violence until the Kennedy administration reluctantly intervened, to prevent further violence and direct confrontation between the federal government and racist southern officials.[18]

Determined to draw national attention to their protest, the riders on the first two buses who were arrested in Jackson, Mississippi, did not pay fines or post bond but stayed in jail for thirty-nine days, the maximum time they could serve and still appeal their convictions for "breach of peace." To maximize the impact of its campaign, CORE decided to fill the jails and so put out a national call for Freedom Riders. By the end of the summer of 1961, 328 had been arrested in Jackson; two-thirds were college students. Three-fourths of the 328 Freedom Riders were men; half were Black.[19] Among the Black women were leaders like Ruby Doris Smith of Atlanta. Among the white women who revered them were a number of Jewish women, including recent University of Chicago graduate Carol Ruth Silver.

On June 4, 1961, three weeks after the first Freedom Rides, Silver went south for the first time, stopping in Richmond, Virginia. Before meeting her team of Freedom Riders, she stayed overnight with Sue

Harmann, one of two white women on the third Freedom Ride from Birmingham to Montgomery. She told Silver about the white mob that ambushed and attacked everyone on the bus, regardless of race, age, or gender. Undeterred, Silver moved on to meet her fellow Freedom Riders in Nashville. She went with the knowledge that her presence as a white woman—and the only woman—riding with a biracial team of male students was certain to inflame the white racists waiting in Jackson.

On June 6, Silver waited in the Nashville SNCC office to meet her fellow Freedom Riders—three Black male college students from the University of Virginia and two white male divinity students from Yale University. She listened there to the "war stories" of the Fisk University students who had participated in some of the first sit-ins and Freedom Rides.

Silver and her five male colleagues left the Trailways bus station at 1:15 A.M. in the presence of a lone United Press International reporter. They stopped for breakfast in Memphis, but Silver sat by herself because they did not want any trouble before arriving in Jackson. In her "Diary of a Freedom Rider," she writes, "We were afraid that if there was anything liable to [create an incident], it was a white girl sitting with Negro men. Southerners are so chivalrous!" [20]

They reached Jackson at 1:10 P.M. Uniformed police and a few reporters and bus drivers were waiting in the station. The group allowed all the other passengers to disembark first, shook hands with one another, and then moved on toward their destinations—the Blacks to the waiting room marked "White intrastate," and the whites to the "Colored intrastate." A reporter said to Silver, "We were told there was a white woman in the group, but that she probably wouldn't go through with it." Silver pushed past him contemptuously.

Inside, their "reception committee was more police, all of them white, all armed, all looking terribly serious." Then, in an elaborately choreographed scene, the police asked the young people if they would move on. Refusing, they were arrested and taken to jail. When a reporter asked the policemen how many Freedom Riders there were, one answered, "There's three Black niggers and three white niggers." Silver had stepped over the line deemed appropriate for women by southern white "chivalry." For that moment, at least, her gender and race mattered less than her politics. By virtue of her action, she was identified as a "nigger." [21]

SURVIVING IN JAIL

Arriving at the prison, Silver shook hands with her male comrades, who were taken to segregated men's cells. She was photographed and fingerprinted, deprived of her personal possessions, and locked in a cell labeled "adult white female." In Mississippi's segregated prison system, her race and gender once again did matter.

Silver soon met with Jack Young, one of Mississippi's premier Black civil rights lawyers. Then she made her one permitted telephone call, collect to her mother. She recalls, "Up to this point she had been with me all the way, but when this call came through, her anxiety got the better of her. I talked and she cried about ten dollars' worth. Then I was conducted back to my cell."

For the first two days, Silver shared a cell with a southern white woman there for rowdy drinking. On June 8, 1961, however, four new young women (whom she refers to as "girls" in her diary) were thrown into the cell. They also were Freedom Riders: Helene Wilson, 26, from Washington, D.C.; Teri Perlman, 19, from New York City; Joan Trumpauer, 19, from Macon, Georgia; and Jane Rossett, 18, from Durham, North Carolina. The six women shared a cell measuring 13 by 15 feet, including a 4-by-6-feet shower. During the day, detectives questioned the women, asking Silver if she had ever dated Negro boys and if she would be willing to marry one. She defiantly told them yes, that she had been engaged to a Negro boy once—a lie. They inquired into her religious beliefs and were intrigued with her self-definition as agnostic, a term new to them.

After what Silver describes as a four-minute hearing, the five women were convicted of breach of peace and sentenced to four months in jail, two suspended, and a $200 fine. They were moved across the street to the Hinds County Jail, to a cell even smaller than the cell they had occupied in the Jackson City Jail. They shared that cell with two white women arrested for drinking and another Freedom Rider, Betsy Wychoff. Wychoff, forty-six, a former Mount Holyoke College professor, had been the only white woman Freedom Rider in jail prior to Silver's arrest.

On the afternoon of June 9, jailers threw in two more mattresses and two more Freedom Riders, Del Greenblatt, a Cornell University student in medieval history, and Winona Beamer, from Dayton, Ohio. One week later, there were fourteen white women Freedom Riders sharing the cell. The newcomers included Lee Berman, 18; Claire O'Connor, a 27-

hunger strike

year-old nurse; Kathy Pleune, 21; Jo Adler, from the University of Wisconsin; Kay Kittle, from Oklahoma; and Elizabeth Slade Hirschfeld, from Cornell University. Silver's diary points out that more than half the women in the cell were Jewish.[22]

On June 13, the three cells of women (one for whites; two for Blacks) discussed going on a hunger strike to protest the stated intention of sending the male Freedom Riders to Parchman Prison (the state penitentiary), where, it was rumored, they would be put to picking cotton. When the women learned on June 14 that the young men were taken to Parchman, they decided "to go on a hunger strike until either the boys come back or we are sent there." They elected Pauline Knight (a Black woman) to speak for the hunger strikers in all three cells. Long before the advent of widespread feminist consciousness, these women were united in their belief that they should not be treated differently than the male activists.

One of the immediate effects of the hunger strike was that Winona Beamer passed out and was unconscious for a short while. After the young women complained and screamed, the jailer called a doctor, who gave her a respiratory stimulant. In her diary, Silver notes, "After a while she was okay. Still weak, but able to sit up and make [self-deprecating] comments about *zaftig* [Yiddish for "plump, buxom, well-rounded"] girls who faint when they don't eat for a day."

NEGOTIATING CULTURAL CLASHES

The brief hunger strike also caused conflict between Pauline Knight and some of the white Jewish women. After hearing lawyer Jack Young's advice that hunger strikes would do no good, Knight decided that the strike should be called off and announced that to the other two cells. Ruby Doris Smith's cell decided almost immediately to follow suit, but the white women's cell had a long and "upsetting meeting" to discuss whether or not they too would do so.

Most of the white women resented Pauline Knight for not consulting with the other groups before telling the jailers about the strike and then for deciding to end the strike. Silver notes in her diary:

> We had all felt very strongly that the spokesman for the strike and the leadership from it should come from one of the Negro girls rather than from one of us in this cell, but we also felt that as individuals equally

with them involved in a democratic movement, we had at least the right to be treated equally.

Georgian Joan Trumpauer, a devout white Christian, tried to mediate the conflict. She explained to the other white women that lawyers carried great weight with Black southern students in the movement, so that when Jack Young said there was no point to the strike, they decided to call it off. Trumpauer also said of Knight's refusal to give a statement to the jailers about the reasons for the strike that Knight had felt that any statement would have gotten no further than the jailers

> except in the form of garbled and perverted releases to the local press. [Trumpauer] explained that the civil rights movement had a firmly religious nature with Gandhi's principles of nonviolence and passive resistance grafted onto Christian morality and brotherly love. Pauline, firmly rooted in these principles, felt that no other decision was possible, that this should be obvious to everyone, and that discussion was not only unnecessary but ridiculous.

Winona Beamer, one of those angry at not being consulted about the hunger strike, objected that she was not interested in mystic faith in a movement that precluded democratic processes, that what had happened was at odds with what she had thought she had committed herself to for the summer. Silver pointed out that the difference between the two attitudes was philosophical.

Silver explained that the civil rights movement was spearheaded in the North by the American Civil Liberties Union (ACLU), which deemed it a "distinctly individualistic and libertarian fight for civil rights." Led by the Southern Christian Leadership Conference (SCLC), in the South the movement was religious, based on love and brotherhood, with nonviolence as a tactic.

Struggling to understand the differences between her fellow Freedom Riders, Silver wrote to her mother on June 18:

> Only one of the girls here is a real Southerner, Joan Trumpauer. The rest of us are damn Yankees. Joan told us some of the experiences she has had on picket lines and sit-ins, and distinguished for us our own liberal, intellectual commitment to the civil rights movement from that of the Negro girls in the other cells, almost all of whom were inspired with the religious aspects of this movement and who had come to

Jackson prepared to suffer anything—mobs, beatings, death itself—before turning back.[23]

Silver's diary charts her efforts to accept her place in the movement. She wrote that northern, liberal, democratic whites are welcomed by the Negro movement in the South, but "they must recognize that it is essentially both Negro and Southern, that they may join, but must not attempt to lead it."[24]

On June 21, four more Freedom Riders, from California, were added to the whites' cell, bringing the number to eighteen. There was not enough room for all the mats on the floor, so they slept three women to two mats, and five to four mats. The same day the Black women in two cells of six and seven each were put into a single cell to free the second for a drunken white woman, presumably to protect her from both racial and political contamination.

The young women entertained themselves in jail by reading, exercising, studying ballet steps called out by Del Greenblatt, and playing chess on a set Silver had fashioned from pieces of white bread. For the ballet class, "six of us hung on the bars and onto the wall doing pliés and relevés," notes Silver in her diary. Betsy Wychoff taught them Greek; someone else, French. At one point they had a party where they did folk dances, including the *hora* (a Jewish folk dance). Having timed her anticipated jail stay to fit into the summer before law school, Silver enjoyed the irony (and privilege) of mailing her financial aid applications with the return address "Hinds County Jail, Jackson, Mississippi."

On June 23, the jailers added two more white women Freedom Riders to their cell of eighteen. That same day came the news they had been anxiously awaiting: they were going to be transported to Parchman Prison, where the male Freedom Riders were being held. Silver describes the four-hour ride to Parchman in the hot paddy wagon as more frightening than any previous part of the whole jail experience. Twenty-three girls, white and Black, were crowded into a truck with no springs:

> [It] bounced along towards an unknown future. Many of us had black and blue marks when we arrived because the drivers delighted in stopping and starting suddenly which threw us against each other and the sharp corners of the seats. But the most terrifying part of the ride was the three occasions when the driver suddenly jolted off to the side of the highway and stopped. We imagined every horror from a waiting ambush of the Ku Klux Klan to mined roads.

In the maximum security unit at Parchman, the women were less crowded and better fed, but they lived in a more menacing environment. One incident affected both Silver and Hirschfeld profoundly; Ruby Doris Smith was physically abused by jailers for refusing to take a shower unless she was given shoes to prevent her from getting athlete's foot. Three women guards took her to the shower area in handcuffs, put her in the shower, and scrubbed her with a floor brush, concentrating especially on sensitive areas of the skin. They also knocked her down a few times while holding onto the handcuffs. At this time, Smith was suffering from a bad case of ulcers and vomiting after every meal.

When Smith returned from the shower, Silver and her cellmates were "burning with anger and frustration" at the sight of the dark welts on her wrists. Then Ruby's voice came from her cell, where she was lying down. She spoke of Christian brotherhood and love, and "how we must not hate because that is victory for the evil forces which we are fighting. She talked of mental nonviolence, which is just as important as physical nonviolence—a returning love for hate, sympathy for oppression." It was very hard for Silver to accept this approach, but she spent a lot of time thinking about it.

Several weeks later, when she had been freed and was asked to give a speech about her experience, Silver recounted what she had learned from Ruby Doris Smith in jail:

> We were furious, we were outraged, we were seething with anger. But she, from the depth of her belief in nonviolence as a way of life, as well as a policy as expedient action, from her deep commitment to tenets of Christianity and the brotherhood of all mankind—it was she who ministered to our pain, it was she who urged us not to feel so badly about her beating, it was she who turned this physical defeat into a victory of love over violence and oppression.

Young Jewish women like Silver, raised in progressive Jewish households, had to make a major cultural leap to understand and embrace nonviolent passive resistance. Progressive Jewish culture valued active Jewish rebellion against oppressors—whether in Egypt or in the labor movement. "Love-thy-neighbor does not come easily to me," Silver writes in her diary.[25]

So Silver attempted to bring her own heritage in line with what was required of her as a civil rights activist. In a letter from jail, Silver asked her mother not to worry about her.

> If I have a social conscience, I inherited it from you, and if I must speak out for the causes of justice, freedom and truth, I learned to do so from you. You must not fear for me when I am in physical danger. It is better that I live a shorter or longer life and live it well and fully than that I live to senility from vain and meaningless existence. But forgive me for being so serious. I love you. Carol.

On July 11, 1961, eight new female Freedom Riders came to Parchman, bringing news that bail was going to be available to some of the women who had been in longer. On July 15, Silver was part of a group that was released. She recalls joyfully, "We were taken to the house of Reverend Mays where some of the church ladies had prepared a dinner of fried chicken, cole slaw, potato salad, the works. . . . Then these wonderful ladies of Jackson treated each girl to a hairdressing in the beauty shop around the corner. It made me feel like I belonged to the human race again."

Founded by Clarie Collins Harvey, Womanpower Unlimited organized this caring treatment. Present when the first Freedom Riders went to trial, Harvey quickly organized women from local churches to support the riders. Womanpower Unlimited grew into an interracial group of three hundred women who provided food, clothes, blankets, and other necessities to the jailed Freedom Riders. They also contacted parents and provided housing for freed activists.

Southern Black women were among the few who welcomed the civil rights activists into their homes like family. When they were released from jail, one of the Black Freedom Riders, Shirley Thompson, invited Silver to stay with her family in New Orleans. Silver created quite a stir as the only white person in the Black neighborhood.

In New Orleans, Silver called a Jewish relative who owned a drugstore there. "He wanted me to come and see him . . . until, that is, he found out that I would be accompanied by a couple of Negro girls. We left it that he would come over to Shirley's house and see me when he got through work, but of course he did not come." Most southern Jewish small-business owners, like Silver's uncle, felt their vulnerability as outsiders keenly. As we will see in chapter 3, the vast majority kept as far away from the civil rights movement as possible. In contrast,

Womanpower Unlimited defied "stereotypes of gender, social class, and race . . . [and] effectively mustered support for the Freedom Riders at a time when it was unpopular if not dangerous to do so."[26]

Silver describes her visit to her own family at home as "a quintessentially Jewish reunion. . . . I felt like the prodigal returned, and the whole family killed a fatted Chinese dinner in my honor." Apparently, the ritual eating of Chinese food made it a "a quintessentially Jewish reunion."

On August 13, Silver and a number of other early Freedom Riders went back to Jackson for their trial. Silver felt a great deal of confidence in their lawyer, William Kunstler. "Aside from the fact that he was both concise and precise, he looked something like my father." In Jackson, she also "saw Jean Kitwell and Rose Rosenberg, the two female attorneys from Los Angeles, and got their confirmation that Kunstler seemed to be fully in control."[27] It must have been comforting for young Jewish civil rights workers to see progressive Jewish "elders" involved in the cause.

Local activists held a mass meeting in Jackson to honor the Freedom Riders. In her speech, Clarie Collins Harvey announced that Womanpower Unlimited was going to work on literacy and voter registration. Silver expressed gratitude for what the organization had done for the women in jail and said admiringly of Harvey, "[T]o me she represented the whole of what I had come to Jackson for, the essence of the civil rights movement and of the validity of Northern participation in essentially a Southern fight."[28]

Northern Jewish women internalized the validation they received from local communities in ways that reinforced and furthered their activist commitments. After returning to the University of Chicago for law school, Silver recruited fellow students to go to the South each summer to work with the NAACP, the Lawyers Constitutional Defense Committee, and other legal organizations working on civil rights.

In 1963, during her second summer of law school, Silver attempted to take a job in South Africa offered by one of her professors. Because of her "criminal record" as a Freedom Rider, she could not get a visa. Not one to be daunted by obstacles, she wrote to all the English-language law firms in Africa requesting a summer job and ended up in Kampala, Uganda.

Upon her graduation in 1964, Silver pursued a one-year internship sponsored by the Law Students Civil Rights Research Council (LSCRC). She went south again, this time to North Carolina to work with civil rights lawyer Floyd McKissick, who later became the head of CORE. When McKissick saw that she could manage the office ("it was just my kind of general pushiness"), he "took the opportunity to travel around the state trying civil rights cases and protecting civil rights workers who were being harassed and arrested." Like a number of Jewish women, Silver's managerial prowess eventually gave her extraordinary access to the kind of meaningful civil rights work to which she aspired.

TESTING THE LIMITS IN THE ALBANY MOVEMENT

After the mass participation of the sit-ins and the Freedom Rides, a small group of SNCC workers went to smaller Black communities to test the two major strategies of the southern movement: nonviolent direct action and voter registration. Late in the summer of 1961, Bob Moses established the first such SNCC project in McComb, Mississippi, one of the poorest areas in the state. Moses, a twenty-six-year-old Harlem native and Harvard graduate, had already visited this part of Mississippi to meet longtime activist Amzie Moore at the urging of his mentor, Ella Baker. A SNCC leader who shunned the spotlight, as Baker did, Moses would provide a model of radical activism tempered by a loving spirit that would inspire and sustain those who worked with him. At this point, SNCC workers and staff "began to see themselves, and were seen by others, as a unique group within the civil rights movement. They were courageous and dedicated organizers, with a revolutionary élan if not a revolutionary ideology."[29] For the first time, northern Black and white students began to work in the field with "local people," the real backbone of the movement.

In the fall of 1961, two SNCC field secretaries—Freedom Rider Cordell Reagon and divinity student Charles Sherrod—arrived in Albany, Georgia. The stakes were high in what would become the Albany Movement because this was the first attempt to attack all forms of racial domination in one location and to involve large numbers of community people in nonviolent direct action certain to result in arrest. That year it was the greatest mass movement in the entire South.[30]

In Albany, during the following summer of 1962, SNCC had a precursor of the much larger 1964 Mississippi Summer Project, with a few northern students coming down to work in southwest Georgia. Among them was Peggy Damond, a young Black woman whom Faith Holsaert knew from the Harlem Brotherhood, an interracial group of students who worked against housing discrimination. Holsaert stayed in New York that summer doing fund-raising and making phone calls for SNCC. However, when, at the end of the summer, three churches were burned in southwest Georgia, Holsaert decided to go south. As she recalls, in the autumn of 1962, "Albany had, not long before I was arrested, erupted in the first mass marching kinds of demonstrations which became a pattern in other parts of the South."

In *While We Were Singing*, Holsaert describes her first two weeks in Georgia, where she met some of her coworkers, including Freedom Singers Rutha Mae Harris (Louise in her story) and Bernice Johnson Reagon, who had been expelled from Albany State College in December 1961 for student activism.[31] Holsaert arrived after a successful bus boycott and a conflict about how to conduct the Albany Movement between SNCC and the more-established SCLC, led by Martin Luther King Jr. A gentle and relatively shy person, Holsaert had to find the right way to enter the SNCC community in Albany.

> A girl who looked to be my age came and sat in the Freedom House kitchen. Without saying a word, she read the newspaper, sweat rolling down her throat. "Look at that—Compton State, threatening to put out more students, like they did us," she fumed. Her eyes met mine. "Louise," she said, "my name's Louise," and she shot me a smile through a mouth of crowded teeth.
>
> "What's yours?" she asked. She dropped the ash off the end of her cigarette, and I thought how pretty a heavy girl's hand can be. We both knew she knew who I was, the only white girl in the Movement in southern Georgia.[32]

Although Penny Patch, another white woman organizer, was the first white woman field-worker in the early southwest Georgia movement, Holsaert almost always worked in settings where she *was* the only white woman present. In Albany, Holsaert worked on a voter registration campaign that involved canvassing, record keeping, and working with high school students.

Because Albany was the center of the southwest Georgia project (headed by Charles Sherrod), the Albany staff also dealt with the U.S. Department of Justice, the newspapers, and the Atlanta SNCC office. Holsaert recalls, "There was a fair amount of telephone work and report writing and that kind of stuff." One of the few times Holsaert remembers rebelling was when Sherrod told her to do bookkeeping and she said he was discriminating against her because she was female. Sherrod said he wasn't discriminating because nobody wanted to keep the books.

Aside from the minor controversy, Holsaert emphasizes that her experience (and that of women who worked in the movement before the 1964 Summer Project) was much more egalitarian than has generally been portrayed. Holsaert has stated, "My quarrel with [historian Sara] Evans and what I understand her thesis to be is that her work reflects neither the complexity and the power of the SNCC experience for women, nor does it reflect the genuine anti-sexist stands taken by many of our brothers."

She continues:

> I think particularly of my program director, Charley Sherrod, sexist to the core, and yet it was Charley who said, "Faith, I don't care whether you grew up in Greenwich Village where no one drives a car. To be a soldier among equals in this movement, you must learn to drive a car. Faith, I don't care whether you want to speak in mass meetings. Soldiers in this army are public speakers, and so you must learn to do this."[33]

The need to get a learner's permit led to another incident Holsaert recalls:

> I walked into this long narrow cinder block building that was divided down the middle with just a piece of twine and white people were on one side and Black people were on the other. I just couldn't bear to walk down the white side so I went down the Black side and got a so-called "colored" permit. Then he [Sherrod] wouldn't let me use it because he thought it would be even worse to have me picked up and have the wrong race on my permit. So actually, I never did learn to drive that year.

In her description of the incident, Holsaert conveyed her revulsion at being confronted with a physical manifestation of segregation. Rather than being channeled into collusion with this system, she re-categorized herself racially. This symbolic action was more important to her in that moment than the pragmatic need to get a driver's license. It was in keeping with the spirit of Sherrod's philosophy of interracialism. "As in Albany, Sherrod continued in rural Georgia to stress the symbolic importance of the actions of his staff." Sherrod believed in interracial teams of civil rights workers because he wanted to "free southern blacks from their fear of whites."[34]

As a member of such a team in the spring of 1963, Holsaert went to work in Terrell County with Prathia Hall, a Black woman SNCC staffer from Philadelphia. They lived and worked closely with Carolyn Daniels, a hairdresser and a formidable organizer, "who was really the center of SNCC activity in Terrell County. Carolyn's house was shot into in the summer before I got there. . . . We couldn't have made any inroads in Terrell County without her support. She was one of the local leaders who just was invaluable. She knew everybody and everybody knew who she was. She had grown up in the county. She's very, very feisty."

Holsaert's short story "Moving Fast" illuminates some of the challenges and joys of being one of the very few white women working in the field in the pre-1964 southern civil rights movement.[35] The story begins with Rachel (based on Holsaert) and Augusta (based on Hall) making humble organizing inroads with a small but promising group of citizens willing to try to register to vote. When their program director calls them back, the two women are sorry to leave but obey orders. The movement needs more "bodies" for major demonstrations.

After admonishing her to "get that wild Jew hair up," Shephard, a minister and project director (based loosely on Sherrod), tells Rachel in preparation for a demonstration in which they'd be arrested, "[w]hen they call for marchers from the pulpit, don't you be among the first or among the last. . . . You're the only white woman, and don't you forget it for your own good." Rachel replies, "How could I?"

This consciousness of her vulnerability becomes more poignant when Rachel is arrested and separated from her Black movement coworkers in the segregated jail. Surrounded by five hostile policemen, with her friends screaming from their cells to try to protect her, Rachel summons all her inner reserves to maintain the open, loving stance toward her jailers that the movement asks of her.

> One of them moved toward her. His legs brushed hers as his hand patted her breasts. Reaching inside her brassiere, he removed her cigarettes and toothbrush. She could smell the skin of his hand. Rachel. Rachel. Rachel. Screams continued from the cell block. He ran his hand over her ribs. She looked full in his face.

They shrieked. They shook the jailhouse bars. Her cigarettes and toothbrush lay on the desk. His hand moved down to her hips, paused on the fastening of her skirt. Below, she wore nothing but cotton panties.

The policeman searching her was her height. He had beautiful skin, the color of tea with milk in it, and hair that had been peppered with silver. He wore a wedding band. Time to look in his eyes. Breathe easy. She was handling herself poorly. Breathe easy. Open and absorb. She could do it.

The people whistled, shrieking whistles, and pounded cups, and screamed her name.

His hand slipped inside the skirt.

'Stop,' said one of the men.

He continued to reach inside.

The other policeman moved.

'Stop,' they said.

He withdrew his hand.

'Take her back to the cell, boys,' the Chief grumbled.

She was led through a barred door back to the concrete corridor.

'She's coming.' The word passed.

Rachel raised her head.

Through an open door, she saw hundreds of dark hands draped through tiers of bars. 'She's coming.'

Later, the same policeman touches her cheek with his club through the cell bars. His harassing questions reveal the contempt in which white male southerners held white women who dared to be allies of Blacks. "You pregnant girl? . . . You white or colored bitch? Let's go in there and get her." Any white woman who is an ally of Blacks must be sexually promiscuous, running from trouble in her own community, or racially mixed. Knowing the dangers of interracial relationships in the South, both Faith and her character Rachel choose a year of "front-line chastity," necessary in what was akin to a state of war. As was true in the South one hundred years earlier, the sight of a Black man with a white woman could endanger the man's life.

Though the calls of her coworkers and fear of negative publicity keep Rachel from being sexually abused by the cops, she struggles inwardly with fear and self-doubt. "She wished she could weave a peace like that of [fellow movement workers], the Calloways, about

her. Contradictorily, she also longed to wreak vengeance on every policeman who had bothered her the night before." Meeting violence
with "Christian" love was a basic tenet of the movement, one that
was not part of the culture of northern Jewish volunteers.

Holsaert struggled with the same feelings that Carol Ruth Silver experienced when Ruby Doris Smith was beaten in jail during the freedom rides. Dottie Miller Zellner, who also had to face violence "nonvi-
olently," describes her concept of Judaism: "People were out to get you,
they were going to kill you and it was a mark of honor to fight back, yes,
to resist." Such a concept made it difficult to stand still and accept abuse
in jail and demonstrations. And yet, because they knew it was not their
movement, Jewish women accepted the discipline and strategies of
Black leaders, based on what James Cone calls "A Black Theology of
Liberation."[36]

Such a theology had to provide comfort in the early movement,
when there were few concrete victories on the ground, particularly in
Albany, where the federal government prosecuted civil rights workers
and not those who were violating the law and terrorizing people. What
also compensated northerners like Holsaert was the sense of interracial
community and shared struggle expressed, for example, in the warmth
of the local Black women who fed her, took care of her when she was
sick, and "watched her back" in dangerous situations. "The people that
I was closest to on a day-to-day basis were people in the community,
most of whom were women." In her story "Freedom Rider," she writes:
"We had to protect one another in a deep sense, regardless of the daily
bump and grind of sheriffs and feds, understanding we could never
protect one another from the physical blows." She writes lyrically,
"There's a public record. And there's a record in our bodies, in our
hearts, river shadows below rock cuts, dark moats in the sun."[37]

One night, while sleeping in the Freedom House, Holsaert saw a
man's face outside her bedroom window. She told her coworkers and
scrambled onto the floor. He smashed the window and reached through
it to feel for her on the bed. Finally he left. But in her 1993 story, Holsaert
writes, "Over the years I have maintained my composure, but that
scream I didn't scream that night has never stopped swelling. Doctor
calls it reflux. I call it that unscreamed scream. . . . I am who I am because
I am still there." Later she reflects, "I have been afraid much of my life,
even though I have done some courageous things."[38]

Ill with hepatitis, Holsaert returned home after a year in the South.
Although she was "pretty traumatized" by having been ill and afraid

for much of the year, she regrets not staying. She remembers feeling very gratified when Sherrod said "that I had become a valuable staff member." The transition back to college was very difficult. Working on the SNCC staff in New York helped maintain some connection.

During the time Holsaert was in Terrell County, Joni Rabinowitz joined the Albany Movement. Daughter of radical lawyer Victor Rabinowitz, she was a student at Antioch College and went to Georgia after spring break in 1963. She was the only white defendant in the "Albany Nine," a group of movement activists indicted by the federal government for allegedly conspiring to picket the store of a white juror who voted against a civil suit brought by a Black prisoner against a local racist sheriff. In the federal indictment, Rabinowitz was painted as the ringleader of the Albany Movement because of her father's "alleged Communist past." This was another of J. Edgar Hoover's attempts to discredit the movement, with the complicity of the Kennedys, who wanted to quell southern fears about their support of Black rights. Among the lawyers briefing the defendants was a young Jewish woman law clerk and future member of the U.S. House of Representatives, Elizabeth Holtzman. Filling in at one meeting for movement attorney C. B. King, Holtzman almost got indicted herself.[39]

Faith Holsaert recalls that when Joni Rabinowitz joined the SNCC staff, the Albany Movement was almost totally male. Rabinowitz turned out a "stinging series of reports" to indicate that as early as 1963, women were critical of their being relegated to second-class status in SNCC. She wrote in one report, "The attitude around here toward keeping the [freedom] house neat (as well as the general attitude toward the inferiority and 'proper place' of women) is disgusting and also terribly depressing."[40] Holsaert remembers that when Rabinowitz arrived,

> she found the restrictions on her movements really onerous. . . . They seemed very functional to me. They seemed to make sense but she felt they were onerous. I think she had a set of sensitivities in terms of what people might be feeling about her presence. She may not have been as aware of how it really was inflammatory for young white women to be living with Black people. I don't know what experience Joni brought to that situation. In some ways, she may have been a more assertive person than I was, but at that point, looking back on it, I think the fact that I was quite soft spoken and quiet acted to my advantage in the sense that it gave me more time to factor in what other people were thinking and feeling.[41]

Miriam Cohen, who joined the Albany Movement that summer of 1963, was in jail with Joni Rabinowitz and seven other white women (in a cell meant for four). She recalls that Rabinowitz

> had been down for a while and was due to leave in a week to go see her boyfriend up the East Coast. She was desperate to get out and she talked all of us into going on a hunger strike because she figured we'd get out faster. So there I was, the last one arrested because I hadn't wanted to leave the Freedom House, and they all announced to me that it was my choice, but that they were all on a hunger strike.

Cohen could not bring herself to "eat in front of them, so I went on this hunger strike. It was horrible. I had cramps for the whole week. I remember my trial. C. B. King was the lawyer and the judge put his head down and went to sleep for forty minutes."[42]

Cohen's father, editor of the *National Jewish Post and Opinion*, had been dismayed about her going to Albany. Nevertheless, he did fly down during the hunger strike and was terribly scared when he first saw his daughter: "I must have weighed just over 100 normally then and I lost 10 or 11 pounds. As a mother now, I can tell you that that would be very scary. As a young woman of twenty-one, I was not at all worried. I was totally unsympathetic to his fears." Despite his ambivalence, her father helped break the national press silence on the Albany trials. The visibility that Cohen's father helped create for the Albany Movement came at a turning point for SNCC. Critical confrontations were heating up in several places.

DEMONSTRATING IN DANVILLE

One of the most volatile movement sites in that period was the textile town of Danville, Virginia. The Danville movement aimed to secure equal access to municipal jobs for Blacks. On June 10, 1963, a day known as "Bloody Monday," police used clubs and fire hoses to attack demonstrators who were praying at City Hall. Dottie Miller, who had been clubbed, was the first to call a report into SNCC's Atlanta office. In one of the most brutal police actions in the movement up to that point, forty-eight of the sixty-five demonstrators were hurt.[43]

Miller was in Danville to write a pamphlet about the movement there for SNCC. When asked how she got the nerve to be the only white person in a march with sixty-five Black people in a movement already known to be dangerous, she says:

> I didn't have any more nerve than they did because I was the only white person. That's what I am trying to say. I had as much nerve as they had. In fact, some of them had much more nerve than I had because after all, I was going to leave there. I had already graduated from college. I was not likely to be going on welfare. The fact that I was there with sixty-five Black people was a moment of total, thrilling pride for me.[44]

Miller was not really thinking of danger when she participated in the first demonstration in Danville. It was night and "all of a sudden, the hoses came on and then a cop hit me over the head with a club but I really didn't know he was going to do that. I'll never forget this guy— he hit me when I was down. I weighed 106 pounds. I was lying on the ground. What was I going to do to him?"

Despite the experience, Miller returned a few days later with SNCC executive secretary James Forman and several hundred demonstrators. They vowed to stay all night on the front steps of City Hall. On the steps, Miller clutched a rail with all her might, looking at the coiled high-volume fire hoses, waiting to be killed. She felt certain that something terrible was going to happen; it was not the way she had felt in earlier demonstrations. She credits Forman with saving their lives because he stepped right in front of the police and asked what was going on, thereby defusing the situation.

Miller and SNCC photographer Danny Lyon attended a mass meeting the final evening they were in Danville and learned that the police and a tank were waiting up the road. According to Lyon, "The SNCC staff, divided by sex and packed into two cars, were the last to leave. . . . The police, having beaten up so many demonstrators had now turned to the state National Guard for more powerful weapons. They had also buried the entrance to the police station with sandbags. The more violence they committed, the more violence they seemed to expect."[45]

The police stopped the SNCC cars, and the passengers stood spread-eagled against the vehicles as men holding shotguns searched them. Lyon, who is Jewish, thought of Camus's description of the execution of French Resistance workers who were told to run into a field as Nazis shot them. The Danville police allowed them to pass but that night issued warrants for the arrest of twenty-two SNCC workers under a state law passed after Nat Turner's rebellion and used to hang John Brown. Lyon and Miller were among those indicted for "inciting the colored population to acts of war and violence against the white population." Lyon writes that at the time, the "crime" was punishable by death. Dottie Miller Zellner recalls that the penalty was five years in prison. Either way, the prospects were frightening.

Forman told Lyon and Miller to return immediately to the Atlanta office. The next morning, they climbed out the back window of the church where the SNCC workers were under siege. A movement woman arrived in a large, pink Cadillac to drive them to the airport. Lying on the floor of the car, covered with newspapers and blankets, Miller began to laugh hysterically. That crazy laughter brought to mind her mother, who found disaster funny. "[T]hat was one of the times I laughed the hardest in my whole life." Although they made it out of Danville safely, she never traveled through Virginia after that because she was, technically, a fugitive from justice.

Danville, Virginia, was just one of many movement sites where SNCC activism came alive in 1963. That year was a turning point for the organization. In the period from May to September, thousands were arrested in communities across the South. SNCC's 1963 income was $309,000, supporting a staff of 12 office workers, 60 field secretaries, and 121 full-time volunteers (staff and field secretaries lived on $10 a week). By August 1963 (the month of Dr. King's March on Washington), SNCC had established projects in Danville, Virginia; southwest Georgia; Selma, Alabama; Pine Bluff, Arkansas, and more than a dozen Mississippi communities. The increasing focus on Mississippi toward the end of the year turned up the heat during a period that historian Taylor Branch has called "The Firestorm."[46]

During this period, Jewish women activists continued to play a vital role in SNCC and in movement projects independent of SNCC. Their participation as the movement intensified in Mississippi would place them at the center of SNCC's greatest victories and most vexing challenges.

NOTES

1. See Charles Payne, "Men Led, but Women Organized: Movement Participation of Women in the Mississippi Delta," in Vicki L. Crawford, Jacqueline Anne Rouse, and Barbara Woods, eds., *Women in the Civil Rights Movement:*

Trailblazers and Torchbearers, 1941–1965 (Brooklyn: Carlson Publishing, 1990), 1–11; and Sara Evans, *Personal Politics*. Though most historians agree that Baker was a catalyst in the founding of SNCC, a full description of her involvement may be found in Joanne Grant, *Ella Baker: Freedom Bound* (New York: Wiley, 1998), and Barbara Ransby's forthcoming biography.

2. Carson, *In Struggle*, 20.

3. Morris, 215.

4. Grant, 126.

5. Rhoda Lois Blumberg, *Civil Rights: The 1960s Freedom Struggle* (Boston: Twayne Publishers, 1991), 77; and Grant, 127–128.

6. Interview with Barbara Jacobs Haber, February 20, 1994.

7. Morris, 140.

8. Carson, *In Struggle*, 26.

9. Ibid., 42–43.

10. James Forman, *The Making of Black Revolutionaries* (New York: Macmillan, 1972), 241.

11. Powledge, 526–527.

12. Cited with Julian Bond's permission.

13. Faith S. Holsaert, "Resistance U," unpublished essay; used with author's permission.

14. Forman, 241–242.

15. Powledge, 526–527.

16. Similarly, Jewish women translators played a critical role in disseminating Marxist ideology in Eastern Europe. See Naomi Shepherd, *A Price Below Rubies: Jewish Women as Rebels and Radicals* (Cambridge: Harvard University Press, 1993), 124.

17. For a riveting account of the attacks on the first three buses of Freedom Riders in Alabama, see Taylor Branch, *Parting the Waters: America in the King Years* (New York: Simon & Schuster, 1988), 412–450.

18. John Dittmer, *Local People: The Struggle for Civil Rights in Mississippi* (Urbana: University of Illinois Press, 1994), 92–95.

19. Ibid., 95.

20. Carol Ruth Silver, "The Diary of a Freedom Rider," unpublished, 18; used with author's permission.

21. Emphasizing the shifting process of racial categorization as linked to social, economic, and political control, Ruth Frankenberg asserts: "Given male dominance within white culture, the 'protection' or 'salvation' of white women and their supposedly civilized sexuality from men of color and their 'primitive' sexuality has been the alibi for a range of atrocities from genocide and lynching to segregation and immigration control." Frankenberg, 76.

22. Silver, "Diary," 53.

23. Ibid., letters section, 12.

24. Ibid., 51–52.

25. Ibid., 110.

26. Dittmer, 98–99.

27. The role of Jewish women lawyers in the civil rights movement needs further research.

28. Silver, "Diary," 136.

29. Carson, *In Struggle*, 45.

30. Morris, 243.

31. Dick Cluster, ed., *They Should Have Served That Cup of Coffee: 7 Radicals Remember the 60s* (Boston: South End Press, 1979), 28.

32. Faith S. Holsaert, *While We Were Singing* (Glens Falls, N.Y.: Loft Press, 1986), 11–12.

33. Interview with Faith S. Holsaert, March 19, 1994; and Faith S. Holsaert, "Women in SNCC: Their Impact on the U.S. Women's Movement of the 1970s and '80s," speech, Charles County Community College, LaPlata, Maryland, March 8, 1994.

34. Carson, *In Struggle*, 75.

35. Faith S. Holsaert, "Moving Fast," unpublished short story.

36. James H. Cone, *A Black Theology of Liberation*, 20th anniversary ed. (Maryknoll, N.Y.: Orbis Books, 1990).

37. Faith S. Holsaert, "Freedom Rider," unpublished essay.

38. Ibid.

39. Branch, 864–868.

40. Sara Evans, *Personal Politics*, 77.

41. Interview with Faith S. Holsaert, March 19, 1994.

42. Interview with Miriam Cohen Glickman, February 11, 1994.

43. Danny Lyon, *Memories of the Southern Civil Rights Movement* (Chapel Hill: University of North Carolina Press, 1992), 63.

44. Interview with Dorothy Miller Zellner, January 4, 1994.

45. Lyon, 68.

46. Carson, *In Struggle*, 71; Branch.

2

Moving In On Mississippi, 1963–1965

I was able to do things I never thought I could do.

—Harriet Tanzman

FURTHERING THE FREEDOM VOTE CAMPAIGN

SNCC's increasing focus on Mississippi in 1963 accelerated the southern movement's impact and visibility. Recognizing the need for new, more drastic tactics in that state, Bob Moses, after some soul-searching, decided to use white workers in the Jackson Freedom House in the summer of 1963. Moses had just met former Stanford University dean Allard Lowenstein. A Jewish New Yorker by origin, Lowenstein had a long history of student and antiracist activism. The two discussed the idea of a Freedom vote campaign, which would allow Blacks to vote for their own candidates and to become more familiar with the voting process.[1] The staff endorsed the plan although there was some ambivalence about Lowenstein in particular and white workers in general in SNCC.[2]

In the fall of 1963, Miriam Cohen asked Bob Moses if she could go down to Mississippi to work on the Freedom vote campaign. He agreed to a two-week visit but said she couldn't stay. At the end of the two weeks, Moses said, "When are you leaving, isn't it time?" Cohen told him that her money had been stolen from the Freedom House. Known for his easygoing nature, the legendary Moses "shrugged and walked away." Cohen interpreted this as permission to stay.

She was soon to have a specific assignment. Matteo "Flukey" Suarez, a veteran of New Orleans CORE and director of the Meridian project, invited Cohen to come to Meridian to work on the Freedom vote campaign. She agreed happily. Later, she learned that Moses had "asked Flukey if I was working or 'working out' [sleeping around]. I had to ask Flukey what that meant because I didn't know. But I *was* working. Bob decided it was all right I guess. I didn't hear any more about it and he didn't offer me the bus fare home."

While *working* in Meridian, Cohen would learn many new things and have to reexamine some of her basic assumptions. Initially unattuned to the implications of being the lone white woman in a civil rights project in Mississippi, she found others around her projecting meanings onto her gender and race. First, there was the question of whether she was in the South to sleep around and not to work. Second, they could not believe a young white woman would risk the violence in Mississippi to fight anti-Black racism, so they assumed she was a light-skinned Black person. Finally, working in the Freedom vote project, Cohen was shocked to find that "the people there had no concept of what it meant to vote. We used to vote in school, [there were] all kinds of ways we knew about voting." Thus in 1963, Miriam Cohen learned that the right to vote, sacred to American Jews, was not universal and could not be taken for granted, even in the United States. This fueled her commitment to fighting for Black voting rights.

By going south, Jewish women activists defied midcentury American Jewish cultural norms. They had to confront Jewish cultural and political ambivalence about becoming visible as critics of American society. Assimilation seemed to require conformity. In the first part of the twentieth century, American Jews identified with and benefited from the liberal state. Thus, for young Jewish activists, critiquing the Kennedy and Johnson administrations, as SNCC often did, required a definite challenge to the Jewish community's liberal Democratic politics. But the conditions they witnessed buttressed their new consciousness.

In addition to a handful of white students like Miriam Cohen who found their way independently to Mississippi in 1963, Allard Lowenstein brought down one hundred Stanford and Yale students to assist the SNCC staff in the two weeks preceding the November 1963 Freedom vote election. The mock vote campaign was a success with more than eighty thousand Blacks voting.

A precursor to the 1964 Freedom Summer Project, which would bring one thousand white volunteers to Mississippi, the Freedom vote campaign demonstrated some of the pros and cons of white students' participation. Though they were concerned that white volunteers would inhibit the development of local Black leadership, the SNCC staff generally agreed that the Mississippi movement needed the visibility white students would bring. Their presence would raise national consciousness and force concessions from the government.

Miriam Cohen's participation in Albany, Georgia, where her father broke the national press silence on that movement, and in Meridian, where local people saw that a white Jewish girl would risk being their ally, suggested the early promise of such a strategy. Unfortunately, the inherent risk of violent backlash would become increasingly apparent, as Mississippi's white supremacists added "outside agitators" to their enemies' list.

PROVIDING SUPPORT IN THE NORTH AND SOUTH

One role that was clearly appropriate for whites was as supporters of SNCC in the North. A sharp demarcation between North and South does not serve to convey the mobility and interconnections among movement workers in both regions. Black and white workers went back and forth—sometimes to accomplish specific tasks like fund-raising in northern urban areas or delivering food to local communities. Some white workers who started out in the northern support movement could not resist going south eventually. Roberta Galler, executive secretary of Chicago Friends of SNCC, was one of them. But before she went south in the fall of 1964, she played multifaceted roles from her base in Chicago.

In 1963, Friends of SNCC groups began to make direct interventions as confrontation escalated in Mississippi. For example, to punish voter rights activists, the Leflore County Board of Supervisors voted to omit the traditional distribution of federal commodities—basic foods— to needy people in winter. Galler responded immediately, organizing major food drives for Mississippi. On February 19, a truck arrived in Greenwood, SNCC's state headquarters, with nine thousand pounds of food and clothing.[3]

Galler saw the drives not only as support for besieged Greenwood activists but as an organizing tool for the political development of Chicago's Black community. "When we were doing food drives, we were recruiting among the Chicago Black gangs and kids . . . as a way of doing political work with them too. We wound up organizing our very first school strike in Chicago."[4]

In Greenwood, SNCC also used food and clothing distribution to educate local people about organizing and voter registration. On February 28, threatened by the accelerating organizing in Greenwood, local white racists ambushed a SNCC car driven by Jimmy Travis, a young

Black activist. When they shot into the car, Travis was wounded in the shoulder and neck; he came close to dying.

Travis spent some time in Chicago recovering. There he and Roberta Galler became very close friends, as she displayed her caregiving talents, in addition to her organizational skills. These and other ties would help Galler become "very close friends with a lot of the central southern Mississippi folks. . . . Support wasn't just fund-raising. It was really deep involvement. So they are still fundamentally like my family even though I don't see them for years."

Despite the physical distance between Mississippi and Chicago, this affinity would enable Galler to play a critical role at a very dangerous time in Mississippi. In June, she took action that has led SNCC leader Lawrence Guyot to credit her repeatedly with saving his life. On the ninth of that month, legendary organizer Fannie Lou Hamer was arrested, jailed, and beaten viciously in Winona, Mississippi. SNCC sent Guyot to investigate. When he finally found Hamer and her colleagues in Winona, the local police arrested and beat him too.

When Guyot failed to check in with the SNCC office (which was standard practice because of constant danger), Galler stayed up all night with a map of Mississippi at hand and called every jail in the state until she located him. Then she alerted the national media and called jail personnel back to threaten them with nationwide exposure of their illegal detention of Guyot. He was released.

During the same week, on Tuesday, June 11, 1963, longtime NAACP leader Medgar Evers was murdered in Jackson. In the devastating aftermath, Galler talked repeatedly by phone to Willie Peacock, a young but veteran Black SNCC activist. Like everyone else in Mississippi, he knew that the perpetrator was white supremacist Byron de La Beckwith, who went scot-free at the time. Peacock would call Galler and say:

> Look, I don't want to die. If I see Beckwith, I'll kill him and if I kill him, I'll be killed. I can't even go into the bus station without them hanging out there and he's bragging about what he's done. If I try to leave town and take a bus, I'll see him and I'll kill him.

Roberta Galler spent many nights on the phone talking with Peacock about his grief and rage and desire for revenge. He did not act on it. Thirty years later, Beckwith was retried and convicted for the murder of Medgar Evers.

Roberta Galler's caring work—nurturing Jimmy Travis, tracking down Lawrence Guyot, and bearing witness to Willie Peacock's despair and rage—is invisible to history. She saved lives and soothed damaged spirits, not an insignificant contribution to a small, radical organization working in a violent, extralegal region. Such work, most often performed behind the scenes by women, helps keep movements alive.[5]

SETTING THE STAGE FOR FREEDOM SUMMER

In the summer of 1963, Dottie Miller married Robert Zellner. Alabama-born Zellner, the son of a former Klansman and SNCC's first white field secretary, was no stranger to Mississippi's violence. Originally hired in the fall of 1961 on a Southern Conference Educational Fund (SCEF) grant to work with white students, Zellner soon joined SNCC pioneers like Bob Moses in direct action. In the fall of 1961, he was attacked in a McComb demonstration protesting the murder of civil rights activist Herbert Lee. To Dottie Miller, Bob Zellner personified the ideals and action she expected of antiracist white people.

In the fall of 1963, Dottie Miller Zellner went with her new husband to Massachusetts, where he was enrolled in a graduate program at Brandeis University. Her assignment was to work with the nascent Boston SNCC office, where she raised money and coordinated shipments of donated food and clothing for Mississippi. She also worked with Kate Clark, whose father, Professor Kenneth Clark, was an early SNCC supporter. An interracial team of women entrusted with a critical task, Kate Clark and Dottie Zellner were primarily responsible for screening volunteers for the Mississippi Freedom Summer Project—reading applications and conducting interviews. Zellner describes their criteria:

> We wanted to screen out any lunatics basically. We wanted to screen out people who thought they were going to go down there to have an exciting time, to have fun, to visit the natives, all of that stuff we screened out.[6]

Given the vast potential for violence in Mississippi, the work of screening volunteers was vital. Zellner initially dismissed the sacrifice she made in leaving her communications and outreach work in Atlanta at such an important point in the southern movement. "I was married. You had to go where your husband went." Insisting that it didn't bother

her because "there was no question in my mind. This was 1963," she describes what it was like to be married to a movement star:

> In a way it was good for me. I'm actually kind of shy. It was sort of like being with an ocean liner. He was ahead of me when we went to a party—he would come in, shake everybody's hands and I would trail along after him and then I'd find some interesting person to talk to. Of course, I would end up knowing them a whole lot better. He was making his rounds. My consciousness was, at the time, very low. It never dawned on me the contribution that I was making was equal, was as important. Believe me, it did not dawn on me.

Being the wife of a movement worker had several advantages. It legitimized one's work in the movement, forestalled unwanted sexual advances, and helped confer more respectability in relations with the white community.

Another husband-and-wife team, Mickey and Rita Schwerner, two key players in what would become Mississippi's tragic visibility, were heading toward Mississippi as the discussion of the role of whites in the movement continued in the winter of 1963–1964.[7]

Married in June, the Brooklyn-based Schwerners were members of CORE and veterans of the organization's protests and sit-ins. In an account of the Schwerners' decision to go south, Seth Cagin and Philip Dray state, "The mid-September [1963] church bombing in Birmingham [that killed four girls] convinced [Mickey Schwerner] that he must act. He applied to the national CORE office asking to be considered for a post in the South. Rita was scheduled to receive her college degree in January 1964 and after that they would be free to go."[8] Cagin and Dray's account subtly removes moral agency from Rita Schwerner: he "must act," but she will be "free to go" with him. In the early 1960s, as Dottie Miller Zellner notes, wives assumed they would follow their activist husbands. However, the women were still activists in their own right.

In her application to go south, Rita Schwerner highlighted her partnership with Mickey in a way that also articulated her own hopes and goals:

> As my husband and I are in close agreement as to our philosophy and involvement in the civil rights struggle, I wish to work near him,

under the direction of CORE, in whatever capacity I may be most useful. My hope is to someday pass on to the children we may have a world containing more respect for the dignity and worth of all men than that world which was willed to us.

She also wrote:

> Since I have become active in CORE here in New York, I have become increasingly aware of the problems which exist in the Southern states. I have a strong desire to contribute in some small way, by the utilization of those skills which I possess, to the redress of the many grievances occurring daily. I wish to become an active participant rather than a passive onlooker. Realizing that northern newspaper and radio accounts are often distorted . . . I wish to acquire first hand knowledge of existing conditions in the South.[9]

Rita Schwerner's statement demonstrates self-confidence, awareness of her skills, humility about her potential contribution, and, most passionately, a desire to witness and know the truth in order to make a difference in the South.

In November 1963, immediately after the assassination of President Kennedy, the Schwerners learned that they had been accepted as CORE field-workers. SNCC would not accept a white couple on staff in Mississippi—the leaders believed it was less effective and too dangerous. But SNCC worked with the Schwerners under the aegis of the Council of Federated Organizations (COFO), an umbrella organization coordinating the Mississippi voter registration efforts of all the major civil rights organizations in the state.

Rita and Mickey Schwerner drove to Mississippi in January 1964. Bob Moses of SNCC, Dave Dennis of CORE, and Matteo Suarez of COFO decided to ask the Schwerners to develop a community center in Meridian, the state's second-largest city. Rita describes the center's quarters as "five cold, empty, dirty and decaying rooms. But we were both very happy. . . . [W]e only saw the rooms as we hoped to make them: colorful, filled with books and the sounds of music and happy people working to become better and more useful citizens of Mississippi and the United States."[10]

Rita's vision for the community center required material resources that simply were not available in the Mississippi movement. Looking at the chronic shortages as an affront to the cause, she used her organizational skills and northern contacts to address the problem.

> Her orientation was one that would prove critical to the movement's ultimate success. Yet Rita's determination to set things right rubbed some movement veterans the wrong way as if her zeal to fill the need she saw was an implied criticism. Still there was no doubting her commitment and it became clear to Moses and others . . . that she and Mickey were a team. His warmth was a foil to her cool intensity, her rigor a curb on his expansiveness. They struck their new colleagues as a solid couple genuinely in love who would support each other in the trying days ahead.[11]

Rita Schwerner's righteous indignation, fervor, rigor, and "cool intensity," qualities that many organizationally skilled Jewish women possess, discomfited some of her coworkers. Rita Schwerner did not fully inhabit the customary gender role for women of the time. Though her working partnership with her husband was central, she did not hesitate to take the initiative on matters she could resolve. Her serious demeanor put the cause first. Defying women's socialization, she spent more energy on political work than on taking care of others' emotions.

From the moment she arrived in Meridian, Rita Schwerner faced harassment, physical deprivation, and death threats. The Klan was obsessed with Mickey, whom they thought of as that "nigger-loving Jew Communist." Because the couple were anathema to the white community and dangerous to the Black community, the Schwerners had great difficulty in finding housing. During frigid weather in January and February, they often had no heat. When they resorted to sleeping in the community center, the water, gas, and electricity were cut off.

In late February, when the phone was installed, they immediately received threatening calls. Because she spent more time in the Freedom House, Rita Schwerner received many such calls there, often obscene, accusing her of having sexual relations with Black men. When Mickey was out, she had to field calls informing her that her husband was dead. When Mickey answered the phone, he was told that Rita was dead or would be soon. Despite the physical and psychological hardship they endured, the Schwerners worked diligently that May to prepare for the arrival of the summer volunteers.

DEALING WITH THE DISAPPEARANCES

On June 21, 1964, Rita Schwerner and Dottie Zellner were among the COFO staff in Oxford, Ohio, helping to train the second group of volunteers who would soon go south for the Mississippi Freedom Summer Project. Zellner recalls, "She had to be the tiniest person I ever saw. I mean, her hips were like this. She couldn't have weighed one hundred pounds." In fact, Rita Schwerner was five feet tall and weighed ninety pounds.[12]

That same day, after setting off to investigate a church bombing in Philadelphia, Mississippi, Mickey Schwerner, James Chaney, and Andrew Goodman disappeared. They were picked up and held briefly in jail by Sheriff Lawrence Rainey and released into the night to face a prearranged Klan ambush, where they were brutally murdered. At first, the three were simply reported as missing. Earlier that morning in Oxford, Bob Moses had cautioned volunteers to think carefully about the fact that they would be risking their lives to go to Mississippi. Later in the day, he announced the disappearance at an assembly.

Rita Schwerner then took the stage. One observer described her as "a thin white girl in shorts":

> She paced as she spoke, her eyes distraught and her face quite white, but in a voice that was even and disciplined. . . . Rita asked us to form in groups by home areas and wire our congressman. . . . We composed telegrams, collected money and sent them, and tried to rub out the reality of the situation with action.[13]

No one embodied this coping mechanism more than Rita Schwerner did. She called President Lyndon Johnson but could not get through. When the Secret Service officer refused to wake the president, Schwerner told him that she would hold him personally responsible for whatever happened to her husband and his two colleagues. The officer noted in his written report that Mrs. Schwerner sounded quite serious and could possibly cause embarrassment to the president.[14]

Dottie Miller Zellner met Rita Schwerner for the first time immediately after the announcement and struggled to find the right words to say to her. She recalls:

> After they disappeared, my first thought wasn't that they were killed. One of the Black guys, Jesse Morris, whom I liked a lot, said, "Of

course you know what happened." Then I knew what had happened, but there still was a glimmer of hope. Rita was unbelievable. That's her conscience. Here Rita was telling the press right from the beginning, "You wouldn't be here interviewing me if my husband was Black."[15]

Rita Schwerner insisted on leaving Ohio for Mississippi immediately. Dottie Miller Zellner says that "the idea was to keep searching on because right after they disappeared, the FBI was there in force. The idea was to pressure. I think Rita must have [had] to do something. She's an unbelievable fighter."

SNCC leaders then asked Bob Zellner to accompany Schwerner. Zellner was a southerner, the first white SNCC field-worker, and a trusted veteran. He was the obvious choice for negotiating this extremely dangerous situation. Dottie Miller Zellner had her own response:

Me, the big civil rights heroine, I'm sitting on the steps crying, begging my husband not to go because he's going to get killed also. Oh my god, oh when I think about it—Bob and Rita going back to Mississippi. . . . By the way, even if it hadn't been that he was my husband, I still didn't approve of the concept. I didn't think it was productive at all.

Dottie and Bob Zellner discussed the decision in the middle of all the staff's activity. She recalls:

I sat on this sofa and I knew that people were looking at me from afar. I'm sure these people were thinking, is she going to convince him not to go? I can't remember what I said but believe me I tried everything. It was one of my nice memories about him. He didn't put me down for feeling that way. I guess he felt I'm just going to sit here and wait until she stops crying and then, of course, he went.

Dottie Miller Zellner tells this story with an emphasis on what she considers her lack of courage, particularly in comparison to Rita Schwerner. She felt she broke a movement taboo by crying and appearing to resist the staff's decision. Nevertheless, she accepted her husband's return to Mississippi, managed her feelings, and continued her work at the Oxford training sessions, helping volunteers, who now knew the seriousness of their endeavor, to leave for Mississippi.

Both Rita Schwerner and Dottie Miller Zellner demonstrated bravery in that historic moment because each made a choice. Not only did

Schwerner choose not to collapse into the role of grieving widow, she used her national press visibility to raise consciousness about southern racism. Zellner's choice was perhaps less dramatic but motivated by the same commitments. Despite her fear, she put the needs of her activist community first—soon accepting her husband's departure and returning to her own work.

Bob Zellner and Rita Schwerner arrived in Mississippi on Wednesday, June 24, the third day after the men were reported missing. At the Cincinnati airport the night before, Schwerner spoke to reporters who told her that the men's burned car had been found in Neshoba County. Thus began a weeklong journey in which Rita Schwerner would charge every major authority figure—from the local sheriff to the president of the United States—with not doing enough to investigate the disappearances.

On Thursday, June 25, Schwerner and Zellner went to the state capitol to confront Governor Paul Johnson and the visiting Alabama governor, George Wallace, at a press conference. With Schwerner standing ten feet away, a reporter asked Johnson if there had been any developments in the case of the civil rights workers. Unaware of Schwerner's presence, Johnson quipped, "Governor Wallace and I are the only two people who know where they are and we're not telling."

As Dottie Miller Zellner recounts it, Bob Zellner's thick southern accent enabled him to get close to the Mississippi governor "because when he opened his mouth, they were disarmed." He gripped Johnson's hand to shake it and then introduced the tiny woman standing next to him as Rita Schwerner. Johnson tried to free himself from Zellner, but Zellner wouldn't let go and said, "We feel it's reprehensible for you to joke about this situation." State troopers stepped forward to release Johnson and then escort the two interlopers off the grounds, with Rita Schwerner all the while demanding in vain an appointment with the governor.

Moving up the chain of authorities investigating the disappearances, Schwerner and Zellner next met with former CIA director Allen Dulles, who had been sent to Mississippi by President Johnson. Schwerner told him that she had learned that there was no significant search for the men under way in Neshoba County. Dulles replied that the federal government was doing all it could. When Zellner described their encounter with Governor Johnson, Dulles insisted that he must have misunderstood the joke. Reflecting SNCC's contempt of federal authorities who refused to protect civil rights workers, Schwerner interjected,

"You may be sure that before we brought you any information, we would check it out since we know you will try to discredit it." A nearby FBI agent remarked that Schwerner was impertinent. Dulles, eager to end the interview, extended his hand to Rita in sympathy but she pulled away.

In interviews with the press, Schwerner described her encounters with Johnson and Dulles, but although copy was filed with various wire services and news agencies, the accounts appeared in few newspapers. Schwerner complained that the press had not used her numerous statements because she refused to be "maudlin or sentimental" about the disappearance of her husband and instead dealt with issues.[16] Once again, she defied traditional gender roles. And with each subsequent encounter with federal authorities, she simultaneously used and subverted the traditional image of a grieving wife to question their integrity, trying to shame them into action.

On Friday, June 26, Schwerner and Zellner risked their lives to confront Neshoba County's Sheriff Lawrence Rainey. Despite their experience, they underestimated the power and arrogance of the Klan in that area. Driving down the same road that Chaney, Schwerner, and Goodman had taken, Schwerner and Zellner saw white vigilantes in cars and pickup trucks guarding the bombed church the three activists had gone to investigate. When the local men saw Zellner's vehicle, one of the trucks pulled across the driveway to cut it off. Zellner hit the accelerator and swerved back onto Longdale Road, the truck in pursuit. As they raced toward Highway 16, a long flatbed truck was pulled across to block the narrow road surrounded by woods. The pickup behind them seemed to close the trap. Zellner jerked the wheel to the right, sending the car crashing into the woods, where he somehow found a way through the trees and to the road on the far side of the roadblock.

They had just narrowly missed becoming the second cohort of civil rights workers to disappear in Neshoba County, but Schwerner and Zellner were not deterred in their mission. They drove back into town to the FBI's temporary motel headquarters and they spoke to a lone FBI agent, who was angry with them for driving into the county. Then Rainey himself pulled into the parking lot with a posse in pickup trucks.

Opening an almost unimaginable conversation, Rainey walked to where Rita Schwerner stood, looming over the tiny but resolute woman. He drawled, "What in the goddamned hell are you doing here?" Schwerner said she wanted to see her husband's car. Rainey shook his head and suggested that she leave the county immediately. More pickup trucks kept arriving in the motel parking lot. "I'm not leaving until I see Mickey's car and I don't care how many pickup trucks show up to intimidate me." Rainey invited the young woman and her companions into the back seat of his patrol car so they could talk. Despite her suspicion that she was placing herself in the hands of someone complicit in her husband's murder, Schwerner got into the car. Then she said she thought Rainey knew where her husband was. State patrolman Charles Snodgrass, Rainey's flunky, explained that the sheriff had been in Meridian by his wife's bedside when Mickey Schwerner was arrested and couldn't possibly know where he was. "I'm not leaving here until I learn what happened to my husband," Schwerner persisted, addressing herself to Rainey. "I'm going to keep drawing attention here until I find out, and if you don't like it you'll just have to have me killed too."

Rainey's body tensed with suppressed rage. "I'm very shocked," the sheriff said quietly. "I'm sorry you said that. I'll give you five minutes with the car." Several white mechanics hooted and gave rebel yells when they learned who had just walked into their garage. Zellner and Schwerner had accomplished what they had set out to do: visiting the ruined church, speaking to Rainey, and seeing the burned-out car. But they would not learn what happened to the missing men until much later.[17]

On Monday, June 29, Schwerner went to Washington accompanied by Zellner and Forman. Congressman William Fitts Ryan of New York helped them set up a meeting with Deputy Attorney General Nicholas Katzenbach. The discussion, which began pleasantly, deteriorated quickly after Schwerner, frustrated by the previous week's events, charged that no serious search for her husband seemed to be under way. "It's only a P.R. job," she asserted, "and not a very good one at that." "What makes you qualified to say whether or not an investigation is under way?" Katzenbach replied angrily. "I haven't been bought off like you by southern politicians," Schwerner retorted.[18]

Later that day, Congressman Ogden Reid arranged for Schwerner and Zellner to meet briefly with President Johnson. At a press conference at the Washington SNCC office, Schwerner described the encounter. In their five-minute meeting, she had told Johnson that the two hundred local naval cadets searching for the men in Bogue Chitto, Mississippi, were inadequate and demanded that he send five thousand men. The president had replied that there would be nowhere near thousands of men but assured her that the federal government was doing everything it possibly could. "The statements seemed somewhat contradictory to me," Schwerner remarked defiantly. "When the federal authorities pull out of Meridian, Mississippi," she added, "I tremble at what is going to happen to the Negroes in the area."

Schwerner closed the press conference by appealing to all Americans with a conscience to come to Meridian and organize into citizen search parties; "go out and do the job which the federal government feels it cannot do."[19] It was a rare occurrence in 1964 for a woman to criticize the government publicly, let alone invite citizens to override its efforts. Like Fannie Lou Hamer, who would give her famous speech at the Atlantic City Democratic National Convention just two months later, Schwerner had the audacity to say, "I question America."

Of course, neither citizens nor federal troops descended upon Mississippi to engage in the search. Several months after the bodies of the three men were found in August 1964, federal authorities arrested twenty white men, including Sheriff Lawrence Rainey and Deputy Sheriff Cecil Price, and tried them for "conspiracy to deprive the dead men of their civil rights."[20] In 1967, seven men (Rainey and Price not among them) were convicted and sentenced to prison. They were never tried for murder (a state offense) because it was deemed highly unlikely that a Mississippi jury would convict them.

ACCEPTING ASSIGNMENTS FOR FREEDOM SUMMER

The Mississippi Freedom Summer Project was a comprehensive assault on the country's most rigidly racist state. It required the staff and volunteers to take on a variety of roles, but the two areas targeted were voter registration and the Freedom Schools. Though the (predominantly white) women who went south in the summer of 1964 had more activist experience than did the men, they played more limited roles.[21] When asked their work preferences on project applications, 48 percent of the women designated teaching in the Freedom Schools (a highly gender-defined task); 56 percent of the women were so assigned. In contrast, 20 percent of the women requested the more dangerous and respected voter registration work; only 9 percent of the women were so assigned. However, Freedom School teachers often joined voter registration workers late in the day for canvassing, so they participated in both major aspects of the summer project.[22]

The first week of training for the project, in Oxford, Ohio, focused primarily on voter registration workers; the second week, on Freedom School workers, the majority of whom were women (including, of course, Jewish women, for whom teaching had long been a primary profession). Thus, a considerable number of these women were among the volunteers who had to reaffirm their commitment to go south after it was considered likely that the three civil rights workers had been killed in Mississippi. The risk was real and they took it.

The murders of Chaney, Schwerner, and Goodman were the opening shots in what became a violent summer. Bob Zellner was director of the Greenwood project when SNCC moved its headquarters there for the Summer Project.[23] For Dottie Miller Zellner, who dutifully went with him, it was one of the most "horrible, most miserable nerve-wracking experiences" of her life. The project faced bomb threats and mass arrests (111 arrested at the July 16 Freedom Day). After several attempts to desegregate the local movie theatre, local activists Silas McGhee and family were harassed, beaten, and shot at by a mob of two hundred whites. The mob held a siege at the hospital where the injured Jake McGhee had been taken. Dispatched by Bob Zellner to the hospital, SNCC worker Judy Richardson was shot at by whites. Another SNCC worker, Jesse Harris, persuaded local Blacks not to take up arms.[24] COFO's list of "hostile incidents" for the Summer Project includes 4 COFO workers killed, 4 people critically wounded, 37 churches bombed or burned, and 30 Blacks' homes or businesses bombed or burned—plus 1,000 arrests.[25]

ASKING QUESTIONS: TEACHING AT THE FREEDOM SCHOOLS

In August 1964, Florence Howe coordinated and taught at the Blair Street Freedom School, one of nine such schools in Jackson. There were more than forty other schools in twenty other towns. Initially, she was very impatient with southern culture and the movement's way of doing things:

> I couldn't understand why we would talk round and round and round and round and round everything and never make a decision and why everybody spoke very slowly. I wasn't attuned to the South and I couldn't understand why we couldn't get on with things. And I was

saying that and Staughton [Lynd] and Howard [Zinn; both historians and Freedom School Project directors] talked to me each privately to say (a) to shut up and (b) to have some patience. . . . I learned quickly. It didn't take long.[26]

Lonely for Mississippi after she returned to "my simple but privileged life in Baltimore,"[27] Howe wrote an essay to convey what she had learned in her transformative experience. She shared it with Lynd and Zinn, who helped get it published. The first lines of her first published essay, which appeared in the *Harvard Educational Review* in January 1965, declare, "All education is political. In Mississippi, at least, it is impossible to find this trite." The lessons learned by Florence Howe and other Freedom School teachers—"the teacher's main problem was to learn to keep quiet, to learn how to listen, and to question creatively rather than to talk at the students"—have informed the development of women's studies and feminist pedagogy. Howe, founder of The Feminist Press, would go on to play a catalytic role in the international women's studies movement.

Liz Fusco, née Aaronsohn, taught first in Indianola, Mississippi, before becoming the post–Mississippi Summer coordinator of the Freedom Schools from 1964 to 1966. The daughter of a rabbi and a veteran of the Peace Corps and Seattle CORE, Fusco heeded the call for Freedom Summer volunteers as she was leaving a bad marriage. Upon arrival, "I soon learned that I knew nothing of value." She had to "unlearn" the internalized values of her Ivy League education: white supremacy and academic superiority. This was not easy and, like Florence Howe, she struggled with her own impatience:

> It took me the two years I was there, after much downright interrupting, rushing, violating, and stepping in front of people, to finally see my own arrogance. It was hard, but transforming, for me to hear the one person who had the courage and caring to tell me, "Liz, you walk around here as if you think you're better than us."[28]

In a 1964 essay on the Freedom Schools in Mississippi, Fusco argued that they were as transformative a force for social change in the state as the voter registration drives:

> It was the asking of questions . . . that made the Mississippi Summer Project different from other voter registration projects and other civil

rights activities everywhere else in the South. And so it is reasonable that the transformations that occurred—and transformations did occur—out of the Freedom School experience occurred because for the first time in their lives kids were asking questions.

In the "Citizenship Curriculum" (one part of the whole), the predominantly northern, white (and female) teachers engaged students with such questions as "Why are we (teachers and students) in the Freedom Schools? What is the Freedom Movement? What alternatives does the Freedom Movement offer us? What does the majority culture have that we want? What does the majority culture have that we don't want? What do we have that we want to keep?"[29]

As many Summer Project veterans have commented, they learned more than they taught. This was especially true of Freedom School teachers. When Liz Fusco left Indianola to go to Jackson to coordinate the schools, she "learned for the first time in my life that with kids you love to disconnect is to suffer. So the teachers were transformed too."[30]

Another way Jewish women intersected with the southern Black movement was as teachers and students at historically Black colleges. Temma Kaplan, a future feminist historian, taught at Tougaloo College in Jackson, Mississippi. Karin Kunstler, daughter of radical lawyer William Kunstler, went to Tougaloo as a student in 1962.[31] She subsequently was a SNCC field-worker.

In May of 1964, Radcliffe College junior Elaine DeLott joined a group of Harvard University graduate students conducting an exchange program with Tougaloo College faculty. She taught sociology and art history during Tougaloo's summer session. At the same time, she began working with the Jackson COFO office on a survey design for Freedom Summer. In the fall, she continued working with COFO's federal programs project. In November, DeLott went to Canton, Mississippi, to work on the ASCS (Agricultural Stabilization and Conservation Service) elections, where she was jailed for trespassing. During the fall and winter, she traveled throughout the state as a resource person for COFO's federal programs project.

From March through May 1965, DeLott was in Batesville, Mississippi, where she helped farmers organize an okra marketing cooperative, financed through federal poverty funds. Her work with local people in various areas provides examples of early welfare rights organizing.

In addition to teaching, other Jewish women brought specific expertise with them down south. Among the relatively small number of women professionals was physician June Finer. She went south as part of the Medical Committee for Human Rights' (MCHR) work in the Mississippi Freedom Summer Project. She was one of approximately one hundred physicians, nurses, and psychologists MCHR sent out in teams to COFO centers. Finer spent two weeks at SNCC headquarters in Greenwood and returned to the North to finish her residency.

> We did educational stuff with the SNCC people who I think probably resented us to some degree. We would try to do public health teaching about not sharing cups and spoons, and stuff that isn't that popular. I think the white northern students who had come South to work in the civil rights movement had no patience for that. They felt we were being patronizing. Maybe we were.

There were roughly 150 lawyers and law students (including some women) handling civil rights cases during the summer of 1964. Passage of the 1964 Civil Rights Act gave movement workers a taste of victory on the legislative front that summer. The act forbids discrimination in public accommodations, employment, and educational facilities receiving federal funds. It delivered a major blow to the Jim Crow system.

ENDORSING THE MISSISSIPPI FREEDOM DEMOCRATIC PARTY AND COORDINATING THE CONGRESSIONAL CHALLENGE

The Mississippi Freedom Democratic Party was founded in April 1964 to help Mississippi Blacks use voter registration to gain control over the political decisions that affected their communities. It would also attempt to influence public policy in the South and nationally to raise consciousness about the nature of southern Black disenfranchisement.[32] Its immediate goals were to register all Blacks in a "freedom party," while continuing a parallel effort to register Black people in the state's official Democratic Party. Seeking to empower Black voters to choose their own candidates, the MFDP sponsored a "mock" statewide election, thus creating a political structure that would challenge the all-white Mississippi delegation at the August 1964 Democratic National Convention in At-

lantic City, New Jersey. MFDP's premise was that the all-white delegation did not truly represent all Mississippians.

Three Black women—Annie Devine, Fannie Lou Hamer, and Victoria Gray—constituted the MFDP delegation seeking floor seats at the
convention. MFDP worked tirelessly to gain recognition for them.
Though that effort did not succeed, former sharecropper Hamer's riveting speech caught the attention of the nation. She challenged the
United States to live up to its ideals and helped create support for passage of the 1965 Voting Rights Act.

The SNCC/COFO/MFDP workers who had gone to Atlantic City
with high hopes returned demoralized and disorganized.[33] Most of the
summer volunteers had gone home, and SNCC lacked human and material resources. SNCC began to move a good portion of its operations
and resources to Alabama, where the famous Selma to Montgomery
march would take place the following year. Nevertheless, the MFDP
initiated "the Congressional Challenge." In December 1964, MFDP
lawyers filed a notice contesting the election of the "official" Mississippi
congressional delegation on the grounds that Blacks had been excluded
from the electoral process.[34] In January 1965, Elaine DeLott organized
meetings of Mississippi community people and representatives of federal agencies in Washington, D.C., in connection with the MFDP challenge effort.

Janice Goodman, a veteran of the Mississippi Freedom Summer
Project who had gone home to New York after the first attempt to seat
the MFDP delegation, felt a pull to continue the work. She returned to
Mississippi for the month of November 1964 and was then sent to the
new MFDP Washington, D.C., office, directed by Michael Thelwell. The
office organized a nationwide lobbying initiative, and Goodman
worked there until the end of 1966.

Florence Howe also worked in the Washington office. One of her
tasks was to take Black Mississippians to congressional offices to lobby.
She remembers most vividly "the sheer ignorance of the congresspeo-
ple and/or their terrible racism."

In the fall of 1964, MFDP chairman Lawrence Guyot invited Roberta
Galler to come to Jackson to work on the Congressional Challenge.
Through her work at Chicago Friends of SNCC, Galler had built up re-
serves of goodwill through personal relationships, including with
Guyot. This enabled her to gain greater levels of trust and leadership
than most white women in SNCC. Also, as Galler notes, "the center was

gone there for a while. One of the reasons I was able to be in the position I was in was that there was a kind of vacuum, a tremendous need for people. On the other hand, you had to be careful not to supercede and take more authority."

Galler's immediate assignment was to set up MFDP offices around the state, to create a state office in Jackson, and to set up political education workshops—all of which aimed to empower local people and provide ways to include their voices in the Congressional Challenge.

This was not an easy time to come down to Mississippi. "There was still a lot of violence going on towards us," Galler recalls. "It was quite dangerous and terrifying to move around the state." And the women's Freedom House in Jackson, where Galler lived, reflected the disorganization of the moment. It was not really a collective where an ongoing group of coworkers built community and shared resources; it was the movement's state headquarters and people would just come and go.

> They would drop in because they needed to go to the doctor or to see the lawyer or to see me. . . . After a very long day and night of working, you would come home and there would be somebody else in your bed. You didn't want to turn on the lights to wake up other people, so you didn't know who [was in your bed]. . . . I would just say, "Move over." I would also see my clothes walking around on other people— there was no way of having your own clothes.[35]

A church sponsored Galler's work, so she received a monthly salary of twenty dollars.

> It was a very small amount of money, out of which I also fed other people. I didn't eat pig ear sandwiches myself, but they were ten cents a piece. "Splits," a little crawfish sandwich, was also ten cents. In the Freedom House, we did do some cooking, but there was the same problem. You couldn't keep food in the refrigerator.

Under these conditions, Galler worked around the clock to coordinate different facets of the Challenge in Mississippi. She didn't realize she had contracted pleurisy and was trying to function normally with walking pneumonia. "We were all in terrible shape, but at that time, we were coordinating busloads of people statewide to go to Washington to testify."

The MFDP's next step was to recruit 150 volunteer lawyers through the National Lawyers Guild, under the direction of radical lawyer Morton Stavis, a founder of the Center for Constitutional Rights. During February and March 1965, the lawyers and MFDP staff traveled the state, taking depositions from Blacks who had been threatened economically and physically, and blocked from attempting to vote. The lawyers and local activists also took testimony from white officials who denied there was a problem.

Attorneys compiled six hundred depositions—three thousand single-spaced pages—which they submitted to the House of Representatives as evidence that the 1964 congressional elections were unconstitutional.[36] Despite this major achievement, the goals of Galler and the SNCC staff centered much more on engaging Black participation in a democratic experiment. Galler reminisces:

> This was quite an extraordinary process. What we were doing was that *the people themselves* from around the state who had been subject to the most gross beatings and injustices were giving depositions and were taking depositions from the various officials who had beaten them.

Not surprisingly, there was a culture clash between the lawyers and SNCC/MFDP staff over the process and priorities for taking depositions. "For the lawyers, this was an extraordinary experience and opportunity to put themselves on the line. However, they came down with their practice—being lawyers, they were used to being in charge of things and making deals . . . and getting on the phone with judges and shmoozing the way they did in the North." The lawyers' priority was to get the material before Congress as quickly as possible; the local MFDP activists' priority was to create a process that publicly "gave people an opportunity in their own communities to absorb power and to be the ones who were actually taking the depositions from their oppressors."[37]

This conflict of styles emerged in the making of arrangements for the depositions. Many local people did not want to give depositions in white-controlled official buildings where they had been harassed, beaten, and prevented from voting. Hence, Galler and her coworkers scheduled some of the depositions in Black churches and "in one case where we had no other place to do it, right in the middle of a cotton field." When white officials resisted, some of the northern lawyers would call local judges to try to enlist their support for the whole process. Galler's perception of the southern judges as "really oppressive, racist bastards" gave her the nerve to confront the lawyers: "You can't shmooze with a judge and agree to do something."

Trying to explain to the lawyers that they were in a support role and could not act independently of the movement, Galler and her coworkers precipitated a crisis in which they came close to "firing" lead lawyer Morton Stavis. She recalls, "We were audacious because we were doing it on behalf of the people." Lawyers Stavis and William Kunstler flew Ella Baker in from Atlanta to try to mediate the crisis. She listened carefully and was sympathetic to both sides. Baker, whose philosophy of grassroots empowerment was the foundational ideology of SNCC, helped Galler "with my style of leadership." With such mentoring behind her, Galler could make compromises to get the depositions done while preserving her and SNCC's priorities of building community, empowering local people, and leaving behind an organizing culture after the depositions had been taken.

Jan Goodman vividly remembers January 4, 1965, the day the U.S. House of Representatives was to vote on a resolution to "unseat" the Mississippi delegation. In addition to presenting the depositions, the MFDP had brought six hundred Black Mississippians to lobby on Capitol Hill.

> We had one of the most beautiful demonstrations of all. A silent vigil on the day of the vote to unseat. It was led by Stokely Carmichael in his early days—this was slightly before full-blown Black Power, probably around six months. They had this very peaceful, nonviolent demonstration in the tunnels of Congress. It was really incredible to watch. When the congressmen, and they were all men, came through, they had to go through a phalanx of two lines of Black groups who were totally, totally silent. And just glaring at them. It was quite dramatic and quite terrific.[38]

Though one-third of House members voted against seating Mississippi's elected delegation, they were sworn into office. However, the statute on contested elections did leave open the possibility of taking further depositions on the issue for forty days. That set the stage for the MFDP's next phase of work.[39]

The MFDP planned a major voter registration drive for the summer of 1965. However, in June, the governor announced a special legislative session to overturn the state's discriminatory voting laws. Johnson was actually trying to undermine the Congressional Challenge and Black enfranchisement. In response, the MFDP launched major demonstrations in Jackson. On June 14, chair Lawrence Guyot led five hundred demonstrators from a church to begin a one-mile march to the state capitol. At its halfway point, police stopped the march and arrested hundreds of people for "parading without a permit." Over the course of the next two weeks, the marches continued and more than one thousand participants were jailed in cattle barns on the state fairgrounds.[40] There were reports of police brutality. White women were taken first to the fairgrounds and then to the Hinds County Jail. Among them was Roberta Galler, who joked that she got arrested so she could rest.

But one reason Galler decided to stay in jail longer rather than post bail was that she wanted local people to act in accord with SNCC's philosophy. "I felt that by going [on the demonstrations], not only would I get arrested, I would somehow precipitate a crisis that would have to get solved by getting other people to assume more leadership and take a different role in the office." Though more staff began to work in the MFDP state office in Jackson, Galler still felt discomfort about her leadership role.

Galler remembers Carmichael telling her not to be so obviously efficient. He "wanted me to be efficient but it shouldn't show too much—he wanted both things from me. He wanted me to work around the clock, he wanted all of my efficiency and, at the same time, for it not to show in ways that could be intimidating to other people who may not have developed the same level of skill." Unlike some white women volunteers, Galler did not take this personally because her goal was to work herself out of a job. "So this wasn't contrary to either my political beliefs or philosophy. It's just sometimes hard personally when you are working like a dog around the clock." Galler simultaneously had to be diligent, put aside her desire for appreciation, and monitor her self-presentation. It required "a funny balance."

Unable to resolve this contradiction, Galler soon left to do direct organizing with John Buffington in Clay County, Mississippi. Then she began working intensively on the Freedom Information Service with SNCC veteran Curtis Hayes, using materials generated locally to run political education workshops.

The Voting Rights Act passed in August 1965, enabling federal examiners to register Black voters turned away by state officials. Jan Goodman says, "When the Voting Rights Act was passed, the Mississippi delegation was officially seated and that ended the Challenge per se. We kept that office going though as sort of a lobbying focus for the next two years. We were lobbyists, a lobby and activist arm." Goodman worked in the Washington office for two years, yet never felt completely integrated into its work:

> Definitely not. There were clearly a variety of pecking orders, as any organization has, but certainly the bottom of the pecking order was women. And I don't know that I would say white women were at the bottom. I don't know whether Black women or white women were at the bottom. It's very hard. It's very painful to think about [the gender and racial dynamics]. It certainly is what propelled me further into becoming a feminist.

Goodman speaks of her resentment at being expected to do mimeographing and at the subtle dynamics that she felt reflected her uncertain status as a white woman worker.

> I remember always being tested. I smoked at that point and you always had these guys taking cigarettes off you. They never bought their own cigarettes but you were there to supply them with cigarettes. I don't know why that always stuck in my craw. It was so silly but it was symbolic for me. Yeah it was very tough. It was very, very tough. [41]

Despite some of the difficulties, for Goodman, "working at the MFDP office was something that you continued doing for a variety of reasons. One, because even though I found some of the treatment of women really demeaning, I still think it's one of the most significant things I've done in my life."

MOTHERING THE MOVEMENT

A number of the women interviewed worked the front lines; others maximized the younger generation's efforts. Trudy Orris's civil rights work continued in the framework of mothering. As head of the New York Parents of SNCC, she worked with James Forman, SNCC's executive secretary. During the Mississippi Freedom Summer Project, she spent much of her time on a WATS line with the Atlanta office. Orris worked with a small group of mothers that included Carolyn Goodman (now Eisner), Andy Goodman's mother; Lisa Foner, mother of historian

Eric Foner; and Gladys Blum. Blum's son spent the summer of 1964 in Hattiesburg, and her daughter went to Mississippi for the Mississippi Freedom Democratic Party election in November 1964.

As did a number of other parents' support groups that first engaged in lobbying, fund-raising, and educational outreach in the summer of 1964, the New York Parents of SNCC continued to work for SNCC after the project.[42] Trudy Weissman Orris hosted and coordinated the visits of young Black activists from all over the South to the New York area, arranging for housing, medical care, and fund-raising opportunities. Up to twenty at a time would stay at the Orris home for their first night, and she would give them an orientation about the upper-middle-class families they would be staying with for fund-raising house parties. She also oriented the host families to the young people's experiences with segregation, violence, and activism.

Such activities underscore the role Orris played as mediator between two groups that differed in terms of class, age, race, political orientation (young radicals v. older liberals), regional culture, and probably religion (many of the host families were Jewish; and the young people were mostly Black Christians). Among the topics she covered for the southerners were use of a host's phone for long-distance calls home (out of bounds) and their hosts' sincerity. "'Yes they're all middle-class, but they are very interested in you . . . and your equality. This is a chance for you for educational reasons.' The whole shmear I gave them." The parties raised $25,000 and made new connections for SNCC. Another form of invisible women's work, the "bridging" done by Orris not only helped raise money but sought to demonstrate in the North, the kinds of cross-racial "beloved communities" young people were enacting in the South. In this way, she challenged her own community to live up to its ideals.

Gladys Blum (b. 1914) helped place the "SNCC kids Trudy brought up" with families in Roslyn and Great Neck, Long Island. An engineer who graduated from Cornell University in 1934, Blum was told she had two strikes against her professionally: she was a woman and a Jew. She had worked on several projects as an engineer (including locks and dams in Mississippi) before joining her husband to work in his furniture factory. Members of the Communist Party in the 1930s and of the NAACP, she and her husband were politically active in integration issues when they lived in Corona, Queens, and later when they moved to Roslyn (a quintessentially Jewish suburb) in the late 1940s.

They started the first civil rights group on Long Island and worked to help Blacks buy houses in their neighborhood in the early 1960s. "That was some struggle."[43] In addition to hosting the "SNCC kids," Blum raised thousands of dollars for the MFDP Congressional Challenge by organizing a dinner in a local synagogue—despite her militant atheism and vehement lack of Jewish identification.

In addition to overt political organizing, radicals Orris and Blum contributed to antiracist movements like many other white, more generally liberal mothers through "the socialization of their children to humanistic values."[44] However, they took it a step further; they sent their sons and daughters south.

SETTLING IN FOR THE SELMA MOVEMENT

After the Mississippi Summer Project, the Selma movement of 1965 was one of the last large interracial initiatives of the civil rights movement. Designed to engage federal protection of voting rights, it was multifaceted and had a large educational dimension. But as violence and repression increased in Selma, the movement inevitably became more confrontational. Prior to the Selma march in 1965, there had been relatively few white civil rights workers in Alabama. Among them were Harriet Tanzman, who spent a year working for the Southern Christian Leadership Conference (SCLC) and Dr. June Finer, who spent five months as southern coordinator for the Medical Committee for Human Rights (MCHR).

Tanzman arrived in Gadsden in September 1964 and spent her first few months working with a veteran Black organizer from New Orleans, Bené Luchion. The two covered northern Alabama for SCLC though neither had a driver's license. They drove anyway, highly vulnerable as a Black man and a white woman organizing together. Aware of racist paranoia about interracial sex, Tanzman states plainly, "We worked very much as brother and sister. I mean we just did the work."

Because SCLC was gearing up after Martin Luther King Jr.'s January 1965 speech for a major voting rights campaign in Selma, recruiting "a nonviolent army," it ordered a number of its field-workers back to Selma. Tanzman and one other married white woman were initially the only white women staffers there. Tanzman did not experience any sexual tension as a single white woman. She attributes this to the fact that she was seeing a SNCC organizer who spent some time in Selma and that she was completely devoted to her literacy work.

So much of my self was put into the work that . . . it was enormously emotionally satisfying. It was incredibly satisfying. I mean I've never met people quite like some of the people I met in Selma and in the South, and at a certain point there were hundreds of people involved. And you're talking about mass meetings every night of the week. And enormously courageous people of all ages—very little ones to elderly. So for me, I was just always learning . . . I really had a lot to learn.[45]

The SCLC literacy program had begun at Highlander Folk School (a movement educational center), and was further developed by Septima Clark and Annelle Ponder. Tanzman tells of

teaching people who knew an enormous amount about survival, about caring, about giving, about seeing old people as neighbors and family, but who didn't have some of the basic skills at all. So I taught but I also taught them to teach. You know, neither of these things did I know how to do beforehand. And I was able to do things that I never knew I could do. I mean it took the best of us, the movement, whether we were eighteen or twenty-five. It empowered our lives. We felt that we could do many things that none of us knew we could do before. And we were always surrounded by many role models.

Among the things the women who attended these classes learned were practical skills, like opening bank accounts and handling legal papers, and some Black history. Those who participated in Tanzman's classes in 1965 "still worked in kitchens for a couple of dollars a day." Some went on to leadership training programs to set up their own classes.

Tanzman lived with a Black family during the tumultuous first six months of 1965. "Selma was the first time that I was ever around death in my life." The first funeral she ever attended was for Jimmie Lee Jackson, a twenty-one-year-old Black man who had been shot by a trooper at an SCLC night march in February, as he was trying to protect his mother. "The funeral was very much a Baptist funeral . . . we all sang all the way to the cemetery. And I was enormously affected by it. You know here a whole community had come out in the streets, no security or anything."

As the Selma movement was heating up, Dr. June Finer arrived as a paid southern coordinator for the Medical Committee for Human Rights, setting up MCHR-funded offices in Baton Rouge, Montgomery, and Selma. In quieter times, she sought to contribute to local public health needs. For example, Finer interviewed some of the Selma doctors to ascertain their attitudes toward Black patients. She and her medical colleagues visited the hospitals and talked to public health officials, trying to improve the treatment of Black patients. They also taught about health matters and first aid to a variety of groups, including church groups, which were often centers of movement support.

Primarily, however, Finer focused on emergency medical needs that arose during demonstrations, dispatching incoming medical teams from the North to places where they were most needed.

> We were always on standby for demonstrations. We wore red cross symbols—a white armband with a little red cross to identify us. It was felt that our presence at demonstrations was of some importance although in fact there's not much you could do [for tear gas].[46]

During the larger demonstrations, when people were jailed, Finer and her colleagues would "go to the jail and demand to see them, thinking this might perhaps prevent them from being beaten up because a medical person had viewed them at some point. If subsequently they appeared to be damaged in any way, one could make a testimony about that."

Jimmie Lee Jackson's death was the impetus for the Selma to Montgomery march on March 7, 1965, which came to be known as "Bloody Sunday." The marchers, led by SNCC's John Lewis and SCLC's Hosea Williams, were brutally set upon on the Edmund Pettus Bridge. Among the supporters who flew in after seeing the attack on television was the Reverend James Reeb of Boston, who was clubbed as he was leaving a Black restaurant and subsequently died.

After some wrangling over whether to march again without federal protection, Martin Luther King Jr. struck a compromise: he would lead a symbolic march of fifteen hundred persons to the bridge, where they would pray and turn around. After Judge Frank Johnson ruled that Blacks had the right to this protest, President Johnson federalized the Alabama National Guard and thousands flew in to support the march from Selma to Montgomery.[47]

Orris, much to her family's distress, insisted on going down to Selma for a week. "They kept calling, they were so worried about me they wanted me to come [home]." She had made up her mind to go—alone or not—"because it was an issue. I had to. That was one of the things I had to do. So I went by myself." Orris stayed with the doctors' group in Selma, which had its own house. "During the day we would go to the march. We were responsible for the medical staff on the march. There were people walking distances, and so we would wash feet, we would put Band-Aids on. They were the doctors and I was helping the nurse. Then I would go back to the house and I would do the cooking. Somebody would've shopped, and I would make some of the meals. A lot of them went out to eat. We'd stay in the Black community."

During the march, Viola Liuzzo, a Detroit mother of five, was shot to death by the Klan as she was driving a young Black man, Leroy Moton, who survived the attack by playing dead. Harriet Tanzman, who knew Moton, was "in an interracial van a half hour later going down the same road." She knew she was risking the same fate.

LIVING WITH LOCAL PEOPLE: MISSISSIPPI, 1965

The Jewish women in this book who stayed after the 1964 Summer Project, who went south for the first time in 1965, or who returned to Mississippi in the summer of 1965 faced hostility to whites in the movement and escalating violence. Every project created elaborate security precautions—regular communication by two-way radio, rules against going out at night or walking downtown in interracial groups—to try to prevent COFO's list of "hostile incidents" from getting any longer.

Despite this increasingly violent milieu, Jewish women continued to go south. The passion of Jewish resistance comes through in the voice of eighteen-year-old Vivian Leburg, the child of Eastern European Jewish refugees. As she wrote to her mother in a loopy handwriting that underscores how young she was, "I'm going because I have to, Mom. Because at last I feel dedicated to a movement. Don't be mad."

With her boyfriend, Greg Hicks, Leburg was one of three hundred northern students who went south in the summer of 1965. She went first to the Jackson COFO office and participated in demonstrations that sent one thousand people to jail. Then, in Leake County, she worked on voter registration and school integration.

"Greg and I have half-way decided to work together. One reason is that as a white woman I can get more respect and therefore be more useful if I am not a single girl by myself in a community."[48] Accompanied by a protective boyfriend, she will be seen as "a woman"; without him, she knows she will be seen and taken less seriously as "a girl."

On June 30, Leburg wrote to her mother:

Yesterday I was sent to Leake County to work in the new office started
there. We are out in rural Mississippi. The closest store is about 5 miles
and the closest town about 25 miles. It's beautiful country, and it's
quiet and green. Greg is here too, and I think we may be working here
all summer. There is no movement around here yet, and if one starts it
will be through the efforts of three of us volunteers and about four
local people. The office is a tiny shack and was given to us after the
man who lived in it died. Water comes from an old pump, and we use
an outhouse which belongs to the family next door. . . .

Yesterday I went into Canton with the Movement people down there
and integrated a white park. It was really weird. The white people are
like animals here. They hate especially us white folks, because they
can't understand us at all. It was the first time I have come face to face
with any white southerners besides the police. The white people were
yelling at us and spitting, but we have a court order which makes the
integration protected by the court, so they couldn't beat anyone up.

In mid-July, Leburg had to go it alone, when her boyfriend's
mother, Florence Hicks, came down for a visit and persuaded him to
move to another project. The young woman wrote, "I feel she is jealous
[of our relationship] and must work to destroy it." But Leburg continued her work: establishing a Freedom School; teaching young people;
testing local segregated restaurants; fighting for better conditions at the
local "Negro" school; and advocating school integration.

Leburg's next challenge was to acquire a driver's license. She had
tried for days but kept running into harassment and bureaucratic obstacles because "the officials hate outside agitators." Her next move for
getting what she wanted nimbly combined the stance of defiant outsider with that of "entitled" insider. It drew on a subtle intergenerational cultural transmission that helped Leburg stand up for herself in
the South. She wrote to her mother:

After taking the especially hard test they give to civil rights workers,
and being told I failed it when I obviously did not, I used some of your
tactics. You know when you get mad, you threaten a person and tell
them you will tell all your friends about the poor service? Well, I told
this highway officer that he was obviously harassing me and that I

would not stand for it any longer and that he must give me my test because I was going directly to the commissioner of public safety to show him how the officer had lied. For about half an hour I yelled at this man and finally he got so scared that he gave me a license. I didn't expect he would. But I guess I really scared him badly—thanks to you who taught me how to scare salesladies and people who are supposed to serve you.[49]

Leburg's use of her mother's "tactics" for getting what she needed bespeaks the ability of newly upwardly-mobile groups, such as American Jews, to use class and educational status to get appropriate "service" and deference—from working-class white men in the South or working-class saleswomen in Los Angeles. But it is also a tactic of the socially vulnerable. Leburg's mother, a single parent and Jewish refugee, used verbal skills to create a safety net for her family when she lacked the material resources to do so.[50]

Verbal bravado, which a number of the Jewish women in this book consciously claimed and/or enacted, served to manage fear. In *Personal Politics*, Sara Evans describes how Leburg slept on a porch next to a rifle she didn't know how to use when local whites began to ride through the Black community she was working in. Evans remarks, "Middle-class women learned to live with an intensity of fear they had never known before. . . . Vivian Leburg summed up the feelings of hundreds when she explained, 'I learned a lot of respect for myself for having gone through all that.'"[51]

Going south gave Jewish women a sense of agency and self-respect as women who demonstrated physical and moral courage. It showed them that there were alternatives to marrying a "nice Jewish boy" and moving to the suburbs. And it provided a sense of community and meaning that they did not find within the Jewish communities available to them. Yet it also put things in perspective for them. It reminded them of their relative privileges as young white people only a generation or two removed from immigration and poverty.

Moreover, their experiences in the South gave Jewish women a more realistic sense of the joys and difficulties of being in an interracial movement fighting for social justice. That many of these women remain actively committed to the elimination of racism and poverty suggests that these difficulties, while painful, did not fundamentally alter their visions of social justice. In most cases, working in the southern movement strengthened the women's commitment to fight discrimination.

As the next chapter makes clear, Jewish women's experiences as allies of African Americans during this era also raised questions about their own identities and histories. Working and living in the South highlighted the complexity of being white American Jewish women fighting for Black civil rights.

NOTES

1. Carson, *In Struggle*, 97.
2. Chafe, *Never Stop Running*, 180–186, 201–210.
3. Dittmer, 146.
4. Interview with Roberta Galler, December 10, 1994.
5. Only with the development of the multidisciplinary field of women's studies can we see, name, and value such radical applications of women's traditional care-giving role. See Joan Tronto, "Care as a Political Concept," in Nancy Hirschmann and Christine Di Stephano, eds., *Revisioning the Political: Feminist Reconstructions of Traditional Concepts in Western Political Theory* (Boulder: Westview Press, 1996), 139–156.
6. Interview with Dorothy Miller Zellner, January 4, 1994.
7. The following account of the Schwerners' experiences is drawn from Seth Cagin and Philip Dray, *We Are Not Afraid: The Story of Goodman, Schwerner, and Chaney and the Civil Rights Campaign for Mississippi* (New York: Macmillan, 1988), and William Bradford Huie, *Three Lives for Mississippi* (New York: Signet Books, 1968).
8. Cagin and Dray, 257–258.
9. Cited in Huie, 37–38.
10. Ibid., 44–45.
11. Cagin and Dray, 257.
12. Huie, 39.
13. Sally Belfrage as quoted in McAdam, *Freedom Summer*, 70.
14. Cagin and Dray, 368.
15. Interview with Dorothy Miller Zellner, May 6, 1997.
16. Cagin and Dray, 357.
17. Ibid., 360.
18. Ibid., 366.
19. Ibid., 368.
20. Carson, *In Struggle*, 115.
21. Doug McAdam, "Gender as a Mediator of the Activist Experience: The Case of Freedom Summer," *American Journal of Sociology* 97 (March 1992): 1230.
22. McAdam, *Freedom Summer*, 108.
23. For a personal account of the movement in Greenwood, see Sally Belfrage, *Freedom Summer* (Charlottesville: University of Virginia Press, 1990).

24. Dittmer, 276–279.

25. Rothschild as cited in McAdam, *Freedom Summer*, 96.

26. Interview with Florence Howe, December 1, 1993.

27. Florence Howe, *Myths of Coeducation* (Bloomington: Indiana University Press, 1984), 1.

28. Elizabeth Aaronsohn, "Justice, Justice Shalt Thou Do," in Christine Clark and James O'Donnell, eds., *Becoming and Unbecoming White: Owning and Disowning a Racial Identity* (Westport, Conn.: Bergin and Garvey, 1999), 201.

29. Liz Fusco, "Freedom Schools in Mississippi" (1964) reprinted in *Radical Teacher* 40 (Fall 1991): 37. This issue also contains Charles Cobb's original call for Freedom Schools and the entire Freedom School curriculum.

30. Ibid., 40.

31. Chafe, *Never Stop Running*, 190.

32. Steven Lawson, *Running for Freedom: Civil Rights and Black Politics in America since 1941* (Philadelphia: Temple University Press, 1991), 147.

33. Carson, *In Struggle*, 149.

34. Dittmer, 338.

35. Interview with Roberta Galler, December 10, 1994.

36. Dittmer, 340–341.

37. Interview with Roberta Galler, December 10, 1994.

38. Interview with Janice Goodman, October 21, 1993.

39. Dittmer, 340.

40. Ibid., 344–346.

41. Interview with Janice Goodman, October 21, 1993.

42. McAdam, *Freedom Summer*, 158.

43. Phone interview with Gladys Blum, December 16, 1993.

44. Rhoda Lois Blumberg, "White Mothers as Civil Rights Activists: The Interweave of Family and Movement Roles," in Guida West and Rhoda Lois Blumberg, eds., *Women and Social Protest* (New York: Oxford University Press, 1990), 173.

45. Interview with Harriet Tanzman, October 15, 1993.

46. Interview with June Finer, December 7, 1993.

47. This brief summary relies on Blumberg, *Civil Rights*, 128–133.

48. Vivian Leburg Rothstein, letter to her mother, June 28, 1965; used with author's permission.

49. Vivian Leburg Rothstein, letter to her mother, August 21, 1965; used with author's permission.

50. Leburg, her mother, and the women in this book can be seen within the reclaimed category of "Jewess." Amy-Jill Levine traces the history of the term and suggests a submerged tradition in which "Jewesses" (as strong Jewish women) are noted for their sexuality, intellect, sophistication, and attempts at self-determination and assimilation. "Therein lies her threat, for she penetrates the dominant group easily, without its realization." Amy-Jill Levine, "A Jewess,

More and/or Less," in Peskowitz and Levitt, 151. Riv-Ellen Prell notes the complex and contradictory nature of Jewish ethnic stereotypes, which Jews themselves help perpetuate. Prell has documented the gendered nature of American Jewish stereotypes in the assimilation process, citing of particular relevance here, the "vulgar Jewish woman" known for "loud and nasal voices and for an absence of good manners." However, the availability of such popular culture images also enabled Jewish women to invoke aspects of the stereotypes to protect their families and achieve their goals. See Riv-Ellen Prell, "Stereotypes," in Hyman and Moore, 1324–1332, and Riv-Ellen Prell, *Fighting to Become Americans: Jews, Gender and the Anxiety of Assimilation* (Boston: Beacon Press, 1999).

   51. Sara Evans, *Personal Politics*, 72–73.

3

Crossing Boundaries

Jewishness in the South, 1960–1967

> Either all of us are your people or none of us are your people.
> —Roberta Galler

DURING HER STAY in the Hinds County Jail in June 1965, Roberta Galler first encountered the Jackson Jewish community in the form of Rabbi Perry Nussbaum. Nussbaum, who had been quietly supporting civil rights against the wishes of his congregation, came into the cell where Galler and several other Jewish women were jailed. Holding up toothbrushes, soap, and other small necessities, Galler recalls that he said, "Okay, who in here are my people?" Galler stepped forward and said, "Either all of us are your people or none of us are your people."[1]

Galler's defiant declaration highlights both the self-righteousness and the universalist spirit in which young Jewish activists saw their civil rights activism. She did not know that Nussbaum was going out on a limb to visit civil rights workers in jail, nor could she have known that his decade of efforts addressing civil rights questions would lead to the bombing of his home and synagogue two years later. With little patience for the situation of southern Jewish communities and little desire to be identified as Jews themselves, young Jewish activists in SNCC recoiled from any sign of what they saw as Jewish ethnic particularism. Nevertheless, they had walked into a landscape where Jewishness mattered.

Most of the northern Jewish women who went south for the movement came from urban centers with large Jewish populations. Although they had encountered mild anti-Semitism while growing up, they could take Jewish identity for granted. Growing up in the 1950s, Jewish women activists internalized mixed messages about Jewish identity from their families and the mainstream culture. One should be proud to be a Jew but not act "too Jewish." Consequently, most of the women were ambivalent about Jewish identity as girls and young women. They felt revulsion at the "backwardness" and sexism of Orthodox Jewish practices, and aversion to what they saw as the materialism and spiritual bankruptcy of suburban Jewish life. Living in the contradictions of midcentury American Jewish culture, they developed their own critiques and chose whether, when, and where to identify themselves as Jewish. However, once in the South, they had the same choice Jewish southerners had always faced: to "pass" or to "come out" as a Jew.

Whether they chose to identify as Jewish or not, the Jewishness of the northern civil rights workers already had a host of meanings to the southern Jewish community, to the Ku Klux Klan, and to the southern Black community, including movement activists. Determined to cross racial, ethnic, and gender boundaries, Jewish women civil rights workers could ignore these meanings and the dynamics they produced only at their peril. The environment in which they worked was laden with tensions born of both the past and present. An understanding of that environment begins with an overview of southern Jewish history.[2]

CONTEXTUALIZING SOUTHERN JEWS

In 1913, Leo Frank was convicted of killing Mary Phagan, a thirteen-year-old from Marietta, Georgia, who worked for him at the National Pencil Company in Atlanta. Frank, who was of German-Jewish background, raised in Brooklyn and educated at Cornell University, had moved south to go into business. In 1915, Georgia governor John Slaton commuted Frank's sentence from execution to life imprisonment on the basis of inconclusive evidence. Taking matters into their own hands, a cross-class group of local men formed a mob. Calling themselves "the Knights of Mary Phagan" and implicitly defending the sexual honor of southern white Christian women, they took Frank from his Atlanta jail cell and lynched him in Marietta on August 17, 1915.[3]

Nativism, the Frank lynching, and the rise of the Ku Klux Klan in the 1920s "encouraged the expression of latent anti-semitism in Atlanta and in the deep South generally."[4] W. J. Cash's influential 1941 book, *The Mind of the South*, reveals the stereotypical view of Jews held by many southern whites. In what sounds like a classic case of "blaming the victim," Cash wrote:

The Jew, with his universal refusal to be assimilated, is everywhere the eternal Alien; and in the South, where any difference had always stood out with great vividness, he was especially so. Hence it was perfectly natural that . . . [the "Jew" should,] as he passed in the street, stand in the eyes of the people as a sort of evil harbinger and incarnation of all the menaces they feared and hated—external and internal, real and imaginary.[5]

One of those menaces was industrialization, in which Jews did play an important role, notably in manufacturing, banking, railroads, and wholesaling. Several decades of anti-Semitic propaganda set the stage to scapegoat Jews for industrialization. Southern Populists such as Tom Watson had disseminated images of Jews as sexual perverts who desired virtuous southern white Christian women. To poor, rural, white southern Christian men, "Jews symbolized the worst evils of an industrial system that subjected them to poverty and forced them to send their women to work in factories where they were at the mercy of crazed Jewish sex fiends."[6] This racial/sexual paranoia paralleled the long history of similar white projections onto Black male sexuality. Just as they would later focus their fears about change on northern Jewish civil rights workers, many white Christian southerners in the early twentieth century sexualized and obsessively blamed northern Jewish capitalists for changing their economy and way of life.

Southern Jews reacted defensively to these attacks by blaming the recent influx of Eastern European Jewish immigrants for outbreaks of anti-Semitism. In a pattern of internal class tensions replicated elsewhere in the Jewish community, Atlanta's more established and wealthy German Jews tried to dissociate themselves from several thousand unassimilated, working-class Eastern European Jews who immigrated to the city between 1890 and 1910. These internal tensions, the rise of populist anti-Semitism, and the Leo Frank lynching were enough to send southern Jews looking for cover. Thus ended the most active period of southern Jewish political and civic involvement before World War II. After World War II, anti-Semitism in the South was manifested mainly in social discrimination.[7] Southern Jews in general did not openly challenge the region's political system. Thus, Jews who cooperated with traditional local politics and were economically productive could expect religious tolerance from the community.

This uneasy trade-off sometimes led Jews to overcompensate in their zeal to fit into the southern way of life. For example, the head of the American Jewish League Against Communism, Rabbi Benjamin Schultz of Clarksdale, Mississippi, was a great supporter of Senator Joseph McCarthy.[8] Some Jews joined White Citizens' Councils, the first of which was founded in 1954 in Indianola, Mississippi.[9] Although these local entities dedicated to preserving segregation often worked with the Klan, the councils had a more respectable civic appearance. Southern Jews joined the councils for complicated reasons ranging from economic blackmail by local white elites to the desire to ensure personal and communal security at all costs.[10]

The southern Jewish community, which was less than one-half of one percent of the total population of the South, consisted mainly of merchants who depended on local communities for their livelihood.[11] Between the 1940s and the end of the 1960s, the Jewish population, already minuscule, decreased in such Deep South states as Alabama, Arkansas, Louisiana, Mississippi, and Tennessee,[12] areas in which the southern civil rights movement would concentrate. Given their ambiguous status in southern society, southern Jews were afraid that support for civil rights would threaten their physical and financial security. There is modest evidence of southern Jewish merchants subverting the racial order by serving and/or, less frequently, hiring Blacks, but the community's overall stance was one of cautious self-preservation.[13]

Despite the pressures against progressive Jewish political involvement in the South, a small number of southern Jews, including women, did contribute to antiracist politics. In Birmingham, Marge Gelders (b. 1922), daughter of southern Jewish progressive leader Joseph Gelders, joined the Young Communist League at age thirteen. During the 1940s, she became active in the Southern Conference on Human Welfare (SCHW) and the League of Young Southerners (LYS), where she and her husband, civil rights lawyer Laurent Frantz, participated in interracial meetings, risking arrest to promote interracial culture.[14]

In Montgomery, Alabama, one source of support for the radical Sharecroppers Union (in which Black women were particularly active) came from a small group of white liberals who had formed a Marxist study group in the 1930s. "Composed of some of the most prominent and richest people in Montgomery," the largely female group included teachers, social workers, and wives of upper-middle-class Jews interested in world peace and domestic social reforms.[15]

Although the majority of southern rabbis avoided political controversy throughout the twentieth century, some did address civil rights issues with a variety of approaches ranging from cautious to defiant.[16]

In the 1930s, Rabbi Benjamin Goldstein of Montgomery's Temple Beth Or was forced to leave Alabama because of his support for a Communist Party–led group, the International Labor Defense (ILD). "Faced with boycotts and Klan threats, Jewish merchants and other leading members of Montgomery's Temple Beth Or congregation not only asked Goldstein to resign, but issued a statement to the press repudiating any outside interference in southern affairs and pledging their unequivocal support for segregation."[17] It was a response many southern Jewish communities would replicate as a number of rabbis sought to reconcile their Jewish consciences with the questions raised by the emerging civil rights movement.

Speaking out definitely involved risks. Even in a large and relatively tolerant city like Atlanta, Rabbi Jacob Rothschild was threatened and in October 1958, his temple, the Hebrew Benevolent Congregation, was bombed. Writing in 1981, his wife, Janice Rothschild Blumberg, recalled that Rabbi Rothschild tried to combat what she called "the Leo Frank syndrome." He wanted to show his congregants that they should not be afraid to publicly identify as Jews involved in current issues. The support of local, state, and federal leaders, and the denunciation of the bombing by President Eisenhower, relieved some of the Atlanta Jewish community's anxiety that, as in the Leo Frank case, they had few allies outside their own community.

Nevertheless, there was reason to fear violent anti-Semitism in the civil rights era. Ten percent of the bombings from 1954 to 1959 were directed at synagogues, rabbis' houses, and Jewish community centers. Southern congregations attempted to muzzle activist rabbis such as Perry Nussbaum of Jackson and Charles Mantinband of Hattiesburg. Mantinband, perhaps the only southern-born rabbi involved in civil rights activism, tenaciously defied both segregationists and his own congregation. Mantinband risked attack by defending the NAACP, speaking at Black colleges and meetings, and socializing with Black colleagues.[18] Unlike most Jewish southerners, Mantinband explicitly connected his religious beliefs with an obligation to fight racism.

The actions of Rabbis Rothschild, Nussbaum, and Mantinband were relatively unique. When the South braced for an influx of northern white student activists, most southern Jews, eager to differentiate themselves from their northern counterparts, saw their Jewish brethren as "outside agitators." Southern Jews' perceived need to protect their physical and financial security, and thus the status quo, set them apart from the northern Jewish activists whose explicit mission in coming

South was to make trouble. It is hardly surprising that interactions among northern Jewish activists and local southern Jews engendered hostile feelings on both sides. Northern Jewish women's encounters with the southern Jewish community exemplified these tensions.

MEETING THE SOUTHERN JEWISH COMMUNITY

In 1964, the year Mississippi waited for the arrival of one thousand northern students volunteering for the Freedom Summer Project, the state's Jewish population was quite small. For example, there were 700 Jews living in Greenville; 420, in Jackson, the state capital; 385, in Meridian, where Mickey and Rita Schwerner opened a community center; and 140, in Natchez, which Florence Howe experienced as "a hell-hole for civil rights workers." Even compared to other Deep South states, Mississippi's Jewish population was small. In Alabama, Selma had only 210 Jews, but Birmingham's Jewish population was 4,145. In Georgia, there were 525 Jews in Albany and 14,500 in Atlanta.[19]

Hattiesburg, Mississippi, a community of fewer than 50,000 (including 180 Jews), was the site of one of the larger summer projects: an estimated 650–675 summer volunteers. There, on July 10, 1964, two men attacked Rabbi Arthur Lelyveld of Cleveland, Ohio, and two volunteers. Emerging from the hospital, Rabbi Lelyveld said Jews in Mississippi should "stand up for decency and freedom with all the risks involved" or leave the state.[20] Hattiesburg's Rabbi Charles Mantinband had done just that, having been driven by hatred and racial intransigence to accept a position in Texas in 1963.

Northern Jewish women activists expressed similar frustration and outrage with the southern Jewish community they encountered through local synagogues and rabbis. Reflecting their own experiences in which Jewishness could be taken for granted, they were unprepared for the level of isolation and fear southern Jews felt. As young people risking their lives for civil rights, they were unsympathetic to southern Jewish fears. Further, they did not want to be reminded of qualities in some northern Jewish communities that they were seeking to escape— such as an emphasis on upward mobility, keeping up appearances, and insularity.

The civil rights movement threatened the tentatively "safe space" some Jews had made for themselves in southern life, and they reacted defensively. During her brief 1960 stay in New Orleans with fellow civil rights workers from the Miami CORE training, Dottie Miller asked how she could help. One of the things they asked her to do was to visit local clergy. The priest she met with was very open, but not so Rabbi Julian Feibelman. "I said, 'Rabbi, I'm Jewish, I'm down here to help.' He said, 'Get out,' so this left me a very bitter girl, very bitter." In contrast, Eli Evans portrays Feibelman as "a complex man who grew up in Mississippi," a founder of the anti-Zionist American Council for Judaism in the 1940s, and the host of the first large integrated meeting in New Orleans. In 1949, Ralph Bunche spoke at Feibelman's temple.[21] Zellner's reaction to Feibelman suggests the tendency of a young person ignorant of the complex histories of Jews in the South to see things in terms of moral absolutes. Feibelman's response to her introductory remark could be attributed to sexism, in addition to displeasure with northern Jewish intervention in southern Jewish affairs.

Another "bitter girl" was Barbara Jacobs Haber, who in the early sixties "encountered a lot of Jewish racism in Baltimore, which was more racist than New York." In 1962, the local CORE leadership asked Haber to go to local synagogues with a Black CORE member to request support. "We didn't get it and I remember my rage at these disgusting racist or wishy-washy rabbis we went to talk to."

Faith Holsaert recalls that her colleague in the southwest Georgia project, Larry Rubin, "went to the synagogue in Albany once, and there were no friendly dealings with the local Jewish community and SNCC people in Albany." Miriam Cohen Glickman relates that "they were not very happy to see me at the temple in Albany."

Florence Howe uses the word *horrible* to describe her forays into the white Jewish community in Jackson, Mississippi, to raise money for COFO's food and clothing drives. "I was assigned because I was the only available proper Jewish lady, because I was an assistant professor at Goucher who could speak nicely." Much to her chagrin, COFO sent Howe as often as possible on these missions.

Howe's use of the term *white Jewish community* underscores her alienation from the Jewish community and her identification with the Black struggle. Because they were not part of the solution, Howe considered southern Jews to be part of the problem. They were complicit with the racial system she was challenging. Their conversations only heightened her sense of herself as an outsider. Assuming she would share their racial views because of shared Jewishness, southern Jews Howe approached would ask, "'How would you feel if your daughter married one of them?'" She would say, "'I'd feel honored' and they would really want to lynch me. I never knew the right things to say. The COFO people thought I was great at this, but I really was terrible because I didn't want to listen to them, I didn't want to hear them say all their racist stuff. . . . Those were the most unpleasant evenings I ever had to spend anywhere."

Howe's disappointment may have been heightened by shame that "her own people" seemed just as racist as did southern white Christians. Like Carol Ruth Silver's uncle, who would not venture into a Black New Orleans neighborhood to see her after the Freedom Rides, southern Jews appeared to betray their northern activist kin by keeping a safe distance.

In contrast, Miriam Cohen Glickman spent time with a local Jewish family in Mississippi, to whom the Klan had made threatening phone calls. The father bragged that he had told them, "Come on out—I have a gun."[22] Such open defiance seems to have been relatively rare among the southern Jewish community, but anecdotal evidence suggests that some southern Jews supported civil rights in more guarded ways.[23]

For example, June Finer had an experience that exemplifies poignantly the bind in which civil rights protests placed the southern Jewish community. During the summer of 1965, there were several Jewish medical people from the Medical Committee for Human Rights assigned to Selma for one- or two-week periods. Finer recalls:

> With a couple of Jewish kids who were in the group at that time, we decided to put on our proper clothes and go to *shul* [synagogue] on Friday. In Selma there was a small Jewish congregation probably of no more than 50 or 60 people. The main *shul* had been closed off, and they had the services in a smaller assembly room. After the service they had coffee and cake. It was very strange meeting this group of southern Jews who were very fearful of us because they were trying to keep a low profile. They were clearly worried that our very presence might label them as radicals and revolutionaries.

Only one family reached out to the Jewish civil rights workers and invited them to their home. Given the family's own hardships due to civil rights work in Selma, they were certainly going out on a limb to do so. As Finer remembers it, the Bartons—mother and daughter—explained

> that a lot of the people were very, very worried about our presence there. The mother was not so southern. She still retained all of her Jew-

ish qualities. The daughter, who was probably my age, was called Betty Faye—Betty Faye Barton. She was like a southern belle but very conscious that she was Jewish. And the father was actually in a mental hospital. He had suffered a severe depression because his shoe store was closed because of the very successful boycott of downtown Selma. It was very strange because here we were as symbols [of what] had in fact demolished their family. The mother was a kindly Jewish lady and she made *rugelach* [a traditional Jewish pastry]. It was a very, very surreal sort of meeting. They were taking huge risks by having us over to their house. They [might] get labeled as "nigger lovers," and they would be even less likely to be able to make a living. I don't know what they were living on with the store bankrupt and the father away. I don't know how they were making ends meet.

This story of Betty Faye Barton and her mother is one of the few accounts of southern Jewish women reaching out directly to civil rights workers during the movement. It underscores the economic and social vulnerability of the large sector of the southern Jewish community who survived as small-scale merchants.

Less economically vulnerable southern Jewish women could afford to take more risks on civil rights. Elaine Crystal of Jackson, Mississippi, for example, wife of the chairman of the board of a large firm, "was even more active and outspoken on racial matters than her husband, having been founder of Mississippians for Public Education."[24]

More wealthy and established Jewish women living in large urban areas, such as Edith Stern of New Orleans, could play a significant role. Daughter of Chicago philanthropist Julius Rosenwald, who gave millions of dollars to build an infrastructure for Black education in the South, Stern inherited some of his fortune. The Stern Family Fund "was one of the few activist sources of money in the South for groups and individuals concerned with civil rights. . . . [It] emerged as a major force for change in the region." Among its grantees was the Voter Education Project of the Southern Regional Council, which "ultimately played the central role in registering three million new Negro voters in the South in the 1960s."[25]

Instances of southern Jewish support for the civil rights movement, however, were more the exception than the rule. Northern Jewish activists admitted to profound disappointment in the organized southern Jewish community's unwillingness to participate in a movement so clearly committed to social justice.

Both southern Jews and northern Jewish civil rights activists were engaged in a struggle about how to enact what Jewishness meant to them. For most southern Jews, their primary struggle was over the right, opportunity, and sense of security to practice Judaism and to publicly identify as Jewish. In other words, they sought the right to be both different from and the same as their southern neighbors. For northern Jewish women activists, who could take their ethnic "difference" for granted at home, the struggle was to infuse meaning into a heritage that seemed to have little place for them. By putting themselves on the line to fight racism, they defied constricting Jewish gender norms and allied themselves with the prophetic Jewish vision of social justice.

ENCOUNTERING THE KLAN

Although Florence Howe and others did not think of their civil rights activism in terms of their being Jewish, other members of southern society—including the Klan—certainly did. In the South, however, Jewish women feared the Klan more as civil rights workers than as Jews.

Encounters with the Klan surface in many of the women's stories. While Miriam Cohen Glickman was driving me to the train, she mentioned casually that a cross had been burned on her parents' lawn in Indianapolis during her civil rights activism. It seemed odd that she had failed to mention this in an extensive transcontinental phone interview, as well as in a two-hour in-person interview on Jewish themes. Odd, given the fact that the rise of the Klan in Indiana in the 1920s and 1930s followed a major increase in the state's Black population, especially in Indianapolis, and that the Klan had also targeted the Jewish community, although much less vehemently.[26] Even so, the delayed, offhand remark underscores the submersion of Jewish identity by Jewish activists in civil rights contexts.

Similarly, after the Selma to Montgomery march, June Finer and her colleagues

> basically got run out of town in Lowndes County after the priest Jonathan Daniels was killed. Some of the civil rights workers had been arrested and we went there to make a doctor visit at the jail. We attempted to go to the jail, [but] as we stood near the courthouse asking where the sheriff's office was, we were surrounded by these guys looking very evil, and we were told that the sheriff was out of town

and we'd better get out of town quickly. We were sort of shuffled back to our car and then basically chased out of town. At one point they had one car alongside and one car right behind us and they would keep trying to cut us off. Apparently what they were doing was quite dangerous, and the driver of our car—I think he was a dentist from San Francisco—really kept his head and got us out of there.

Finer notes that many of the medical and professional volunteers, including the dentist and a psychologist in the car, were Jewish, as is she. When surrounded by men who were very likely members of the Klan, Finer didn't think about her own or her colleagues' Jewishness—either as a comforting bond or a potential liability. Yet, her assertion that many of the volunteer doctors were Jewish suggests that she was aware of this connection on some level.[27]

Florence Howe returned to Mississippi in 1965 with her future husband, Paul Lauter, to work on school desegregation in Natchez, a Klan stronghold in the southwestern part of the state. Because of its potential for violence, COFO had maintained only a very small voter registration project in Natchez in 1964. During that summer in Natchez, two churches were burned to the ground, the police constantly followed SNCC field secretaries and harassed local Blacks, and a tavern owned by an interracial couple living next door to the Freedom House was bombed.[28]

Lauter, Howe, and one of Lauter's students were the only white civil rights workers in Natchez in the summer of 1965. They all worked separately. For Howe, being in Natchez in 1965 was much more dangerous than being in Jackson in 1964 because Natchez "was a hell-hole for civil rights workers. . . . It was very rough, very rough. . . . The only person who would take me in was one of the poorest Black women in the community who had a one-room shack and an outhouse. I slept on the floor."

As they worked on school desegregation, Howe recalls: "We were trailed everywhere by KKK people. We changed cars five times in a month. . . . About every four or five days I would change cars, go to a motel, and take a shower. It was horrible. Really hot. And it was very difficult working." A bomb that Howe believes was meant for their car detonated in a different car. It blew the legs off the man in the car.

Although well aware of the Klan as a threat to her in Natchez, Howe did not feel endangered as a Jew. Because she was not a practicing Jew, she says she did not think of herself as particularly Jewish in those years "unless there was anti-Semitism, or unless people pushed me around." This lack of identification was heightened by "the experience of the Mississippi Summer, in which I was physically safe only in the Black community. The minute I stepped into the white community, I was in physical danger of being killed. I had several very narrow escapes at the hands of white people who were ready to mow me down in a truck."

If Howe had been in Jackson two years later, she would have witnessed the kind of anti-Semitism that might have summoned up her instinct to fight back as a Jew. In 1967, the Jackson area Klan, led by Samuel Bowers, decided to shift its attacks from Blacks to Jews. Bowers, head of the White Knights of the Ku Klux Klan, was obsessed by the idea of an international Jewish-led Communist conspiracy to destroy white Christian society; in the United States, he believed, the cabal's chosen vehicle was the civil rights movement.[29]

The September 18, 1967, bombing of Rabbi Perry Nussbaum's Temple Beth Israel in Jackson underscored how little the Klan cared to differentiate between northern and southern Jews. A few months later, they also bombed Nussbaum's home. After receiving a patronizing response from the Jackson city fathers and Christian religious leaders, Nussbaum and some Jewish community leaders decided on a radical course of action. They financed an FBI scheme to pay Klan informants to set up an elusive fellow Klan bomber who was planning to attack the Jewish community again. The bomber, Albert Tarrants, was only wounded, not killed as planned. Kathy Ainsworth, his female companion on the bombing, was killed.

Terror in the Night, Jack Nelson's account of the Jackson Jewish leaders' campaign, highlights the profoundly different views held by southern Jews and northern Jewish civil rights activists about both the Klan and the FBI. As noted earlier, many of the northern women did not feel that their Jewishness made the Klan a threat to them. They were much less in touch than were southern Jews with the immediate danger the Klan's anti-Semitism represented. Jackson's Jewish leaders who had worked with the FBI to set up the extralegal bomber plot were pragmatists with the financial resources to protect their community ("by any means necessary"). Although the bureau was willing to see the Jewish community's need for self-protection as legitimate in the Jackson temple bombing instance, it clearly did not see the Black community as equally in need. SNCC activists had debated the ideology of armed self-defense internally for some time. However, when some members of

SNCC and the Black Panther Party did arm themselves and/or use the rhetoric of armed self-defense publicly, the FBI's response, through its domestic counterintelligence program, COINTELPRO, was to repress the Black movement.[30]

Many SNCC activists, including the women profiled in this book, would have been horrified at the thought of working with the FBI, which had not protected them throughout the early civil rights campaigns. Indeed, many felt the organization was complicit with the Klan.

The Klan's goal was to preserve the white supremacist racial order, and it targeted anyone perceived to be subverting the order. Moreover, it did not differentiate between "practicing" and "nonpracticing" Jews. Whether Cohen, Finer, Howe, and their Jewish colleagues identified as Jewish or not, the Klan viewed them as part of an invading army of Jewish mongrelizers bent on destroying the southern way of life. Southerners had engaged in a century-long debate about the racial status of Jews, often linking them racially and politically with "Negroes."[31] Although the women did not subscribe to interpretations of their Jewishness by the Klan or the southern Jewish community, they were tolerant of the different meanings that their Jewishness had for local Black communities and movement workers.

TALKING ABOUT JEWISHNESS IN SOUTHERN BLACK COMMUNITIES

Northern Jewish women did not fear the Klan's anti-Semitism and also downplayed any anti-Semitism they encountered in local southern Black communities and the movement. They felt far more betrayed by southern Jews' failure to fight racism than they did by local Black anti-Semitism. The southern Black community's responses to northern Jews who went south included mild anti-Semitism, lack of knowledge of Jews, a sense of religious kinship, and the perception of Jews as a special category of white people.[32]

Dottie Miller Zellner recalls that "if you traveled around the South by car, you'd go to any little town like Greenville or Greenwood and you would see Cohen's Jewelry Store." She notes that local Blacks, especially in the rural areas, had the image that "Jews weren't necessarily rich, but they were store owners or owners of some kind." She remembers explaining to a few people that "where I come from there are Jewish cab drivers. They were very surprised."

Few of the women say they experienced anti-Semitism in the movement. Those who did told their stories without indignation. Their feeling of safety in the Black community and the primacy of anti-Black racism made many Jewish women reluctant to confront whatever Black anti-Semitism they did encounter. As Jan Goodman relates:

> I wasn't aware of it in the South—there you're so involved in the particulars of what you're doing that you become less sensitized, immune to affronts. There was talk about Jews among Blacks in the movement, and I would probably classify it as some level of anti-Semitism, but it's a very conflicted anti-Semitism. At that point [1964–1966], I was much more aware of the affronts to me as a woman than as a Jew.

Other Jewish women's responses to anti-Semitism in the movement were similarly mixed. When asked if she had experienced any anti-Semitism, Dottie Miller Zellner recalls:

> Oh, there were a couple of things. There was a Black Muslim man at the Atlanta office leaning up against his Cadillac, the head minister of the Nation of Islam Mosque in Atlanta, somebody "X," I can't remember his first name. He told everybody that the only thing wrong with Hitler was that he didn't kill all the Jews, he didn't burn them all. And I was standing there. . . . It was one of the first times I ever heard anything really raw like that.

Stunned into silence, Zellner had felt intimidated and afraid: "He was a Black minister and I knew how he felt about white people." No one else in the room spoke out against the minister's remarks.

> [I]t wasn't that they were ready to repudiate what he said, but nobody agreed with him either and it was sort of like, "Oh, this man is saying something I don't want to deal with." Afterwards I pointed out a few things to a few people and I never felt that [the minister's anti-Semitic message] was falling on fertile ground. I think he came over to test the waters.

Though the minister visited the office only once or twice, Zellner admits, "I think I probably could have done better on that occasion. I'm not totally brave."

Although Zellner is critical of herself for not confronting anti-

Semitism in that moment, the story of the encounter has made its way into the literature on Black-Jewish relations in ways that contradict Zellner's own interpretation. For example, Benjamin Ginsberg, in *The Fatal Embrace: Jews and the State*, distorts the encounter by suggesting that it was a direct attempt to intimidate Jewish civil rights workers and to embarrass Black SNCC coworkers for working with Jews.[33] Yet, Zellner clearly chooses to interpret the incident more as a Black Muslim attempt to recruit SNCC to its nationalist point of view than as a direct attack on Jews.

The incident throws into relief the complexity of Jewish identity for Jewish SNCC workers in movement interactions. Zellner's response weighed her Jewish sensibilities against the likely divisiveness of a confrontation with Atlanta's Black Muslim community. In that moment, she gave her SNCC identity highest priority, which did not erase her Jewish identity. Acting in accord with one of several identities in a given political situation does not preclude bringing all of oneself to the situation.

The multiple and complicated expressions of Jewish identity have led to confusion in understanding the role of Jews in the southern civil rights movement. The few civil rights scholars who address the role have done so in less than illuminating ways. These include SNCC activists who became chroniclers of the movement. For example, Mary King writes:

> Despite its traditional emphasis on social justice, Judaism remained in the background. Perhaps in part because its congregations were fighting their own battles against discrimination, its support of the civil rights movement was manifested by individual action. Fellow Jews in the South were not as discriminated against as were Blacks. . . . Few connections compelled those of Jewish extraction or from northern synagogues to go south to take part in a movement so entrenched in the moral suasion and spiritual force of a Black Christian culture closely linked to resistance.

Yet, it is exactly that link to resistance that attracted moderately religious/liberal Jews, as well as secular and radical Jews to the movement. King continues:

> The number of Jews or individuals of Jewish extraction on SNCC staff was perhaps 5 percent, counting Chuck McDew's conversion.

This meant a fluctuating figure of up to one quarter of the white SNCC workers, a percentage showing a concern for justice much higher than their presence in the overall population. No one in SNCC thought of Jews as a separate group, however, they were simply considered white.[34]

Here King seems to contradict herself. She conflates organized participation by synagogue members with the participation of individual Jews. She also underplays the extensive role of Jewish organizations in the civil rights movement. To illustrate, the American Jewish Committee, the American Jewish Congress, the Anti-Defamation League, the National Council of Jewish Women, and Jewish labor unions, among others, provided financial, organizational, legal, and strategic support, albeit often to the more mainstream civil rights organizations. She states that Jews had a disproportionately high presence among white SNCC volunteers in relation to their percentage in the national population but cannot account for that without a better understanding of the secular Jewish tradition.

A more sophisticated historian and SNCC veteran, Clayborne Carson, suggests that it was not Judaism but, rather, radical Jews' alienation from Judaism that enabled them to become allies of their counter-cultural Black SNCC colleagues. It is true that SNCC activists clearly differed from politically conservative, religious Jews; it is not true, however, as Carson later stated during a contentious panel discussion of Black-Jewish relations, that if Jewish heritage motivated Jewish participation in the civil rights movement, "there is no historical evidence for it."[35] (Chapters 4 and 5 treat the nature of that heritage and its links to civil rights activism.) Although his earlier essay seemed to distinguish between Jewish religion and culture, Carson, like many Americans (including Jews), seems to accept and reinforce the hegemonic view of Jewish identity, which defines Jewishness as religion. The delegitimization of a secular Jewish tradition obscures our understanding of the motivations of the significant number of Jews who were actively involved in the civil rights movement.[36]

Zellner and other young Jewish radicals were critical of what they saw as the political pragmatism of the organized Jewish community's motives for civil rights work,[37] but they did respect southern Christians—Black and white—who were moved by religious beliefs to work for civil rights. Of southern white Christians on the SNCC staff, she

Vivian Leburg Rothstein's parents in Holland, 1936, where they lived after fleeing from Berlin, Germany. They subsequently left Holland for New York City under the sponsorship of Rothstein's uncle. Courtesy of Vivian Leburg Rothstein.

Dr. Barney Miller and Dorothy Miller, Stuyvesant Park,
Manhattan, 1939. Courtesy of Dorothy Miller Zellner.

The Galler family in front of maternal grandparents' tailor shop, Chicago, 1942. With uncle Sidney Goldstein, whose Coast Guard ship was subsequently sunk by Germans. Courtesy of Roberta Galler.

Janice Goodman and her mother at summer camp, 1946.
Photo credit: Max Goodman.

Passport photo from 1950. The Holsaerts traveled with Charity Bailey to Haiti. *Left to right:* Faith S. Holsaert, age 7; Eunice S. Holsaert; and Shai S. Holsaert, age 5.

Elaine DeLott, Hebrew School Valedictory Address, Temple TiFereth Israel, Massachusetts, 1952. Courtesy of Elaine DeLott Baker.

Roberta Galler and Ralph Nichols at the office of *New University Thought*, 1962. Courtesy of Roberta Galler.

Barbara Jacobs Haber in the 1960s. Courtesy of Barbara Jacobs Haber.

From an article in the *Southern Patriot*, "Students Challenge Rural Georgia."
SNCC Southwest Georgia project members. *Left to right:* Agnew James of Lee
County, Penny Patch, Faith S. Holsaert, Larry Rubin, and Charles Sherrod,
project director. Photo credit: Patriot Photo.

Dorothy "Dottie" Miller (Zellner) after being clubbed and losing her shoes to high-pressure hoses during a demonstration in Danville, Virginia, June 10, 1963. She gives an affidavit to SNCC executive secretary James Forman. Magnum Photos, Inc. © 1963 Danny Lyons. Used by permission.

Rita Schwerner, Atlantic City, August 25, 1964, speaks to Maine delegates to the Democratic National Convention asking their help in getting the Mississippi Freedom Democratic Party seated at the convention. (AP Wirephoto). By permission of Wide World Photos.

Miriam Cohen (Glickman) in Kiriat, Israel, in the fall of 1964 after working in the 1964 Mississippi Freedom Summer Project. She subsequently returned to work in Mississippi until February 1965. Courtesy of Miriam Cohen Glickman.

Harriet Tanzman assisting two women teargassed on "Bloody Sunday," March 7, 1965, Selma, Alabama. Police on horses charged civil rights activists attempting to cross the Edmund Pettus Bridge. © 1965, 1980, 1990, 2000 Bob Fletcher. Reprinted by permission.

Dr. June Finer, Medical Committee for Human Rights, treats foot-weary Doris Wilson, Selma, 1965. © 1978 Matt Herron/TAKE STOCK. Reprinted by permission.

Jacqueline Levine representing the American Jewish Congress, Selma to Montgomery March, 1965. Courtesy of Jacqueline Levine.

Vivian Leburg (Rothstein) at nineteen and her boyfriend, Greg Hicks, shortly before leaving California for Mississippi in 1965. Courtesy of Vivian Rothstein.

Top: Florence Howe speaking about Freedom Summer; pictured with other activists, Baltimore, January 1965. Courtesy of Florence Howe. *Bottom:* Florence Howe with stepsons David Lauter *(r)* and Daniel Lauter *(l)* and daughter Alice Jackson, Baltimore, 1965–1966. Courtesy of Florence Howe.

Top: Gertrude "Trudy" Weissman Orris at a feminist march, 1978. Courtesy of Trudy Orris. *Bottom:* Trudy Orris at a peace march, 1988. Courtesy of Trudy Orris.

At the Trinity College Conference on the Civil Rights Movement, 1988, singing "We Shall Overcome." *Left to right:* Joyce Ladner, SNCC's second chair Charles McDew, Dorie Ladner, Faith S. Holsaert. Photo credit: David Martin.

Janice Goodman with Mississippi Freedom Democratic Party leader Victoria Gray Adams at the 1988 SNCC Reunion. Courtesy of Janice Goodman.

Friends for more than thirty years, Faith S. Holsaert *(l)* and Amina Rachman *(r)* in 1992. Photo credit: Leonore Gordon.

Vivian Rothstein with Stella and Carien Wilder in Leake County, Mississippi, where she visited them during the 1994 Mississippi Freedom Summer Project 30th Anniversary Reunion. Stella Wilder housed Rothstein in 1965 when she was a civil rights worker. Courtesy of Vivian Rothstein.

Jacqueline Levine and her husband, 1996. Courtesy of Jacqueline Levine.

Miriam Cohen Glickman, 1999.
Courtesy of Miriam Glickman.

Carol Ruth Silver in Birmingham, Alabama, May 2000. Courtesy of Carol
Ruth Silver.

Dorothy Miller Zellner, 1998. Photo credit: André Beckles.

says, "There were very few, very, very few. And all were cherished. The fact that they were southern—we sort of treated them—the analogous situation would be we treated them like righteous Gentiles."[38] The way that Zellner speaks about them indicates she saw herself in a different category, one more identified with Blacks but also resonant with Jewish memory of the Holocaust.

Southern Jews had long endured changes in their racial and ethnic position in the South. Zellner, too, experienced her Jewishness as in a kind of flux, embracing the contradictions with a certain ironic zeal. Having lived in New Orleans for many years after leaving SNCC, she explains, "When I was in the South, I worked out this very complicated way of doing things. If I went to a Jewish hospital and they asked me for Jewish affiliation, I would write 'none.' I found it very annoying and offensive. But if I had to deal with a Gentile establishment, I would always say Jewish because I felt it was important to maintain the honor of the people."

In Meridian, in 1963, Miriam Cohen Glickman discovered that "the local Black community assumed I was Black because there was no concept that a white girl would be down there. . . . They used the term *bright* for light-skinned." She also remembers that "the local people considered the Jewish people not to be white if the Jewish people treated them decently." Cohen's experience is in keeping with a Jewish Anti-Defamation League study of Black attitudes toward Jews in New York, Atlanta, and Birmingham. In citing the study, Eli Evans notes that some of the excerpted interviews indicate "that Southern Blacks don't look on Jews as `whites' but as a sympathetic third race, in contrast to the other whites they encounter."[39]

The above stories and comments draw attention to American Jews' perceived "racial middleness," a concept that highlights the historical nature of American Jewish racial identity. In the postwar era, Jewish assimilation required learning the ways of whiteness. The women in this book were trying to "unlearn" these ways by going south. At the time, most saw their civil rights activism as being motivated by American ideals. But, if, as Toni Morrison argues, the very possibility of being American is predicated on identifying Blacks as "Other," then even these antiracist Jewish women could not escape complicity with assimilated Jewish whiteness in the 1960s.[40] And on some level, they knew it, so they struggled hard to disentangle themselves from the privileges this entailed. Therefore, they must have felt gratified when local southern Blacks saw their Jewish selves as "not-white" because it enabled them to retain a Jewish sense of pride within their larger project of subverting white supremacy.

Clearly, the racial meaning of Jewishness in the southern movement context was difficult for both Blacks and northern Jewish women activists to negotiate. It was far easier for each group to relate to the other by trying to connect the political values intrinsic to the Jewish and Christian spiritual traditions.

Carol Ruth Silver recounts her reactions to a community meeting honoring two hundred Freedom Riders returning to Jackson for trial in August 1961:

> The opening invocation was given by a rabbi from San Francisco, and I was at this point introduced to one of the strangest (to me) aspects of a southern Negro audience, their habit of responding aloud to sentiments with which they were pleased. As the rabbi repeated some of the stock phrases of Jewish ritual, I heard choruses of "That's right," "We believe," and "A-men!" At first I could not help feeling that this was impolite and inappropriate, but as it continued through the evening, I began to get into the spirit too and to shed my northern reserve.[41]

At the time of her participation in the Albany Movement in 1962–1963, Faith Holsaert believed her activism "grew out of ethical and humanist principles that I think are inherent in Judaism." She remembers "talking with people in rural Georgia who never met someone who was Jewish before about why I felt that." Some of the people "were kind of baffled" but others understood because the movement was very centered in the church. "Although it was the Christian church," Holsaert found "it was easier to talk in terms of moral, religious reasons for doing political things." She believes that her project director, Charles Sherrod, a minister, "would have seen Judaism as a spiritual ancestor of Christianity."

In a similar way, Jewish communal leader Jacqueline Levine used the prophetic voice of southern Black Christian spirituality to advance her own progressive Jewish agenda. Levine, who flew in for the March 25, 1965, Montgomery rally at the end of the Selma to Montgomery march, made explicit links between the prophetic aspects of both traditions. Her brief stay differentiates her from the rest of the women in this book, as does her explicit pleasure at the time in participating as a Jew.

As president of the Women's Division of the American Jewish Congress and a vice-president of the Council of Jewish Federations and Welfare Funds, Levine appealed in 1972 to the General Assembly of the Council (the country's most influential Jewish organization) for the greater participation of women in Jewish communal life:

> Seven years ago last March I participated in the glorious march from Selma to Montgomery, a march undertaken for the purpose of securing voting rights for all Americans. I stood, one balmy Alabama night, under a starry Alabama sky, and I heard the never-to-be-forgotten voice of Martin Luther King ring out in his never-to-be-heard-again prophetic cadences as he said, "We are all witnesses together." He did not mean witness as onlooker, witness as voyeur. He meant witness-participant. And so are we women, when we ask to share in communal responsibility, asking to be witnesses, participants, in our own Jewish community.[42]

Seeking community, many of the young northern Jewish women activists felt community's potential in the southern Black churches so central to the movement. As June Finer puts it, "The church was just where you went to meetings all the time, so the churches became very much a warm and friendly part of the whole movement." Often, in more dangerous situations, such as Dottie Miller Zellner's escape from Danville, the churches were the only safe havens for civil rights workers. But deeper feelings of spiritual connection were also at play.

Miriam Cohen connected with and reflected deeply on her experience with southern Black religious practice. She wrote in the December 17, 1963, issue of Brandeis University's student newspaper, *The Justice*:

> The summer in Albany was the first meaningful religious experience in my life. I must have prayed hours each day—for what else were my thoughts about my friends in jail but prayer? Too, there were the mass meetings when an old woman cried out in hysterical seizure (in good Baptist tradition), "Jesus, Jesus, we need you Jesus! Come to Albany, Jesus! . . . Have mercy, Jesus!" Again and again she intoned her plea, to Jesus—the symbol of her suffering. A part of me was with her, for I too cried out to something outside myself, my own suffering [in jail] and my reactions to the suffering of others was more than I could bear within. *The unrehearsed cry of those who have suffered too much had meaning for me that prayers of rote recitation never had.*[43]

For Cohen at that moment in her life, "The Black Church seemed much more emotionally relevant to me."

It is not surprising that young Jewish civil rights workers resonated with the spirit and politics of the Black church. Most Reform and Conservative American Jewish movements, with their emphasis on decorum and respectability, left behind the emotionalism "of traditional European Jewish prayer." Given the imperative to assimilate into American society, such a tradition seemed "chaotic, lacking harmony, and Western aesthetics."[44] Yet, something was lost in the process of Americanizing Eastern European Jewish ways of life. Young Jewish activists rejected the materialism and inauthenticity of suburban Jewish life. Jewish women activists in this book found the culture of U.S. synagogues at best sterile and at worst hypocritical, sexist, and alienating. They sought a community, as Elaine DeLott Baker wrote a friend after returning from Mississippi, where "thought and action had meaning and a kind of totality, which in actuality gives you sometimes a heightened and perhaps dangerous urgency about the significance of both."[45]

Most of the women initially found the community of meaning they were looking for in SNCC. Yet, despite their embrace of universalism and interracialism in SNCC's "beloved community," the Jewish women in SNCC could not transcend the effects of such forces as racism, sexism, and political repression on the movement. These forces drove a wedge between Blacks and whites, men and women in the movement.

WORKING WITH BLACK WOMEN IN THE MOVEMENT

Elizabeth Slade Hirschfeld remembers that during the Freedom Rides, "there wasn't the hostility then between Black and white women. . . . It was too early. The Freedom Ride was the pure time. We really hadn't had to work together." When she got out of Parchman Prison in 1961, Hirschfeld stayed with Cordell Reagon's sister, Joy, and another Black woman who had been jailed with them. She recalls their closeness: "We all had to sleep in the same bed. I was in the middle and we had our arms all wound up against each other . . . and for a second, I couldn't figure out whose arms were whose. We talked about that and about the closeness for awhile."

Later, the night before their arraignment, the three women went to church where people were singing "We Shall Overcome." When they sang the verse that included "Black and white together," everyone held up and linked their arms. Hirschfeld recalls it as "a very spiritual and joyous moment" in which she thought, "at this second, I'm part of history."

Hirschfeld did not realize that she was also part of a history of northern white and Jewish women who went south to fight for racial justice in earlier periods of the twentieth century. One avenue for doing so was through the Communist Party, which was one of the earliest supporters of the twentieth-century Black civil rights movement.[46]

In 1951, Jessica Mitford and four other women from the California Communist Party, including Evie Frieden, the daughter of radical Jewish Hungarian immigrants, drove from Oakland to Jackson, Mississippi, as a "White Women's Delegation." Sponsored by the national office of the Civil Rights Congress, they went to Jackson to sway public opinion on the Willie McGee case. The "White Women's Delegation" visited clergymen, clubwomen, and other prominent white Jackson citizens and did door-to-door canvassing in white neighborhoods.[47] As noted earlier, their efforts and Bella Abzug's advocacy failed.

Later conflicts between some members of the Black and Jewish communities should not obscure stories that remain to be told of Black and Jewish women's activist collaborations for civil rights. For example, there is a history of collaboration between the National Council of Negro Women (NCNW) and the National Council of Jewish Women (NCJW) that dates back at least to the 1940s. Mary McLeod Bethune (1875–1955), founder and president of the National Council of Negro Women from 1935 to 1949, sent the organization's executive director to the National Council of Jewish Women for consultations when the NCNW was planning its governance structure.[48]

One Jewish woman who remained intimately involved with NCNW was Polly Spiegel Cowan. Cowan was very close to Dorothy Height, president of NCNW since 1957. During the civil rights movement, they collaborated on "Wednesdays in Mississippi," an effort that brought groups of prominent northern white and Black women to Mississippi to meet with their southern counterparts in interracial settings to support the movement. Among participants were Pearl Willen, president of the National Council of Jewish Women; Trude Lash (wife of Roosevelt biographer Joseph Lash); and activist/attorney Flo Kennedy.[49]

In July 1964, during one of their visits, Height and Cowan decided to integrate a motel near Jackson. Cowan's son, veteran civil rights worker Paul Cowan, wrote in his memoir, *An Orphan in History*, that when he went to visit them, he noticed some white teenagers drinking beer by the motel pool and making racist comments. His mother and Dorothy Height seemed not to be worried by this:

> After my parents died, Dorothy Height told me that a cross had been burned in front of their window late that night. She and Polly doubted they would survive until the next morning. Polly, who talked about the past, her feelings, her work, and even her sexual attitudes with complete freedom, had never bothered to mention that part of the episode. Why should she dwell on something that might make her seem heroic? She knew that the people in whose name she was acting, Jews in Hitler's Europe, Blacks in the South, had faced far greater dangers than she ever would. Many millions had died. In her mind, where good manners and good taste were inextricably interwoven with progressive politics, it seemed unseemly to dwell on the few minutes of fear she had faced.[50]

Polly Cowan stayed in the civil rights movement until she died, long after many liberals, including Jewish liberals, had left it. She was the only white woman on the board of the National Council of Negro Women. She helped establish a day-care center in Mississippi. She worked for a drug rehabilitation program in New York. She became NCNW's delegate to the United Nations. Paul Cowan wrote:

> Of course she felt uneasy with the polarization that beset the movement; with slogans like "Black Power," which often communicated strong anti-white feelings. Indeed, the polarization was more painful for her than to most people, since it affected her daily as the only white official of a Black organization. But her loyalty to Black allies like Dorothy Height remained unshakeable. . . . Once in a while she mentioned the fact that in Germany during the tough times, many Christians, including liberals, had abandoned the Jews. In her stoic way, I think she retained a deep commitment, almost a spiritual commitment, to the importance of bearing witness to the fact that that need not happen between Blacks and whites in the United States.[51]

Roberta Galler, who went south just as Black Power concepts were gaining acceptance, also sought to heal rifts between Blacks and whites through the authenticity of her personal relationships with movement coworkers. This included sharing her Jewish connection:

I brought some of my Jewishness down with me. I did have my own cultural stuff—it really wasn't religious stuff. . . . When I was living in the Morehouse apartments near Jackson State University, I gave a Jewish soul food party. From very cheap food that I had access to, I made *luchsen kugel* [a dense noodle pudding] for the multitudes. You could make it with noodles and cottage cheese and raisins and all the things I could still get in the South and the food wasn't so strange tasting to a lot of Black people.[52]

Galler was also known, "as hysterical as it was," for traveling throughout Mississippi with cooking equipment and spices. In Mount Beulah, she and movement coworkers lived in an old deserted college dormitory, where they were provided "terrible food" in a big institutional kitchen. Occasionally, they took matters into their own hands. Galler remembers

making a big Thanksgiving dinner there and stirring the biggest vat I ever saw to make cranberry sauce. I also remember—it must have been Chanukah—attempting to make potato pancakes, and grating, grating, grating lots of potatoes. I had never made them before and I didn't know that you had to put them in ice cold water or they would turn black and the potatoes were turning black, but we did make latkes. The people liked them but they were very ugly.[53]

The fact that Galler traveled throughout the state may have mitigated some of the tensions felt between Black and white women in more settled local projects. However, at the heart of SNCC's operations, its headquarters in Atlanta, an effective working relationship evolved quickly between Dottie Miller Zellner and Ruby Doris Smith, the indomitable Black woman leader who had inspired Carol Ruth Silver and so many other Freedom Riders. Zellner recalls, "She was very involved, she was very, very smart, she was great, she was a legendary, fearless person." As SNCC's executive secretary, Smith ran the Atlanta office with devotion and discipline. In Zellner's words, "She was tough as nails but she wasn't just tough with white people, she was tough with everybody. You did not get over with Ruby and there were a lot of people who were really afraid of her."

Though "Ruby was aloof with me," Zellner worked well with her in the Atlanta office. Zellner was surprised when Cynthia Fleming, who was doing research for her biography of Ruby Doris Smith Robinson, called and asked to interview her because she was "one of the few white women that Ruby respected."[54] When asked how she gained Ruby Doris Smith's respect, Zellner replied that it had something to do with their shared work ethic, as well as with Zellner's recognition of her appropriate place in SNCC. As other Jewish women's stories recounted here attest, such awareness came more quickly to some than to others. Knowing when, as Florence Howe put it, "to shut up" and how to follow Black leadership are political skills that deserve recognition.

Ruby Doris Smith Robinson became very ill while on a business trip in New York and was at Manhattan's Beth Israel Hospital for months. Zellner visited her often despite the fact that she had been distant in the Atlanta office. When asked why, Zellner responds:

> She was one of my SNCC people . . . and I felt very sorry for her. She was all alone, [without] her husband, her child, and her sister. She was very close to her sister. I was right there, so whatever suspicions she had of me disappeared because after all, there she is lying there. I'm taking her bedpan. There was a sort of intimacy there. Then, she sort of let me in when she was sick. She was young, she was so young. So it was one of those instances where, like Casey [Hayden] said, "race fell away." I think she knew I was coming to help her and I was very pleased that she trusted me enough. She could easily—and believe me in a second she would—have said, "Please don't come back; you're making me nervous."

In recounting this story, Zellner does not mention that during the time of her hospital visits, SNCC was debating whether whites could stay on staff. Ruby Doris Smith had been one of the advocates of a Black-dominated SNCC.[55] Although Bob Zellner had been the first white SNCC organizer and Dottie Miller Zellner had planned to dedicate her life to SNCC, they would soon be voted out. However, the precariousness of Dottie Zellner's position in SNCC did not stop her from caring for her colleague. Her quiet presence comforted Smith Robinson, who returned home for a few months before she died in 1967, at twenty-six.

The untimely death of Ruby Doris Smith Robinson marked the end of a period when Black and white activists could struggle together in SNCC for social justice, when right and wrong were more clear than they would be for the rest of the century.

Even as white activists worked closely with Black activists in SNCC, often in extremely dangerous situations, racialized dynamics inevitably emerged among movement workers. The interracialist ideal faced its greatest challenges on the terrain of intimate personal and working relationships in the movement. Here northern Jewish women could not deny the whiteness of their Jewishness, nor escape the implications of being part of that controversial movement category "white women." Negotiating interracial sexual relationships and discussions of the role of whites in the movement, northern Jewish women's struggles to transcend the limits of their whiteness failed. But the struggles themselves are instructive, both for the passionate convictions and the false assumptions on which they were based.

NEGOTIATING THE POLITICS OF SEX IN THE MOVEMENT

It is extremely difficult to talk about interracial sex in the southern civil rights movement.[56] Most veterans and scholars alike give the subject short shrift. Clayborne Carson, an African American historian and leading scholar on SNCC, barely mentions interracial sex. White historian John Dittmer believes the extent of sexual activity between Blacks and whites in the 1964 Mississippi Summer Project has been exaggerated. Feminist historians Sara Evans and Mary Aickin Rothschild have been criticized for overstating the "victimization" of white women by Black men, although their actual texts are somewhat more nuanced than critics suggest.[57] Such SNCC insiders/chroniclers as Sally Belfrage and Mary King insist that they never experienced sexual exploitation. Sociologist Doug McAdam portrays a significant amount of sexual activity among volunteers, most often between Black men and white women.[58] Ever protective of the movement, Dottie Miller Zellner says that the question of sex in the movement is "my least favorite question," and skillfully deflects attempts to discuss it.

The long and ugly tradition of lynching as a paranoid response to fear of miscegenation provides the historical background for this reluctance to discuss interracial sex. Well aware of this tradition, movement foes such as FBI Director J. Edgar Hoover attempted to discredit the movement by revealing details of Martin Luther King Jr.'s sex life. As the Mississippi Sovereignty Commission files opened in the 1990s suggest, racists used this tactic against local activists as well.

Thus, negotiating the politics of sex in the movement presented a challenge for northern Jewish women who worked in the South. Like all white women volunteers, Jewish women faced the complex symbolic and actual dynamics of interracial sex. Some sidestepped the challenge by being oblivious to sexual dynamics or by using the cover of a husband or boyfriend to protect them from unwanted sexual advances.[59] Some relished romantic moments of connection, more intimate than sexual. Some, who were simply naive or unaccustomed to the South, learned quickly. In Jackson in the summer of 1964, Florence Howe went out one evening with a fellow Freedom School director, a Black man. "You were lucky to get away with your lives," remarked a movement colleague the next day.

Other Jewish women, sometimes the most politically savvy, confined their relationships with Black men to safer contexts outside the South. Faith Holsaert and her sister, Shai, dated Black men in the North. Joan Nestle had a relationship in New York with a Black divinity student she had met in Selma, Alabama. In law school, Carol Ruth Silver "had a very active romance with a Black African man."

Inside and outside the southern movement, some Jewish women had interracial relationships based on genuine mutual connection. They were not, however, exempt from racialized dynamics. Some had relationships with Black men to experiment with sexuality, to demonstrate their nonracism, and to "connect more purely to the movement" as Elizabeth Hirschfeld phrased it. Some Black men manipulated those desires and sexually exploited some Jewish women.

Mutual projection was inevitably rampant. Melanie Kaye/Kantrowitz's candid account of her first summer as a movement worker in Harlem illustrates this poignantly.

On the bus returning home from the March on Washington, a Black man my age flirted with me and I flirted back and he sang me this song:

> Jew girls from Brooklyn they go wild over me
> and they hold my hand where everyone can see
> oh, they paint their face like whores
> have me leave them at their doors
> they go wild, simply wild over me.

Intensely focused on white racism, utterly unaware of racism against Jews, or of the possibility of Jewish danger (the Holocaust was eons ago, irrelevant), I felt only shame at the label—Jew girl from Brook-lyn—and at the stereotype—hypocrite, liberal in public but won't bring him home to meet the family. I determined not to be like the oth-ers; not to be like myself.[60]

While this encounter comes from the North and not the South, Jew-ish women who went south also shared the desire not to be "hypocriti-cal." Revealing their attraction to Black men exposed them to stereo-types as well. As Ruth Frankenberg comments, "Like the negative stereotypes of [hypersexualized] African American men, images of white women in relationships with men of color frequently reduced them to entirely sexual beings."[61] Such images caused friction between white women and Black women and between SNCC and the local com-munity. They seemed to provide ammunition for local racist whites.

Circulation of a memo critiquing sexism in SNCC heightened ten-sions over interracial sexual relationships in the organization because it highlighted the different perspectives of Black and white women. Au-thored by white women but presented anonymously at the November 1964 Waveland retreat, the memo listed eleven examples of SNCC's sex-ism and defensively asked for a fair hearing on these issues, even though the authors knew the issues would be ridiculed or ignored.

In response to the memo, Stokely Carmichael commented that "the only position for women in SNCC is prone." At the time, most SNCC staffers did not pay much attention to the memo. Many insiders con-sidered Carmichael's comment a joke. Most SNCC men ignored the issue of sexism. Black women leaders, such as Cynthia Washington, while privately annoyed at the comment, had a hard time understand-ing white women's complaints about sexist treatment because Black women exercised many forms of leadership in SNCC.[62] Although the memo resonated with some white women who resented being rele-gated to secondary movement tasks while being pursued sexually, some white women, including Zellner, ignored the memo because they saw it as divisive. For Black women and Black-identified white women, racism was the primary issue in 1964.

Thus, for Jewish women activists, part of the challenge was to struggle with the limits of being white women. This struggle took place on several interrelated planes: in intimate relationships with Black men;

in working relationships with Black women; and in a metadiscussion about the role of whites in SNCC.

The difference in responses by most white and Black women to Carmichael's comment reflected their different locations in the movement and their different histories. The sexism of the times led to disrespect of both Black and white women in the movement, but it took very different forms that meant different things to Black and white women. A variety of forces shaped these forms: the different gender roles white and Black women had been required to play historically; the constraints on the roles white women could play because of southern racial repression; the racial/sexual taboos that made relationships between Black men and white women seem so compelling; the different kinds of pressure Black and white women experienced in the movement; and the intensity of the fight against racism in the South, especially Mississippi.

In the 1960s, try as they might, movement workers could not overcome these racial/sexual tensions, their symbolism, and the histories behind them.[63] According to Elaine DeLott Baker, interracial sexual relationships in the movement were "the vehicle for a complex communication" that has not yet been described in ways that do justice to the depth of peoples' experiences. She recalls, "They needed something and we needed something. It was not okay to trust each other, but the power of the need to be understood, to communicate, and to challenge authority [was very strong]."[64]

When she worked in the Washington, D.C., office of the Mississippi Freedom Democratic Party, Jan Goodman dated director Michael Thelwell. Joining him at the bus station as he returned to the University of Massachusetts, the two encountered Bob Moses. Like most veteran Freedom Summer Project volunteers, Goodman revered Moses. But that day, "[W]e walked over to Bob and he just turned his back on me and he would not talk to Mike as long as I was there. That's the worst thing I ever remember. It was just horrible." After his 1965 trip to Africa, Moses had made a decision to stop talking to white people.[65] Working in the MFDP office, which was still heavily dependent on white support and therefore muted Black Power language, Goodman was not fully prepared for her first encounter with "a Black separatist push."

As Goodman's experience suggests, relationships with prominent Black civil rights leaders could have both negative and positive consequences for women in the movement. Several Jewish women succumbed to the charms of SNCC's first chairman Marion Barry (later the target of scandal and ridicule as mayor of Washington, D.C.). Despite his reputation, Elizabeth Slade Hirschfeld still treasures their relationship and what she learned from him. Barry stayed with her family in Detroit. "It was a real relationship," Hirschfeld insisted, "though," she jokes, "I'm sure he had thirty or forty others at the same time."

Hirschfeld was also involved with the future U.S. congressman John Conyers. When asked about her relationships with women in SNCC, Hirschfeld, who later came out as a lesbian, replies, "I really truthfully didn't care about relationships with women then. I was interested in power and programmatically pulling whatever power there was into what I was doing. And it just didn't lie with women." Was she saying that she "slept up" to get power? Hirschfeld laughs: "It's possible, sure. Certainly not consciously. Less manipulatively than as a way to connect more purely and intensely with the movement. I think that's really what it was, but it was true, I always went up as far as I could."[66] Although Hirschfeld's experience was not necessarily typical for Jewish women or white women in general, it does underscore the historical fact that sleeping with powerful men has been one way women have attempted to overcome the limits of their gender.

Taboos against discussing homosexuality suggest that the civil rights movement often reinscribed the traditional gender roles of its day, even as interracial relationships transgressed important boundaries. Despite the visibility of the contemporary Jewish lesbian feminist movement (which includes many civil rights veterans), few Jewish women were able to locate or name their desire for other women while working in the movement. During the 1965 Selma to Montgomery march, Joan Nestle "never told my comrades that I was different because a secret seemed a little thing at such a time in history." When she did tell her male Black friend/lover that she was a lesbian, she never heard from him again.[67]

Even in the 1990s, lesbianism was still a sensitive issue for civil rights veterans. Faith Holsaert's decision to come out to friends in SNCC was difficult. Although her former boyfriend, SNCC activist Reggie Robinson, had known for several years that she was a lesbian, Holsaert was unsure how others would respond. Support from Martha Prescod Norman, a prominent Black woman SNCC veteran, encouraged Holsaert to expect acceptance from others.

Holsaert's struggle over the decision to come out as a lesbian mirrors the care with which some of the women in this book talk about interracial tensions in the movement. Proud of their ability to cross boundaries in personal and political relationships, they seek to protect the historical legacy of the movement by remaining focused on its main objectives. They also wish to preserve the cross-racial, cross-class relationships forged in the midst of struggle. SNCC's Black Power phase tested these relationships.

A well-honed Jewish survival strategy—the ability to mute or submerge Jewish identity when the context calls for it—helped facilitate the many kinds of boundary-crossings enacted by the women profiled in this book. This strategy has fostered Jewish acceptance into myriad cultures, including the culture of the southern civil rights movement. Not a manifestation of "false consciousness," this "muting" impulse was available to the women who went south. They chose when and where to use it for a variety of reasons, ranging from the desire for acceptance and their sense of primacy of anti-Black racism to their Jewish cohort's ambivalence about post–World War II American Jewish culture. The following two chapters explore the impact of this culture on the women and the ways in which their responses, adaptations, and reactions to American Jewish culture helped move them toward their commitment to the civil rights movement.

NOTES

1. Interview with Roberta Galler, New York, December 30, 1994. For an account of Perry Nussbaum, see Gary Phillip Zola, "What Price Amos? Perry Nussbaum's Career in Jackson, Mississippi," in Mark Bauman and Berkeley Kallen, eds., *The Quiet Voices: Southern Rabbis and Black Civil Rights, 1880s to 1990s* (Tuscaloosa: University of Alabama Press, 1997).

2. For overviews of Southern Jewish history, see Leonard Dinnerstein and Mary Dale Palsson, eds., *Jews in the South* (Baton Rouge: Louisiana State University Press, 1973), and Nathan Kaganoff and Melvin Urofsky, eds., *Turn to the South: Essays on Southern Jewry* (Charlottesville: University of Virginia Press, 1979). For a popular introduction, see Eli Evans, *The Provincials: A Personal History of the Jews in the South* (New York: Atheneum, 1973).

3. Nancy MacLean, "The Leo Frank Case Reconsidered: Gender and Sexual Politics in the Making of Reactionary Populism," *Journal of American History* 78 (December 1991): 917–948.

4. Gerald Sorin, *The Prophetic Minority: American Jewish Immigrant Radicals, 1880–1920* (Bloomington: Indiana University Press, 1985), 167.

5. W. J. Cash, *The Mind of the South* (New York: Vintage Books edition, 1991), 333–334.

6. Benjamin Ginsberg, *The Fatal Embrace: Jews and the State* (Chicago: University of Chicago Press, 1993), 87–88.

7. Sorin, *The Prophetic Minority*, 168; Ginsberg, 91; Steven Hertzberg, *Strangers within the Gate City: The Jews of Atlanta, 1845–1915* (Philadelphia: Jewish Publication Society of America, 1978).

8. Eli Evans, 141; Shapiro, 35.

9. Clive Webb, "Big Struggle in a Small Town: Charles Mantinband of Hattiesburg, Mississippi," in Bauman and Kallen, 217.

10. Mark Dollinger, "'Hamans' and 'Tourquemadas': Southern and Northern Jewish Responses to the Civil Rights Movement, 1945–1965," in Bauman and Kallen, 70–71.

11. Albert Vorspan, "The Dilemma of the Southern Jew," in Dinnerstein and Palsson, 334.

12. Eli Evans, 348.

13. Leonard Rogoff, "Is the Jew White? The Racial Place of the Southern Jew," *American Jewish History* 85 (September 1997): 195–230.

14. Robin D. G. Kelley, *Hammer and Hoe: Alabama Communists during the Great Depression* (Chapel Hill: University of North Carolina Press, 1990), 199, 206–207. In the 1950s, Marge Frantz directed the Independent Progressive Party in Oakland, California, and subsequently became a professor at the University of California–Santa Cruz.

15. Ibid., 48.

16. See Bauman and Kallen.

17. Kelley, 87–88. The ILD's choice of a Jewish lawyer in the Scottsboro case further complicated Goldstein's situation.

18. Melissa Faye Greene, *The Temple Bombing* (New York: Fawcett Columbine, 1996), 5–6, and Webb, 213–229.

19. Figures are from Morris Fine and Milton Himmelfarb, eds., *American Jewish Yearbook 1965*, vol. 66 (New York: American Jewish Committee and Jewish Publication Society of America).

20. The figures on summer volunteers come from McAdam, *Freedom Summer*, Appendix C, 255–256. Arthur Lelyveld, cited in ibid., 262.

21. Eli Evans, 238.

22. Phone interview with Miriam Cohen Glickman, December 1993.

23. See Webb on Hattiesburg's Marvin Reuben, 224–225. In a personal communication, Berkeley Kallen noted that Jewish women were involved in the 1968 sanitation strike that preceded Martin Luther King Jr.'s assassination in Memphis. Future research will likely show that southern Jewish women aided the civil rights cause in modest ways, while enacting traditional female roles. For example, though she does not mention Jewish women specifically, Bernice McNair Barnett writes that southern white women contributed money for civil rights organizing to "their" domestics, Black women involved in such informal groups as "The Club From Nowhere." See Bernice McNair Barnett, "Black Women's Collectivist Organizations: Their Struggles during 'the Doldrums,'" in Myra Marx Ferree and Patricia Yancey Martin,

eds., *Feminist Organizations: Harvest of the New Women's Movement* (Philadelphia: Temple University Press, 1993).

24. Jack Nelson, *Terror in the Night: The Klan's Campaign against the Jews* (New York: Simon & Schuster, 1993), 33.

25. Eli Evans, 307–308.

26. Kaufman, *Broken Alliance*, 52–53.

27. Interview with June Finer, December 7, 1993. I asked Finer how, despite not being attuned to her Jewishness in such moments, she knew that "many, many, many of the medical and related professional volunteers were in fact Jewish. . . . I would say the vast majority were Jewish." She replied: "Just culturally. I had lived in Chicago with the Jewish community to a large degree since 1960, so I had a pretty good sense of who was and wasn't Jewish. A lot of the nurses perhaps were not Jewish, but most of the doctors and psychologists were. Most of the doctors were either Black or Jewish."

28. McAdam, *Freedom Summer*, 75 and Appendix D—Running Summary of Incidents.

29. Nelson, 26.

30. Manning Marable, *Race, Reform, and Rebellion: The Second Reconstruction in Black America, 1945–1990* (Jackson: University of Mississippi Press, 1991), 111.

31. See Rogoff.

32. It is important to distinguish between local Black reactions to northern Jewish civil rights activists in the intense and unique political context of the movement and the general nature of Black-Jewish relations in the South. Jews were a tiny and insignificant minority in the South, whereas Blacks were a majority in many rural areas and, as a group, were integral to the culture and nature of the South. As Deborah Dash Moore argues, the history of Blacks and Jews in the South is one of "enormous contrasts and few similarities," noting differences in demographic, occupational, cultural, religious, and political patterns, as well as widely divergent experiences of prejudice and oppression. Thus, the African American community's overall response to Jews was based less on personal interaction and more on the community's Protestant Christianity, which sometimes lent itself to anti-Semitism. However, personal interaction did engender more complex responses to Jews, as the experiences of the activists described in this chapter suggest. See Deborah Dash Moore, "Separate Paths: Blacks and Jews in the Twentieth Century South," in Salzman and West, 275–293.

33. Ginsberg, 168, superimposes his own interpretation on Jonathan Kaufman's more neutral account in *Broken Alliance: The Turbulent Times between Blacks and Jews in America*. It is important to track such moments of interpretation because scholarship continues to add fuel to the fire of Black-Jewish debates.

34. Mary King, *Freedom Song* (New York: William Morrow, 1987), 274–275.

35. Carson, "Blacks and Jews in the Civil Rights Movement: The Case of

SNCC," in Salzman et al., 37–38. Karen Winkler, "Debating the History of Blacks and Jews: Issue Causes Discomfort at History Meeting," *Chronicle of Higher Education*, January 19, 1994, A11. There was much disagreement among the five panelists at the American Historical Association meeting, some of whom charged that their statements had been misunderstood. One thing they agreed on was the need to avoid sweeping generalizations until there is more basic documentation of Black-Jewish history.

36. Carson criticizes Jewish scholar Murray Friedman for lack of evidence in his assertion that "the Jewish kids who went south were acting out, albeit unconsciously, a Jewish tradition. It is as if these *boys* [my emphasis] were wearing their yarmulkes without knowing why." Although one sympathizes with Carson's critique of Friedman's hyperbole, this book seeks to explicate the experiences and transmitted values that would lead primarily secular Jewish women to go south. Thus, Friedman's invoking of the yarmulke highlights precisely the gender differentiated nature of Jewish women's alienation and motivations for going south, underscoring the need for gender analysis in this complex question of Jewish motivation for civil rights activism. See Clayborne Carson, "Black-Jewish Universalism in the Era of Identity Politics," in Salzman and West, 181–182.

37. Ginsberg, 168. In examining the participation of Jews in the civil rights movement, it is necessary to distinguish between the organized Jewish community and individual young Jewish people who went south without an institutional Jewish context. Ginsberg argues that for Jewish middle-class liberals, support for civil rights was both a moral commitment and a political strategy. Ginsberg notes several advantages for Jewish liberals in alliances with Blacks, working for the enfranchisement of Black voters. These include the delegitimization of conservative southern state and local governments and the anti-Semitic forces that had accused Jews of un-Americanism; greater access to public policy roles for Jewish civil servants, academics, foundation officials, and others; increasing liberal influence in the Democratic Party and the federal government; and greater commitment to the elimination of all forms of discrimination.

38. "Righteous Gentiles" refers to non-Jews who helped protect Jews from the Nazis.

39. Eli Evans, 305.

40. Brodkin, 10, and Toni Morrison, *Playing in the Dark: Whiteness and the Literary Imagination* (New York: Vintage Books, 1993).

41. Silver, "Diary," 135.

42. Jacqueline Levine, "The Changing Role of Women in the Jewish Community," in Jacob Marcus, ed., *The American Jewish Woman: A Documentary History* (New York: Ktav Publishing, 1981), 906.

43. Miriam Cohen, "Integration in the Deep South: Death Goes On," *Justice*, December 17, 1963, 4–6. Emphasis added.

44. Riv-Ellen Prell, *Prayer and Community: The Havurah in American Judaism* (Detroit: Wayne State University Press, 1989), 40.

45. From letter of Elaine DeLott Baker. Reprinted by permission.

46. Jessica Mitford, *A Fine Old Conflict* (New York: Vintage Books, 1956), 134.

47. Ibid., 162–194.

48. Conversation with Susan McElrath, archivist, National Black Women's Archives.

49. Kay Mills, *This Little Light of Mine: The Life of Fannie Lou Hamer* (New York: Dutton, 1993). Conversation with Polly Cowan's daughter Holly Cowan.

50. Paul Cowan, *An Orphan in History* (New York: Bantam Books, 1983), 52.

51. Ibid., 97.

52. Interview with Roberta Galler, New York, December 30, 1994.

53. Ibid.

54. Cynthia Griggs Fleming, *Soon We Will Not Cry: The Liberation of Ruby Doris Smith Robinson* (Lanham, Md.: Rowman & Littlefield, 1998).

55. Sara Evans, *Personal Politics,* 95–96.

56. The women's reluctance to discuss their sexual experiences in the movement challenged my training in using gender and sexuality as categories of feminist historical analysis. However, that training also requires respect for one's "informants," so I did not press them to disclose more than they wanted to. Some told stories that were "off the record," for use only to enhance my understanding of the complexities of this topic for white women civil rights workers. My political and intellectual conviction is that it is up to the women and men veterans themselves to write about their sexual experiences. They may choose to publish this information now or seal it for many years.

57. Fleming, 116–117.

58. McAdam, *Freedom Summer,* 93–96. McAdam suggests the strong attraction between Black men and white women came from breaking the ultimate racial/sexual taboo for each group. He cites Evans's hypothesis that Black men and white women were uniquely able to affirm the other's masculinity and femininity, given the internal gender dynamics of their home cultures. McAdam also suggests that "it would be hard to think of a more sexually potent mixture of feelings than those of tension, fear, excitement, danger, and uncertainty."

59. Those who were married, like Dottie Miller Zellner and Rita Schwerner, faced fewer difficulties, as did women such as Heather Tobis Booth, Vivian Leburg Rothstein, and Harriet Tanzman, whose boyfriends visited them or worked in the movement.

60. Melanie Kaye/Kantrowitz, "To Be a Radical Jew in the Late 20th Century," in Kaye/Kantrowitz, 94.

61. Frankenberg, 87.

62. To explore the controversy over "The Memo," see Sara Evans, *Personal*

Politics; Mary Aickin Rothschild, *A Case of Black and White: Northern Volunteers and the Southern Freedom Summers, 1964–1965* (Westport, Conn.: Greenwood Press, 1982); Mary King; Fleming; and Casey Hayden et al., *Deep in Our Hearts: Nine White Women in the Freedom Movement* (Athens: University of Georgia Press, 2000).

63. For an account of interracial relationships in the Peace Corps, see Jonathan Zimmerman, "Crossing Oceans, Crossing Colors: Black Peace Corps Volunteers and Interracial Love in Africa, 1961–1971," in Martha Hodes, ed., *Sex, Love, Race: Crossing Boundaries in North American History* (New York: New York University Press, 1999).

64. Interview with Elaine DeLott Baker, February 1994.

65. Carson, *In Struggle*, 201, 330.

66. Interview with Elizabeth Slade Hirschfeld, February 1994.

67. Joan Nestle, *A Restricted Country* (Ithaca: Firebrand Books, 1987), 49–67.

PART II

SEEKING THE LEGACY

4

Uncovering Family Legacies

I learned for the first time when I was in my fifties that I had this secret socialist grandfather. My father told me that socialism was spoken
at the dinner table every night.   —Barbara Jacobs Haber

BORN IN THE tumultuous period between 1935 and 1946, the core
group of women in this book were marked by the dislocations and
changes of the Great Depression and World War II. They were the
daughters of first- and second-generation Jews who were striving to ac-
tualize dreams of America as the golden land. As girls and young
women, they experienced the drama of the war and the rocky transition
from a multigenerational urban and ethnic lifestyle to a more isolated
and Americanized middle-class affluence in the suburbs. The upheaval
wrought by this transition would touch their lives on many counts.

Although the women, as girls, were deeply affected by the sweep of
larger historical change, many experienced turmoil on a more intimate
level as well. Home was often the scene of economic struggle and personal adversity. Add to this portrait the fact that many of the Jewish
women who went south for a sustained amount of time came from families that deviated from the normative, cultural stereotype of the 1950s
nuclear family—the young, suburban, middle-class, intact unit headed
by a breadwinning Dad and a full-time homemaking Mom—and the
commonalities of their upbringings begin to emerge.[1]

Taken as a group, their collective experiences included the devastating loss of parents through premature death, living through their
parents' divorce, trying to make ends meet in woman-headed households (including a lesbian household), managing illness and disability,
and attempting to protect radical parents during the McCarthy era.
Such experiences, many combined with the economic and social hardships of working-class Jewishness, made them feel different and made
it easier for them to identify with others who were different. Women

whose families were middle-class often lived with immigrant grandparents or near working-class relatives. Many who experienced family poverty or economic instability were able to perceive the fragility of their privilege, as well as to empathize with others more vulnerable. This sensitivity was just one of the means by which Jewish women activists were able to cross class, ethnic, and racial boundaries.

For many of the women, Jewish, class, and gender identity was never constant or fixed but, rather, often in flux. Oscillating between the outsider status that is often historically attached to Jewishness and the sense of entitlement and "insider" privileges that come with assimilation, the women grew up "in between" classes and cultures. Wavering between reluctantly accepting women's culturally sanctioned passivity on the one hand and embracing the possibility of making a mark on the world on the other, the women grew up "in between" gender definitions and roles. The racial ambiguities of midcentury Jewish identity also located them "in between" the privileges of whiteness (including access to higher education) and a lingering sense of not quite belonging because of anti-Semitism.

How did these shifting positions affect Jewish women's evolving consciousness, eventually influencing the decision to go south for civil rights? Their lived experiences of family struggles, marginality, otherness, and being in between classes, gender roles, cultures, and forms of Jewishness generated alternative ways of knowing the world and its possibilities.[2] These ways of knowing the world—born of and responsive to personal and cultural changes—are presented here as positive "family legacies." By navigating these emotional, political, and cultural family legacies, the women sharpened their ability to perceive contradictions and hypocrisy, to raise difficult questions and access new frameworks, to see the past and envision the future, to tolerate the unknown and to take risks.

NEGOTIATING PERCEPTIONS OF CLASS IDENTITY

The majority of the women's grandparents emigrated from Eastern Europe to the United States in the early part of the twentieth century. They came from Hungary, Lithuania, Poland, Romania, and Russia. A few had more varied backgrounds. Faith Holsaert's Jewish maternal grandparents came from Holland and Poland; her father's family, who were not Jewish, emigrated from the Netherlands in the 1800s.

Florence Howe's grandparents came from Russia, Poland, and Palestine. Elizabeth Slade Hirschfeld's Jewish paternal family came from Germany in the mid-nineteenth century; most of her non-Jewish mother's family can trace its roots back to the Revolutionary War. Trudy Weissman Orris and Dottie Miller Zellner were both children of two immigrant parents. Trudy Weissman Orris's father emigrated from Hungary, and her mother from Austria. All four of Dottie Miller Zellner's grandparents were born in Russia and immigrated first to Canada. Her father emigrated from Canada to the United States in 1929; her mother, in 1934.

If most of the women's grandparents were working-class immigrants, their parents' class identity was in flux. The women saw their families' class status in ways that suggest some of the strains and contradictions for American Jews at that historical moment. Living with her divorced mother, Jan Goodman knew "we were poor, but we still lived a middle-class existence. It was a middle-class mentality although we didn't have money."[3] Such a mentality must have generated both a sense of entitlement and a sense of insecurity.

The life of Trudy Weissman Orris (b. 1916) reflects the economic journey of many American Jewish immigrant families from Eastern Europe.[4] Her early struggles, like those of so many of her generation who came of age in the 1930s, led her to become a radical activist. Her Austrian-born mother, the third of her father's wives, died when Orris was six years old. Her Hungarian-born father remarried "as a convenience" to have a caretaker for his children, Orris and her two brothers. The family was very Orthodox. Orris's father was a fine tailor whose skills were becoming obsolete. They lived in a predominantly Italian and Irish community in Greenwich Village. Her brothers were educated and went to Hebrew school, but she did not. Her father did not believe in educating girls. He did, however, believe in girls contributing to the family income. Orris got her first job when she was thirteen years old, working for a plumber after school.

At fourteen, she got a full-time job in a henna factory, attending continuation school one morning a week, which was mandatory for working children under sixteen. When asked how she made the decision to start working at such a young age, she replies, "My father made the decision . . . I was supporting my father. I had to make enough money to be able to leave home and still support him because he was an older man and people weren't getting homemade suits. They were going out to Barney's and buying suits. He wasn't doing so well."

Orris then worked as a bookkeeper at the Fulton Fish Market, saving money to get her own apartment. In the evenings, she went to night school, read the classics, and enjoyed dancing. When she was twenty, a Marxist roommate introduced her to socialist ideas, with which she immediately resonated. She became interested in union organizing and joined Local 16, an office workers union. She also became involved in the Communist Party and started organizing for Local 55 in the 1930s. After marrying in 1941, she continued to work in a Jewish-owned drygoods shop where she was elected union foreman, an unusual role for a woman at the time.

An early gender rebel, Orris moved from the traditional working-class Jewish immigrant daughter's life of self-sacrifice to a radical milieu where she took the initiative to fight the poverty and economic injustice that plagued her own family. Her life exemplifies patterns that were typical of Jewish immigrant daughters: the need to support their families economically; their roles as buffers between the Old and New Worlds; their passion for education; their resistance to traditional gender norms; and their commitment to progressive politics.[5]

Like Orris, Florence Howe was born into a family facing economic hard times. She believes her maternal grandmother came to the United States without a husband, bringing Howe's father as a baby from Poland. She recalls that he was always embarrassed about not having "proper papers" and not voting. Her grandmother remarried and had two daughters, but still desperately poor, she left the daughters in Howe's father's care (when he was only eight years old) and went to work in a buttonhole factory.

Howe was born in 1929, at the start of the Great Depression. Between 1929 and 1934, Howe, her parents, and a younger brother, born in 1932, lived in Brooklyn with her father's mother, two sisters, and their husbands.

Howe's maternal grandfather, who was from northern Galilee, left a wife and three children in Palestine when he was twenty-one, made his way across Europe, settled in Scotland, and became a Prudential Life Insurance salesperson. He came to the United States when he was about thirty and married Howe's Russian-born grandmother (who was about sixteen), "without ever telling her about the family in Safed." These maternal grandparents were also very poor:

> My grandfather never earned any money. He didn't work in insurance in this country. He thought of himself as a Hebrew teacher and a rabbi.

And he made 25 cents a lesson. So my grandmother took in sewing, which she hid because he didn't want her to work. There was a trunk in which she kept the sewing machine. And the children would watch out for him. If they saw him turn the corner, she would get rid of every scrap of evidence. And he never knew that the household ran on her sewing money.

Similar dynamics existed between Howe's parents. Her father, who left school when he was eight, "told me never to tell anybody that he drove a cab, to say he was in the transportation business." She suspects her father gambled away the tips he earned driving a cab. He did not give her mother enough money to run the household, "and she cried every night." Howe's memory of her family during the Depression is one of tension and difficulty: "[T]here was no money, no jobs, and my father with no education, and my mother who had an education and could have earned money had to take care of me." From 1934 to 1939, when Howe was five to ten, "we moved every year, and I went to a different elementary school every year."

"My father was a typical working-class man who said, 'My wife is never going to work.'" But Howe's mother did eventually go back to work, her way paved by the wartime demand for women's labor. When Howe's mother decided to get a job as a riveter in an airplane factory in 1939, her father "just had to put up with it. Because her last name was Rosenfeld, they called her Rosie." And like the mythic "Rosie the Riveter" representing women who took men's jobs for the war effort, "she resigned without a single pang of anger" after the war, though Howe thinks "she was sad because she liked going to work there." Having worked, like many second-generation Jewish women, before marriage as a bookkeeper, Howe's mother found a bookkeeping job after the war; she earned approximately one-third to one-quarter of her previous salary as a riveter.

Once she rejoined the workforce, Howe's mother never turned back. Like many Jewish women of her generation, she took advantage of a moment in which "there was at once a need, and opportunity, and a new ethos that encouraged women to work after their families had been properly cared for."[6] Yet, once her mother went back to work, Howe had to do three hours of housework when she came home from school. She recalls, "I never played. I don't know what playing is." For working-class families, the standards of being "properly cared for" were different. Children, particularly girls, often bridged the gap.

Poverty dictated the physical movements of Florence Howe's childhood but also accelerated changing gender roles within the family. Preserving the Eastern European pattern in which Jewish women supported their families and their husbands' religious study, Howe's grandfather could pretend he was the patriarch while his wife supported the family by sewing piecework at home. The pretense and the hiding reflects the increasing influence of American gender expectations that men alone were to be the breadwinners. As in her grandmother's case, economic need similarly spurred Howe's mother, who had felt trapped in a traditional female role, to leave the home for the work world. Although her husband objected, this was a culturally sanctioned move from the American point of view. Thus Howe grew up between the Old World and New World Jewish family forms in which women were essential to economic survival yet still disempowered in other ways.

Like Florence Howe, Elaine DeLott Baker transformed her early experiences of being shamed for her family's working-class background into a broad compassion for the disenfranchised. The youngest of three sisters, Baker was born in Winthrop, Massachusetts, in 1942. Three of her four grandparents were from Eastern Europe. When her mother was nine, her family moved from the South, where she did not fit in because she was Jewish, to Chelsea, Massachusetts, a first-generation Jewish ghetto, where she did not fit in because she was southern. Baker's father had dropped out of school in the eighth grade to help support his family and worked as a plumber's helper. Because his mother had been unable to provide for him, he had spent some of his childhood in an orphanage. "Even as a first-generation American, he was expected by his culture to achieve a status higher than a laborer. Within the Jewish community, my father was a failure." Baker's early sensitivity to categorizing people on the basis of material wealth "contributed heavily to my emerging sense of social justice."[7]

Baker grew up in a family in between several worlds. She witnessed her mother's outsider status as a southern Jew transplanted to the North. She experienced the northern Jewish community's disapproval of her father for not moving quickly enough into the middle class. Hence, she matured into a passionate, questioning outsider who would fight her way into an elite college—Radcliffe—only to find that she preferred the outsider's stance.

Issues of class, social mobility, and respectability were fraught with tensions for first- and second-generation American Jews.[8] Like Baker,

Barbara Jacobs Haber was no stranger to these tensions. Haber began her life in the midst of her mother's unassimilated, tight-knit, Jewish family. "My mother was one of eight kids from a very poor family, and her father had deserted the family. This was before welfare, and I'm not sure how they existed. My mother was very close to her family. We moved from Brooklyn to the Bronx because my mother wanted to be closer to her mother and her two closest sisters [who lived around the corner]." They never had a baby-sitter and the family's only social activities were visiting relatives. On these weekend visits "the men played pinochle and drank, and the women gossiped in the kitchen, chain-smoked, and drank coffee."

In Haber's family, internal Jewish class tension was expressed in a fourteen-year estrangement between Haber's father and her paternal grandmother, who disapproved of her son's marriage to a woman "from a lower class. She wanted my father, who was the only one of the five kids to complete college [he also completed law school] to rise in the world." Later, Haber's father and stepmother would become part of "the assimilating generation that moved out to Long Island."

Their path to middle-class security was not smooth. Her father practiced law for two years, hated it, and became a business executive in the venetian-blind industry for many years. He was then fired and unemployed for two years just before Haber went to college.

> It was scary, he was clearly upset, and it just wasn't supposed to happen. My father was always proud that he earned a good living. We were never rich. I think he was a little inflated about the way he talked about himself. I think it was important to him to see himself as a successful executive. I idolized him, and here he was fired and unemployed and it was financially terrifying. You know, we were eating a lot of macaroni. There were five kids.

Although money was tight, Haber's parents somehow found a way to send her to college, thus underscoring the importance of higher education to Jewish families.

Her father soon got a job in another venetian-blind company and commuted to Baltimore for one year. After the whole family moved down there, he was fired again and was unemployed for another two years while Haber was in college. This propelled her stepmother into getting a job at Westinghouse and then at the Social Security Administration (public-sector jobs then being attractive to American Jews for their security). Haber says, "It was a desperation move because the kids were still little and at home. . . . He then got a job at the very bottom of Social Security, and I mean the bottom. He took over the desk that a twenty-four-year-old friend of mine was vacating, and he worked his way up to the top. They both retired from Social Security after having worked there a pretty long time."

Though the family managed to regain its equilibrium, by the time Haber was a young woman, she had experienced her mother's death and her father's economic vulnerability. As Haber puts it, "I had already had a huge blow finding out that my mother could drop dead, and now my father could drop out of the work world. Though it was very destabilizing and brought about feelings of insecurity, I don't think it taught me any big lessons because I certainly haven't lived my life in order to create security." Haber's experience of losing her mother and of the family's fluctuating class status helped her look for security within. Her father's employment history showed her that despite the golden promises of Jewish assimilation, risk was ever present. This perception may have facilitated her self-creation as a risk taker and a boundary crosser.

A number of the women's fathers were unable to follow the career paths they had envisioned for themselves. Like Haber's father, Carol Ruth Silver's father had a law degree but did not practice law because he needed to support his wife and three daughters during the Great Depression. After a stint at the Works Progress Administration (WPA), Silver's father "worked at sometimes awful jobs, one of which was being a door-to-door salesman in poor Irish and Black neighborhoods selling plastic shower curtains and tablecloths."[9] Silver reminisces:

> Financial times were hard. My father was given a job by a relative delivering ice cream. So my father, this very gentle, very intellectual, very sweet person was now a truck driver tooling around Boston in a battered old truck delivering ice cream. I remember going with him on at least one occasion when the windshield wipers in the truck were not working and it was snowing out and he was driving down the road with one hand, trying to wipe the snow off the windshield with the other. I always remember him working very hard, coming home late at night and eating nothing but milk and soda crackers because he had ulcers. I would wait up for him and he would read to me.

Silver's mother left school in eighth grade in order to support her own mother and siblings from her mother's second marriage. The second husband was abusive, "a gambler and a drunk and a child abuser and a wife beater and all those things that Jewish men are not supposed to be." Silver describes him and her grandmother as being "from a very low-class rural setting in Russia." Silver describes her mother as a voracious reader who "was as much an intellectual as my father." Headed by two intellectually gifted parents, Carol Ruth Silver's family was caught in the gap between the American Jewish ideal of education as the ultimate social safety net and the harsh material realities of life.

Issues of class, Jewishness, and disability entwined in painful ways for Roberta Galler as a young girl. Like many of the others, Galler was born into a family that faced an array of economic struggles. Her Russian-born father immigrated to the United States as a very young boy. His grandfather had been a Talmudic scholar. Galler's U.S.-born mother came from a large Lithuanian Jewish family. In a traditionally gendered division of labor, Galler's mother stayed home while her father worked as a chiropodist (known today as a podiatrist). Because her paternal grandfather had money and her father was a professional, "there was always this illusion that we were a middle-class family." At the same time, "there was always a puzzle as to why we were so poor and why we somehow couldn't have all the cousins over to eat the way they had us over to eat." It was a terrible shock when the family later learned that Galler's father "was a secret gambler and had in fact gambled away everything." As a traditional wife, her mother had accepted her father's management of finances and "had no idea what we had, what we didn't have, what was spent. He took care of everything and told her not to worry."

In addition to money, however, there were other things about which to worry. In 1946, at the age of ten, Roberta Galler contracted polio. Initially completely paralyzed, she spent long periods in hospitals for surgery, as well as at Warm Springs, Georgia (the famous healing center founded by Franklin Delano Roosevelt in the 1920s). Graduating from wheelchair to two crutches, to one crutch, she was determined not to be limited by her disability. After a brief stay at a Dickensian "School for Crippled Children," she insisted on going to a regular school, which she was able to do with some accommodation, support from her mother, and sheer will.

Her family had to go into debt to send her to Warm Springs for rehabilitation. Her doctor (himself Jewish) would not give her a referral to Warm Springs because he had already sent his "quota" of Jewish patients and did not want to be perceived as sending too many. Thus, neither the Warm Springs Foundation nor the March of Dimes would pay for her care. She became aware of differential treatment based on class: "I didn't have the new aluminum wheelchair, I had the old wooden wheelchair." When her family became more indebted to her paternal grandfather, they blamed the contradictions between their supposed middle-class status and their actual poverty on Galler's illness. "It was a way of covering up the fact that my father was actually a gambler. That's why we didn't have money. I could feel, therefore, guilty and also indignant that I didn't have what other kids had because I was Jewish." The financial crisis eventually precipitated a divorce. Galler's younger brother went to live with his father. Her mother struggled to make a living and Roberta Galler went to college. Throughout her childhood and adolescence, Galler lived in between middle-class identity and actual poverty, between a strong will to succeed and the fear and "otherness" still projected onto people with disabilities.

Whereas many of the women described their upbringings as working-class, others, including Vivian Leburg Rothstein, characterized their backgrounds as lower-middle-class. Rothstein was born in Jamaica, Queens, in 1946. Her sister was born in 1939. In 1932, her parents had left Berlin for Holland, where they established a business. The Dutch Nazi Party office was next door. Before the rise of Nazism, Rothstein's parents lived "a very artistic, romantic, European life." Her mother worked as a seamstress in fancy shops and her father, a photographer and painter, earned his living designing window displays and making artificial flowers. Neither attended college. It was a middle-class lifestyle.

An uncle sponsored their immigration to New York in 1937. Her parents separated soon after Rothstein's birth, and in 1952, Rothstein, her mother, and her sister moved to California. Her mother worked as a bookkeeper but was always financially dependent on her brother. Growing up in a struggling woman-headed household in a community of Holocaust survivors, Rothstein could not take security of any kind for granted.

Like Vivian Leburg Rothstein and Jan Goodman, Faith Holsaert's class status changed after her parents' divorce. She was born into a middle-class liberal family in Greenwich Village; her father was an editor at Simon & Schuster, and her parents moved in the literary world. When Faith was six, her mother became a single parent raising two daughters in partnership with Charity Bailey. Growing up in an Irish neighborhood in the Village, Holsaert had the sense that "somehow we were less American than our Irish playmates, both because we were Jewish, and also because Charity was a woman of color."

Holsaert remembers asking for credit at the grocery store for most of her childhood. Her maternal grandmother

> saw my mother as the failure of her four children because my mother didn't have very much money. My grandmother got along with Charity but there was also some sense of unease about the fact that Charity was a woman of color and also nobody really knew or would say what the relationship was between my mother and Charity. This is all in retrospect. This is nothing that anybody said to me.[10]

Miriam Cohen Glickman, the eldest daughter in a family of eight children, grew up in a more traditional Jewish family. And, like many Jews in Indianapolis and other midwestern cities, Glickman grew up in relative comfort.[11] Her father established the *National Jewish Post and Opinion* in Indianapolis and published it for more than fifty years. Her mother had earned an associate's degree and worked as a teacher before she married.

Glickman went to an integrated high school "in a changing neighborhood in the inner city, and there was clear discrimination against the Black kids. The Jewish kids were also not in a great position." Although it was not her neighborhood school, it was the high school where all the Jewish kids went, perhaps banding together. Glickman recalls that initially there were no Black or Jewish kids nominated for "junior prom king and queen"—those all-American icons. During her high school years, "there was one Jewish girl nominated, but still no Black kids. The [sports] teams were really well mixed, but the cheerleaders were always white. And one of the gym teachers used to use the word 'nigger' with the kids. I remember Jewish kids were more comfortable than a lot of the other white kids being friends with the Black kids."

Glickman's description captures a moment of transition that many American Jews experienced at midcentury, characterized by Karen Brodkin as "racial middleness." During this period, American Jews were starting to break into the mainstream but their social place was still tentative. This allowed many to feel a greater sense of "belonging" in relation to Black Americans while still feeling marginal in white, Christian America.[12] In urban neighborhoods that their parents would soon desert, young Jewish people like Miriam Cohen Glickman could still traverse the social borders between Black and white.[13]

Also a child of the transitioning Jewish middle class, Harriet Tanzman was born in 1940 in Brooklyn, New York. Her father, in rebellion from his Hasidic family, went to City College of New York at night, later earned a master's degree in French, and became a public school teacher. Tanzman's mother had worked as a secretary since age sixteen, but stopped when her children were young. Soon, the family moved to a predominantly Jewish part of Far Rockaway, Queens. Tanzman remembers Far Rockaway at that time as a somewhat diverse community. The two largest groups were Jews and Blacks, but they lived in separate areas. Thus, Harriet Tanzman's high school experience was a great deal more segregated than that of Miriam Cohen Glickman. Nevertheless, Far Rockaway was not the idyllic white suburb embraced by middle-class Jews in this period. Tanzman was still in between Black and white and experienced being an "outsider" because of her family's progressive politics.

Another child outsider (as the daughter of a Communist father), Dottie Miller Zellner grew up in an "Old World" Jewish, working-class family in the process of moving toward middle-class status. Her Russian-born maternal grandparents immigrated to Canada in 1905 and eventually came to the United States when Zellner's mother was six months old. Owners of a grocery store, they were, as Zellner describes them, "lower-middle-class people." Her paternal grandparents, also from Russia, settled in Leeds, England. Her paternal grandfather was a tailor, and they were working-class. They went to Canada from England in 1910, when her father was eleven.

Zellner's father considered himself a lifelong Englishman and also identified strongly as Jewish. In 1929, he left Toronto for New York because he felt very thwarted in his desire to become a teacher due to discrimination against Jews. He reluctantly became a dentist, the only one in his family to attain professional status. However, he arrived in the United States just as the stock market crashed, so for three years he was unemployed and came close to starvation. Zellner's mother came to the United States from Canada in 1934.

Zellner grew up in Manhattan in a basement apartment with her younger sister and brother. Her father had his dental practice in the front part of the apartment, where her mother assisted him. "The five of us were crammed into three rooms and then he had three small rooms

in the front," Zellner recalls. "Even though my father was a professional, we didn't live like a professional family. I mean it was a mom-
and-pop operation in our apartment."[14] The home-based dental practice coexisted with a family practice of radical politics. As a result, Dottie Miller Zellner learned that moving ahead professionally did not
require giving up the kind of working-class Jewish radicalism that
would nurture her future activism.

Also a daughter of a professional father, June Finer was born in
London, England, in 1935, the eldest of three sisters. Her paternal
grandparents sold men's clothes from a cart in the East End. Her father
became a physician and maintained his practice long after he could
have retired. Finer's maternal grandfather, an artist who had a glass-
cutting business, managed to send his daughter to college for two years.
Finer's mother dropped out of college to help her husband in his practice. It was clear to Finer that her parents were middle class because "we
lived in a working-class neighborhood," in which all the row houses
were small and subsidized, and "the doctor's house was the one indi-
vidually designed house," with a driveway, a garage, and "a garden
about three times the size of everybody else's."[15]

Nevertheless, the war and two bouts of tuberculosis made Finer's
childhood far from idyllic. Despite her family's high-class status in their
community, the bombing of London and the experience of severe illness
showed Finer that money ultimately did not provide security. Her own
physical vulnerability as a child enhanced her sensitivity to others who
were vulnerable, and eventually led to her activist medical career.

Jacqueline Levine and Elizabeth Slade Hirshfeld grew up in relative
material comfort. Levine was born in Brooklyn in 1926 to what she describes as an upper-middle-class Jewish family. Her paternal grandparents emigrated from Poland in 1903, when her father was three years
old. She never knew them. Her father, "who had an academic background," became a businessman. Levine's maternal grandmother was
fifteen when she emigrated from Poland at the end of the nineteenth
century. Described as "very elegant and very smart" by Jacqueline
Levine, she assimilated quickly and became involved in the issues of
the day.[16] She and her daughter marched in suffrage parades. Levine's
mother, a member of the Young People's Socialist League, earned a
Ph.D. in psychology. Both her parents were liberals.

Though Levine grew up in an upper-middle-class milieu shaped
primarily by the assimilationist, secular activist ideals of her maternal

line, she also knew about her father's background. As the child of more recent immigrants, Levine's father, despite his "academic interests," went into business, presumably for economic reasons. Thus, Levine was attuned to the diversity of Jewish economic experience. When she became an activist in her own right, she turned to Jewishness as the lens through which she engaged issues of social justice.

Elizabeth Slade Hirschfeld was born in 1937 in an "old and classy part of Detroit" to a "very upper-middle-class [family], with many generations of professional people behind it."[17] She can trace a large part of her mother's family back to the Revolutionary War and jokes, "[S]hould I be silly enough to choose it, I have six ways into the Daughters of the American Revolution." Her father's German Jewish family was well established in the United States by the late nineteenth century. Her family identified strongly as Republicans.

Hirschfeld went to private school and always expected to attend college, though the only future she could envision for herself was as a wife and mother. Her mother was not Jewish and her father's family actively discouraged him from identifying as Jewish, but Elizabeth Slade Hirschfeld's fascination with her Jewishness grew as she grew older and began to identify with other "outsiders."

Negotiating multiple changes in class, gender, racial, and ethnic norms, these future Jewish women activists embraced their inheritance as critically thinking outsiders. On many levels, being outside and/or in between opened up new pathways and possibilities for breaking the rules. In their relationships with parents, evolving political views, and developing racial consciousness, they would strain against, adapt, and transform aspects of their family legacies.

RELATING TO PARENTS

Like the nineteenth- and early-twentieth-century Russian Jewish and immigrant women radicals Naomi Shepherd describes in *A Price below Rubies,* many of the Jewish women civil rights workers had difficult relationships with their mothers:

> The primary concern of the Jewish radicals was to be as different from their own mothers as possible, even if it is clear that they inherited their mothers' practical energies. The managerial skills of radical

women, both in the middle and working class sectors, appears to have been inspired by their trading, peddling mothers and grandmothers.[18]

Shepherd cites a common theme among the women she studied, "I pitied mother, but my sympathies were with father."[19] Such identification with fathers facilitated their daughters' break with the limitations of a traditional Jewish female role. In the United States, the same was often true for Jewish women radicals.

When asked about the implications of being the eldest daughter in a family of eight children, Miriam Cohen Glickman replies that it was a bad position. "My mother still complains to this day, and here I am in my fifties, that when I was in high school I didn't help her enough—instead I did my homework."[20] Glickman's mother also did not believe in girls going to college. When asked how she negotiated getting to Brandeis, she answers, "My dad and I ignored her." Glickman continues, "She was really out of step there. All the other Jewish girls were going to college, even the ones who weren't so bright."

Also a firstborn daughter, Barbara Jacobs Haber was her father's favorite. Haber felt like "the center of my mother's and my father's universe." This changed dramatically after her mother's death. Haber speaks of the mixed gender messages she received from her father and stepmother. As a girl she "painted and drew pictures, and I was at one point very interested in drawing floor plans of houses, which made my father believe I could be an architect and my stepmother said maybe an interior decorator."

> I remember my stepmother said something to me once, I don't know if it was high school or college. I remember hating her for saying this. She said that she could really envision me married to an academic because I would do well with him in an academic community but I didn't have—I don't know what term she used. It wasn't that I wasn't smart enough, but I didn't have the stick-to-itiveness, the perseverance and the single-mindedness and the discipline to choose one thing and become really knowledgeable. And she was right about me, but I hated her for saying it. Instead, what I would have liked from her was for her to help me to get that so that I could go out there and achieve. She felt that my best bet was to get a guy who was in that world and I would live happily in an academic environment without having to be an academic.[21]

A number of the women expressly criticize their mothers. June Finer said she "never felt terribly fond or admiring of my mother."

> [S]he was an ambitious woman and wanted to see my father recognized for his skills. I think she had a certain amount of envy for a couple of relatives who had made it more in a materialistic sort of way. Her values were somewhat materialistic. My father is much more of a humanitarian and is just a very decent man who is fond of his patients and lets them talk. Even though now his eyesight is very, very poor, his patients still come to him even though they know his limitations.

Florence Howe describes her grandmother, who died in an accident when Howe was seven, as "the one person in my life that I thought actually loved me. My mother didn't really want me. Her life was made miserable by the fact that she had me just nine months after she got married."

Howe remembers knowing before going to kindergarten that she was to be the teacher her mother never could be. When asked what her own dreams were, she replies, "It never crossed my mind to want anything other than my mother said. I was the most obedient, passive [child]." Nevertheless, she did get enraged about what she called "things that were unfair." For example, neither her brother nor father picked up his clothes and put them in the hamper. "So those were the only things I carped about—that Jackie could go out and play and that I had to help my mother with the housework." To this her mother explained, "'Well, girls do this and boys do that.'" When Howe pointed out that it was unfair, her mother replied, "'Life is unfair.' She would never discuss it." Howe was aware that her mother "was the unhappiest of persons especially since my father was not nice to her."[22]

As the family's oldest child, born in 1938, Dottie Miller Zellner was very influenced by her father. Although he was disappointed that she was not a boy, he still enjoyed showing off his precocious daughter. While treating his dental patients, he would call her in to read them the lead story in the *New York Times*. "So I would read it. I had no idea what I was reading, but I was reading it. Everyone was very impressed." Unlike most girls of her age, she felt her father wanted her to be a doctor or dentist and this was his way of giving her "a jump on it." Holding unsupportive mothers at bay and reveling in their father's dreams for them, Jewish women civil rights activists found a small space in which to defy traditional female roles.

INTERNALIZING FAMILY POLITICAL CULTURES

If their families' practice of gender roles seemed to diminish possibilities for these young women, family life simultaneously provided an open space for Jewish women's developing consciousness—through political discourse. From conservative to radical, most Jewish families felt compelled to know about and debate contemporary political developments, if only to ask, in the words of many contemporary jokes, "Is it good for the Jews?" This impulse to know what was going on in the outside world followed Jews from the Old World to the New, though the unforeseen dangers decreased dramatically.

Still, other aspects of Old World consciousness remained. As noted earlier, many of the women's grandparents immigrated to the United States from Eastern Europe in the early part of the twentieth century. The majority of Jewish immigrants in this period had been required to live in what was known as the Pale of Settlement: western Russian provinces and eastern Polish provinces under Russian rule. From the late nineteenth century to the early twentieth, Jews in the Pale experienced increasing economic pressure, political and educational restrictions, and mass violence (*pogroms*). In response, a range of Jewish groups were formed, including revolutionary socialists and Zionists (who saw the solution of the "Jewish problem" in the foundation of a Jewish state in Palestine). The Haskalah, an earlier Eastern European Jewish "Enlightenment," a secular Jewish intellectual movement that rejected religious, political, and social orthodoxy, had influenced them. The *maskilim*, followers of movements for Jewish secularization and modernization, called for increased education for Jewish boys and girls and critiqued traditional gender roles in the Jewish family. As Susan Glenn notes, both the Zionists and the Jewish Workers' Bund, founded in Russia in the 1880s, insisted "that Jews should militantly defend their political, social, and ethnoreligious rights, thus providing their followers with what historian Gerald Sorin calls 'new forms of Jewishness.'"[23] The generation of Jews who immigrated to the United States in the early twentieth century brought these new politicized forms of Jewishness with them.

Many of these first-generation Eastern European Jewish immigrants maintained the idea of having both a leftist political identity and a Jewish identity. Their children, the second generation, were more focused on becoming American, that is, economically successful and socially secure, but historical circumstances once again pushed them in

the direction of a more leftist consciousness. The Great Depression rad-
icalized second-generation Jews; at its height, the Communist Party's
Jewish membership was approximately 30 to 40 percent. In the Young
Communist League (YCL), approximately five thousand of its thirteen
thousand members were Jewish. In the New York area, Jews also pre-
dominated in noncommunist left-wing organizations.[24]

By the time most of the women were growing up after World War
II, postwar prosperity and the drive for economic security had dis-
tracted, if not muted, their parents' radical consciousness. However,
parents, grandparents, and other extended family members still managed to transmit progressive social values derived from earlier or current experiences. In some cases, interactions with classmates and
friends, and in settings such as summer camp, progressive meetings,
and cultural activities, sent a message. The following stories illuminate
this transmission of values, which was often entwined with Jewish
identity in enigmatic ways.

Red-diaper babies like Dottie Miller Zellner, children of Communist Party members or people loosely connected to the Communist
milieu, grew up in families that proudly communicated radical political values. But these same families also suffered from fear, political
persecution (in the form of blacklists and witch-hunts), secrecy, and
ideological rigidity. Nevertheless, red-diaper babies' upbringing instilled a sense of community and purpose that made the call of the
civil rights movement irresistible. Judy Kaplan and Linn Shapiro
identify five common themes that characterize this enabling family
environment: the centrality of left politics to everyday life; an oppositional identity; heightened historical awareness; a feeling of connection to an international activist community; and a belief that one's actions can make a difference, especially when working with others to
radically change society.[25]

In some radical families, two generations were involved with
SNCC. Among Jewish women who went south, Joni Rabinowitz and
Karin Kunstler are daughters of movement lawyers who made history.
Victor Rabinowitz defended his daughter and her colleagues who were
arrested during the 1963 Albany, Georgia, movement. William Kunstler,
an attorney close to SNCC and to Martin Luther King Jr., helped direct
SNCC's 1965 Congressional Challenge.

For these women, family commitment was clearly total. In other
cases, disillusionment with the party set in, while progressive values remained. Harriet Tanzman's parents were members of the Communist

Party, but her father left in 1939 after the Hitler-Stalin pact. Her mother left after World War II when there were struggles within the party over identifying with the Soviet Union. Tanzman recalls, "I think she got sick of the intellectuals. She was much more of a doer. She got tired of all the infighting."[26]

Even Jews who were not politically engaged often came in touch with radical culture through Communist Party–sponsored organizations like the Jewish People's Fraternal Order, which created a network of social programs, schools, summer camps, and of folk dancing and folk singing groups.[27] In 1946, Jan Goodman, for example, went to Camp Taconic, run by Bob Kinoy, a relative of Arthur Kinoy, who also worked with Kunstler for SNCC on the Congressional Challenge. Goodman notes that for "that day, it was considered a radical camp." They discussed politics, including civil rights. "Although there were no Blacks there, everybody talked about these things." Progressive Jewish culture communicated a number of social justice messages. One of them was that anti-Black racism was wrong.

Although there was a sizable number of red-diaper babies among the whites who went to Mississippi in 1964,[28] the majority came from liberal families. The same is true specifically for Jews who went south.

In contrast to Zellner and Rabinowitz, most of the Jewish women in this book came from homes with a more diffuse Jewish progressivism. Jan Goodman, Barbara Jacobs Haber, and Faith Holsaert make it a point to say that they were not red-diaper babies. This was not said with any anti-Communist fervor but to underscore the absence of organized political affiliation that would have channeled them as young people into political activity.

Jacqueline Levine's parents "were nowhere near even neo-Communists at all. They were just plain liberal, which is what I am." She enjoyed discussing "the politics of the day" with her father, who "helped me a lot and shaped me a lot. . . . Everything that goes with a good solid progressive household went on in mine." This family culture imbued Levine with the belief that "one's politics are an expression of your own values, not personality, but of all the things that you hold dear and that benefit the country and humankind. . . . I really don't have time for people who are not liberal."[29]

Although most of the women were not red-diaper babies, they often had a family member who communicated radical political views passionately. Carol Ruth Silver speaks ironically of her aunt Evelyn, a "very rabid Communist in the '30s" who later "fell in love with a very orthodox rabbi and converted from Marxism to Judaism."[30] She had six children and supported the family while her husband studied.

In some cases, an immigrant grandparent directly handed down the legacy of Eastern European Jewish radicalism to future activists. Carol Ruth Silver attributes both of her parents' political consciousness to the influence of Tillie Silver, the "sterling matriarch" of her father's family. Tillie Silver, who had come from Vilna (one of the great centers of Jewish religious and intellectual culture), was widowed early and supported her six children by running the "legendary" Silver bakery in Boston's west end. In her home "there was an enormous table" filled with people engaged in political debate.

For others, like Barbara Jacobs Haber, the heritage was there but suppressed. Haber interviewed her father when he was in his mid-eighties and he "boasted" that he had secretly voted socialist the first time he voted. Haber also learned for the first time "that I had this secret grandfather who was a very active socialist." Because Haber's father loved him so much, it pained him to speak of his father, who "had dropped dead" of a heart attack on the subway at a young age.

Though she did not hear about explicitly radical politics from her family while growing up, Haber always "felt that my father intended for me to become things that he was too afraid to live out. He wanted me to be a radical, he wanted me to be an artist, and he was always very supportive of me even when I was quite obnoxious. He was very supportive of my participation in the civil rights movement. He took me to the church the first time I went on a sort of mini Freedom Ride on the eastern shore of Maryland."

Roberta Galler's parents saw themselves as liberal Democrats, "very big believers in FDR and FDR-type politics." Above all, "they were determined to be American." Galler's grandfather was a socialist, but he spoke more of his atheist beliefs than his politics. Because she was named after her great-uncle's mother, a group of older relatives used to pinch Galler's cheeks as a young girl and call her "our little mother." Among them was one radical great-uncle, who greeted Galler both by pinching her cheek and announcing, "Now here's our little communist." Though she was exposed more to Jewish liberalism than radicalism, clearly the rebellious streak must have shown early.

In Harriet Tanzman's family, "the death of Julius and Ethel Rosenberg was a very big theme." As Judy Kaplan and Linn Shapiro underscore in their red-diaper baby anthology, the execution of the

Rosenbergs in 1953 for the charge of conspiracy to divulge atomic secrets to the Soviet Union was the archetypal event for children of
Communist families.[31] Harriet Tanzman eloquently describes the
feelings this evoked:

> My aunt and uncle were active in trying to save the Rosenbergs. I was
> between ten and thirteen. I didn't understand, but [it had an] impact
> that people could be killed for what they believed in. That had to have
> had a big impact because they were very ordinary people, the Rosen-
> bergs, and so were my family.

Tanzman experienced a sense of "being the 'other,' [though] we weren't
the 'other' in the Rockaways, but we were the 'other' just even in having different points of view during a very dead, repressive time, during
the fifties."

Jewish women civil rights activists thus came from families whose
politics ranged from Communist to "just plain liberal." Yet regardless of
where they fell on a political continuum, their families shared and
passed on the belief that it was important to know, care, and have opinions about what was going on in the world.

BECOMING RADICALIZED

Although the majority of the women were not, then, red-diaper babies,
many did see themselves as "political" by the late '50s and early '60s.
Having had contact with progressive adults and/or radicalizing experiences related to race, they were primed to put their values into action
when the civil rights movement put out the call.

By the time she went to Mississippi, Jan Goodman defined herself
as a political person. She had spent several summers at Camp Taconic
and had attended hootenannies and Pete Seeger concerts in the late
'40s and early '50s. She worked on campaigns against Senator Joseph
McCarthy while a student at the University of Michigan. She chaired
the University of Pennsylvania's chapter of Students for Democratic
Action and started a fair housing committee to address segregated
student housing. Back in New York after graduation, she worked on
Mark Lane's congressional campaign in East Harlem and attended
CORE demonstrations in New York City. Like many other New York

antiracist activists, including Mickey Schwerner, her first demonstration in the South was at Gwynne Oaks, a segregated amusement park outside Baltimore.

Like Jan Goodman, Roberta Galler encountered progressive politics as a girl in the 1940s. The principal of her grammar school held weekly assemblies where she tried to convey the message that it was okay to be different—through songs, stories, and guest speakers, like the great Black Olympic runner Jesse Owens. A number of progressive teachers encouraged Galler, who was an excellent student: "What I didn't necessarily get from my family, I got from some teachers."

A number of Jewish women teachers in her predominantly Jewish grammar school supported Galler, but the tone changed when she entered high school at the height of the McCarthy era. One of her Jewish women high school teachers expressed enormous fear about Galler's politics. Galler and her friend "liked to torment her by being as radical as we could." One time, the teacher "screeched, went to the window, and said if we didn't stop being the way we were, she would throw herself out the window."

This did not impress Galler, who continued to give radical speeches as she fought her way to the top as state champion public speaker. Voted "the girl most likely to succeed," she gave a high school address entitled "Forward with Honor." Galler remembers saying, "as only a sixteen-year-old can, with great arrogance, that it is not the followers but the rebels who propel society forward."

June Finer attributes her radicalization to "the times we lived in," to her exposure to the effects of racism in Chicago, and "to meeting very political people." Nevertheless, she also believes

> I would have slid into civil rights activity anyway even if I hadn't met them because one thing my parents did instill in me was this tremendous sense of fair play. . . . [H]aving a sister close in age, everything had to be divided absolutely equally. And things were not fair. That was such a common thing. I have a big sense of equality and things not being fair. I'm sure that's a whole lot of why I ended up doing the things I did—the inequalities were so outrageous. It just wasn't right.

During her internship and residency in Chicago in the early 1960s, June Finer became politicized through the "very focused" Dr. Quentin Young and his friends and contacts:

There was an interracial organization called the Committee to End Discrimination in Chicago Medical Institutions that had been around for fifteen or twenty years. It was amazing because this was pre-civil rights, pre-everything. There were Black and white doctors in this group for years. Presumably, the Black and white doctors who had been in this group for years all had a somewhat leftist background, and it was a most wonderful group.

Carol Ruth Silver also found a home in the political community in Chicago. A student at the University of Chicago, she recalls jokingly, "I was not afraid to be an iconoclast before Chicago, and after Chicago, I was impossible." In the late 1950s, a tiny percentage of the university's student body was Black. Silver recalls that among her best friends was one of those few Black students.

As an undergraduate in the 1950s, Silver was involved in the mildly left-wing Student Representative Party. She was president of the Documentary Film Society and the Folklore Society, and says that the Film Society "did nothing but hold wingdings" where people came with guitars and sang folk songs. Although "that sounds fairly nonpolitical," for the mid-fifties, it was one of the few ways to express one's dissenting political identity. With the extra money the Film Society raised, the students sent donations to groups on strike and got involved in "all of the pre-sixties liberal, humanitarian agenda."

Although Silver "hung out" with socialists and communists and agreed with their human rights agenda, she rejected Marxism philosophically. She wanted to protect individual rights and disagreed with historical materialism, wrapping her critique in Jewish identity. "As a true Jewish atheist, I did not see the world as having a steady progress, a steady march from anything to anything, [including] . . . the march from feudalism to industrialism."[32]

In the winter of Silver's senior year (1960), she heard about the Woolworth's boycotts and agreed when asked to organize a boycott in Chicago. From this modest engagement with civil rights work, Silver propelled herself down south as one of the early Freedom Riders.

Elizabeth Slade Hirschfeld's first involvement with a political campaign was with John F. Kennedy's presidential campaign. Breaking with her family's staunch Republicanism, she not only worked for the Democratic party but began to feel "that I was kind of a socialist." In a discussion with Freedom Rider Charlie Haney, whom she dated,

Hirschfeld asked him, "'How can you be a socialist?' And he said to me, 'If everybody could be fed and everybody could be housed and every-body could be well educated, would you give up part of your income?' and I said, 'Sure.' He said, 'You're a socialist,' and it was almost that simple." Hirschfeld describes this as "a moment of lightning" in which she first understood that "the world wasn't for everybody the way the world had been for me." Not long after, she was in jail herself as a Free-dom Rider.

Faith Holsaert declares that her first public political act was "walking down my street when I was a child with Charity and my mother, in the sense that people did call us names." Charity Bailey also took Faith to events sponsored by the teachers union. She heard Pete Seeger sing during the time he was blacklisted and attended other benefit concerts, of which she remembers "a tremendous sense of belonging and solidarity."

Holsaert's mother "signed petitions and went to demonstrations for the Rosenbergs." Although she seems to present her mother as an ambivalent liberal, when pressed to describe her mother's politics, Holsaert mentions that her mother and Bailey had the first interracial children's show on television in 1955. At one point, NBC lawyers called her mother in to say that someone had accused her of being "prematurely antifascist" (a euphemism for Communist) because she had signed a petition concerned with Spain in the 1930s. Though her mother was not a Communist, she taught Faith and her sister, Shai, humanistic values, which Faith later came to identify with Karl Marx and Jewish humanism.

Holsaert attended the High School of Music and Art, which at that time, had "a wonderful sense of camaraderie that was pretty cross-racial." There, Holsaert became an activist, attending SANE demonstrations and participating in student leadership programs run by the National Conference of Christians and Jews. Through the NCCJ, she attended a camp in the summer of 1960 in Beacon, New York, where she met some of the students who had been involved in the sit-ins and Freedom Rides. They would later become her "direct entree to SNCC."

Also through the NCCJ, she became involved in the Harlem Broth-erhood, high school and college students who did housing surveys. A core group of five to ten friends grew very close, and Holsaert was one of its few white members. Holsaert took her first trip south at Christ-mastime in 1961 with Peggy Dammond, a brotherhood friend, to take part in a sit-in in Christfield, Maryland. They were arrested and spent a week in jail. Most significant for Holsaert was meeting SNCC staff people who would later form the foundation of the Cambridge Movement, led by Gloria Richardson.

Holsaert was eighteen when she was arrested; nineteen when she went to Albany; and turned twenty when she was in southwest Georgia. Unique perhaps among Jewish civil rights workers, Holsaert attributes her ability to circumvent some of the tensions between whites and Blacks in the movement to having grown up with a Black woman who played a parental role in her life.

In "While We Were Singing," Holsaert's work about her time in the Harlem Brotherhood, she describes her two best friends in the characters Vera and Isobel. On a roof in Harlem, looking down at Columbia University on Morningside Heights, the three girls have the following conversation:

> "Hey, Sis"—Isobel addressed me as Sis for the first time on that roof—"you could pass for black, with your tan."
> "And that just-about-kinky hair," Vera laughed.
> "It's hot up here," I said, unable to say how proud they made me.

Later there is some tension when Holsaert's character is one of the few white girls at a party. Isobel reports that she has been recruited by the Nation of Islam and criticized for hanging around with a white girl. As the three girls prepare for sleep at Vera's, there is a discussion:

> "I got a bone to pick with you," Vera said to Isobel.
> "Don't you say ofay again to me."
> I didn't ask what ofay meant.
> "It's what she is," Isobel said sulkily.
> "She ain't ofay, she white." Vera daintily brushed powdered tempera off the heel of her hand. She got out blankets and pillows, handed them to Isobel and me, and began to undress.

The exchange brings to mind a theme that surfaces in the lives of Jewish women civil rights workers: their pride in passing for Black and being validated for this feeling by Black movement allies. In this case of three young women in Harlem, Vera chastises Isobel for using the term *ofay* because it implicitly indicts all whites as racist. Although everyone acknowledges that Faith is white, she and her friends wistfully joke about her "passing," which would make it easier for Black peers to see and treat her as "one of us," an insider.

Over the years, Holsaert and her two friends went in and out of one another's lives. The character of Isobel is based on Amina Rachman, who became very involved with the Nation of Islam and was featured as Sherron Ten X in a film about Malcolm X. Though she and Holsaert were out of touch from the midsixties to early seventies, she helped Holsaert understand the political necessity of Black nationalism as a phase in the movement. Their friendship, as Holsaert notes, demonstrated that Black Muslims and Jews could understand and respect one another. In the 1990s, Rachman converted to Judaism, as had SNCC activists Charles McDew and Julius Lester, showing that border crossings can go both ways.

LEARNING ABOUT RACE

The ability to be an antiracist white ally in the Black-led civil rights movement required a fairly sophisticated analysis of racism. Most of the women in this study, in addition to becoming aware of their own difference as Jews, learned about anti-Black racism at relatively young ages. Faith Holsaert, however, was the only one to learn about racism in school, at the progressive Little Red School House in New York City. In 1954, she recalls, in a social studies class

> half of the year we studied the history of the Negro people in the United States and the second half we studied Jewish history. So the two histories were explicitly linked there. I learned about Paul Robeson, so-called Negro spirituals along with other music, and about the *Brown v. Board of Education* decision, which happened when I was in fifth grade. There was even a pretty explicit teaching that racism was an important thing to struggle against.

Among those who received strong antiracist messages at early ages were Freedom Riders Elizabeth Slade Hirschfeld and Carol Ruth Silver, who got them from their mothers. Hirschfeld tells of seeing her first Black person when she was two or three years old. "I remember saying the word 'nigger' and my mother washing my mouth out with soap." Later when walking down a street in Detroit, she asked her mother why a Black person she saw there looked different. Her mother replied:

Hundreds of years ago, people were brought to this country who were kings and queens and princesses from another part of the world where everybody is that color. They were forced to do the most terrible things here, and they lost their families. It was terrible what we did to those people, and you must always look at those people with respect.[33]

Silver recollects that while she was in grammar school in Revere, Massachusetts, the first Black family moved into her neighborhood. "My mother extended herself to this one Black family . . . and I'm sure I learned a bunch of things at that moment . . . but I don't recall any specific discussions. It was just in the atmosphere and the culture that my parents conveyed to me."

Not all the women's families conveyed messages about racism as clearly as did Hirschfeld's mother. In many cases, families' mixed messages encouraged deeper probing of the issue. To elicit a contemporary rather than retrospective sense of their childhood awareness of Blacks and race, I asked several of the women, "What's your response when I say the word *schvartzer*?"[34]

Taken aback by my use of a term that exists as a shameful remnant of an era of more unselfconscious Jewish racism, Harriet Tanzman offers a typical reply: "Oy. Well, to tell you the truth, I think my aunt and my grandmother used it a little, and I always thought it was a real bad word. But I didn't hear it a lot otherwise. I didn't hear Yiddish words much, period. She also used *goyim* for Gentile. She said it casually. I guess she meant everybody who wasn't like her."

Florence Howe's family used the same derogatory language, and "even before I was twelve, I couldn't understand my family's fierce hatred of Black people." During big fights with her parents, her father would say, "You only know nice ones, not the ones I meet in my taxi. You only know cultured ones."

Howe's father's racist comments may be understood as a reflection of his status anxiety (as an uneducated Jewish immigrant without "proper papers"). Florence Howe was precisely at the beginning of the process of acculturation that would quell such anxieties for upwardly mobile American Jews. She recalls that her New York accent "got knocked out of me at Hunter College High School when I talked lower-class Brooklyn, and they labeled me speech defect." As higher education did for other Jewish women, it provided Howe with a way out of the working class. While at Hunter College, she had a sociology course with Mary Diggs, the only Black professor on staff. After one of Diggs's lectures, Howe attempted to explain the development of "scientific racism" to her parents, but that did not change their point of view. Few could make the analogy between the social construction of anti-Semitism in Europe (Jews as "other") and racism in the United States. In one of her first acts combating institutional racism, Howe helped found the first interracial sorority at Hunter.

Coming from a similar background, Barbara Jacobs Haber says,

> My family was racist. *Schvartzers* were the people who we had come clean our house. I don't remember if we ever had a maid before my mother died. My aunt [who worked as a teacher] always had a maid referred to as "the schvartzer." You weren't ever supposed to do anything to harm colored people. I was taught that racism was bad and segregation in other parts of the country was bad, but I also somehow got the message . . . that it was the fault of Blacks and Puerto Ricans that they lived in these horrible slums and that they weren't good in school.

Haber, who was a talented child artist, had "this picture of inferiority and superiority" challenged when she recognized that the work of her Puerto Rican classmate, Cruz Roblez, was better than hers. Later on, Haber fought with her parents over their failure to criticize Jewish neighbors who used the word *nigger*.

Jacqueline Levine feels she was aware of racism "from birth because I knew it wasn't right to discriminate against anybody on any basis whatsoever."

> I couldn't stand the language that was used by many people, by many Jews. I hate the word *schvartzer*. I barely can say it. I hate that word and the other word I absolutely cannot say. The "n" word. That I didn't hear, but in the Jewish neighborhoods where I grew up certainly everyone was saying [*schvartzer*]. I am afraid that my grandmother, who was very elegant and very smart, said that, as it was part of her background. She spoke with no accent, and I didn't know enough to stop her from saying it. I knew I didn't like the word, and because my parents were what they were, all bigotry and discrimination was frowned upon. And, of course, anti-Black racism was the prime element of that in those days.

Two of the women, Roberta Galler and Elaine DeLott Baker, had early childhood experiences that connected them more directly with southern racial ways. As a child with polio, Galler stayed for extended periods at Warm Springs, Georgia. She noticed to her chagrin that

> there were no Black patients. Blacks performed only the most menial tasks. Nothing that involved touching or personal care. Not even nurses or anything else, nobody was Black. The servant class was Black and—I don't know that it occurred to me at the time—what happened to the Black kids who got polio, and why were none of them there?[35]

Although she did not spend time in the South as a child, Baker grew up hearing stories about how the Black people in Sparta, Georgia, loved her grandmother because she treated them with respect in her store and everyday interactions. Baker particularly resonated with stories about how the family cook, Dollie Gordon, loved Elaine's grandmother, mother, and sisters. A lonely child, Elaine wrote to Gordon when she was twelve, although they had never met. Gordon replied on September 20, 1954, expressing great happiness about reconnecting with the family that had moved north and with special affection for Elaine.[36]

Without interviewing Gordon, it is difficult to know what feelings she may have had about the DeLott family other than the apparent warmth and concern conveyed in her letter. It seems likely that she played a role typical of Black women domestics in the segregated South: the person who connected southerners of both races to one another. In her study of domestic workers and their employers, Susan Tucker found

> that in the South many people have been brought close to others through the care of Black women. And though such care involved a complicated entanglement of memories, history, psychology, race relations and economics, it also involved maternal love, daily contact, mutual dependence and attention to the needs and strengths of the individuals involved. [37]

From the perspective of a young Jewish girl in the North, what did it mean to have a Black woman who played no real role in one's life except a kind of romanticized comfort? What kinds of questions did it raise? Did Dollie Gordon have her own family? Where did she work after the DeLotts left? Why did she want to stay connected to the family? Fortunately, Baker did have her grandmother as a direct role model, a woman who crossed boundaries and violated southern social norms in order to relate to Black people as her personal conscience dictated.

If Baker's family links to a southern Black woman attuned her to race relations, Trudy Weissman Orris responds to the question of when she became aware of racism as if Jewish antiracist consciousness was a given:

> Well, I always felt that I knew what racism was because of being a Jew and being discriminated against. So racism to me was very much like being a Jew and being discriminated against. And so I felt that I as a Jew had a better understanding and a better feeling of racism than if I wasn't a Jew.

Being of an older generation more directly scarred by anti-Semitism, Orris could make the link between Blacks and Jews because of her own experience. However, the assumption of a *natural* alliance between Blacks and Jews is a myth. Contemporary conflicts and historical analyses show that the relationship between the two communities changes over time, responding to political, socioeconomic, and cultural transformations.[38]

Examples of this fluctuation, as the women's stories demonstrate, are the mixed messages that 1950s liberal Jewish families sent to their children about people of color. On one hand, families taught that racism was wrong and they should not express it, as Elizabeth Slade Hirschfeld learned when her mother washed her mouth out with soap. This ensured external respectability. On the other hand, within the safety of the family, tolerance of the word *schvartzer* in all its patronizing condescension, sent a message that Jews were somehow superior. This clearly reflects the insecurity of a transitional social group going through ethnic, religious, economic, cultural, racial, and social changes. In the 1950s, posits Karen Brodkin, Jews developed their own form of whiteness, which helped them mitigate the anxieties of upward mobility by retaining a concern with social justice.[39]

Once again, Jewish ambivalence, mixed messages, and transitional identities, while certainly not easy to live through, served future Jewish women activists well. Moving between worlds within their own families and local contexts, Jewish women activists developed the flexibility and openness to difference that enabled them to cross borders to go south. As they witnessed relatives' disenchantment with the Communist Party and Aunt Evelyn's conversion from Marxism to Judaism,

they saw that belief systems could and should change according to expanded evidence and perspectives. As young Jewish women reaching
maturity in the restrictive gender regime of the 1950s, their liminal identities gave them license to be bolder than their cultural options seemed
to allow. Drawing on the empowering aspects of family legacies and
leaving some of the more oppressive elements behind, future Jewish
women activists learned to speak out, loudly, for what they believed in.

NOTES

1. May, 7; Breines, 50.

2. As Sandra Harding writes, "[T]ransitional epistemologies are appropriate for transitional cultures." Sandra Harding, ed., *Feminism and Methodology*
(Bloomington: Indiana University Press, 1987), 186. Standpoint theorists like
Harding contend that people from oppressed groups have an epistemic advantage because they must understand both their own ways of knowing and those
of the dominant system in order to survive. In making a similar case for Jews,
the editors of *Insider/Outsider* note the positive aspects of the liminal Jewish position as outsiders who are insiders and vice versa. Historically, this position facilitated Jews' survival for centuries "precisely because they were able to establish themselves close to centers of power and negotiate between competing elite
and popular forces." From a contemporary perspective, this position allows
American Jews to contribute significantly to a multiculturalism that affirms difference. Biale et al., 5–8.

3. Interview with Janice Goodman, October 21, 1993.

4. On Jewish "proletarianization" and the nature of the garment industry,
see Gerald Sorin, *A Time for Building: The Third Migration, 1880–1920* (Baltimore:
Johns Hopkins University Press, 1992), 109–110.

5. Paula Hyman, *Gender and Assimilation in Modern Jewish History: The Roles
and Representations of Women* (Seattle: University of Washinton Press, 1995),
93–116.

6. Henry Feingold, *A Time for Searching: Entering the Mainstream, 1920–1945*
(Baltimore: Johns Hopkins University Press, 1992), 43–45.

7. Elaine DeLott Baker, "A Social Autobiography" (1993); used with author's permission.

8. Andrew Heinze, *Adapting to Abundance: Jewish Immigrants, Mass Consumption, and the Search for American Identity* (New York: Columbia University
Press, 1990).

9. Interview with Carol Ruth Silver, February 9, 1994.

10. Interview with Faith S. Holsaert, March 19, 1994.

11. Kaufman, *Broken Alliance*, 53.

12. Brodkin, 2–3. Brodkin's distinction between "Jewish double vision"

and what W. E. B. DuBois described as African Americans' "double consciousness" is essential because it takes into account the differential socioeconomic
opportunities afforded each group, recognizing many Jews' access to white
racial privilege. See Biale et al., 17, for another perspective on Jewish "double-
consciousness."

13. For an analysis of Black-Jewish urban interactions, see Jonathan Kaufman, "Blacks and Jews: The Struggle in the Cities," in Salzman and West,
107–121.

14. Interview with Dorothy Miller Zellner, November 15, 1993.

15. Interview with June Finer, December 21, 1993.

16. Jewish women who entered the public realm in the early twentieth cen-
tury did so out of a Jewish version of domestic feminism. Faith Rogow, *Gone to
Another Meeting: A History of the National Council of Jewish Women* (University:
University of Alabama Press, 1993).

17. Interview with Elizabeth Slade Hirschfeld, February 10, 1994.

18. Shepherd, 291.

19. Ibid., 290.

20. Interview with Miriam Cohen Glickman, February 11, 1994.

21. Interview with Barbara Jacobs Haber, February 20, 1994.

22. Interview with Florence Howe, December 1, 1993.

23. Susan Glenn, *Daughters of the Shtetl: Life and Labor in the Immigrant Generation* (Ithaca: Cornell University Press, 1990), 35.

24. Feingold, 220–224.

25. Judy Kaplan and Linn Shapiro, eds., *Red Diapers: Growing Up in the
Communist Left* (Urbana: University of Illinois Press, 1998), 9.

26. Interview with Harriet Tanzman, October 15, 1993.

27. Feingold, 222.

28. McAdam, *Freedom Summer*, 131. McAdam has suggested that Communist connections may have been played down because of the red-baiting
of SNCC and the civil rights movement, but contemporary interviews still
suggest that this background was not as common among volunteers as has
been assumed.

29. Interview with Jacqueline Levine, October 1993.

30. Interview with Carol Ruth Silver, February 20, 1994.

31. Kaplan and Shapiro, 4.

32. Interview with Carol Ruth Silver, February 20, 1994.

33. Interview with Elizabeth Slade Hirschfeld, February 10, 1994.

34. Guilty protestations to the contrary aside, *schvartzer* is more than a de-
scriptive Yiddish term for a Black person, at least in the twentieth-century
United States context. The term has an implicitly pejorative—or at best—patronizing ring. As Leo Rosten notes in *The Joys of Yiddish* (New York: Pocket
Books, 1968), 381: "Schvartzer and schvartzeh to mean Negro man and woman,
became 'inside' words among Jews—cryptonyms for Negro servants or em-

ployees. Since the growth of the civil rights movement, these uses have declined."

35. Interview with Roberta Galler, December 10, 1994.

36. Photocopy in possession of author; courtesy of Elaine DeLott Baker.

37. Susan Tucker, *Telling Memories among Southern Women: Domestic Workers and Their Employers in the Segregated South* (New York: Schocken Books, 1988), 16.

38. Interview with Gertrude Weissman Orris, January 21, 1994. Recommended selections from the burgeoning literature on Black-Jewish relations include Ella Baker, "The Bronx Slave Market," *Crisis* 42 (November 1935): 330–331, 340; John Bracey and August Meier, "Towards a Research Agenda on Blacks and Jews in United States History," *Journal of American Ethnic History* 12 (Spring 1993): 60–67; Kaufman, *Broken Alliance*; Kaye/Kantrowitz; Salzman et al.; Joseph Washington, ed., *Jews in Black Perspective: A Dialogue* (Lanham, Md.: University Press of America, 1989); Michael Lerner and Cornel West, *Jews and Blacks: Let the Healing Begin* (New York: Putnam, 1995); Salzman and West.

39. Brodkin, 139.

5

Exploring Many Ways of Being Jewish

I think it's important for people to understand that you can say you're a Jew, you can be ready to go out to the firing squad because you want to say that you're Jewish, and you can be proud of being Jewish without ever having one shred of religious feeling.

—Dorothy Miller Zellner

ALTHOUGH DOTTIE MILLER Zellner asserts an expansive sense of secular Jewishness, the issue of who gets to define Jewish identity is, of course, highly contentious. With its image of the firing squad, Zellner's articulation of Jewishness evokes the resistance of the Warsaw Ghetto. Yet, the narrative of Jewish resistance—including ghetto and concentration camp sabotage and rebellion—has only recently started to include Jewish women.

If, as Isaac Deutscher writes in his classic book, *The Non-Jewish Jew and Other Essays*, it has been Jews' historic marginality that has led to a broader perspective, more clarity about society's injustices, and identification with the oppressed, then what are the implications for Jewish women? Deutscher's statement describing Jews in general—"Each of them was in society and yet not in it, of it and yet not of it"—applies doubly to Jewish women, who have been marginalized in Gentile society and within male-dominated spheres of Jewish life.[1]

Thus, if the activism of Jewish women profiled in this book was, to a significant extent, born of their experiences of difference and marginality, it is important to see those experiences through the lenses of both Jewishness and gender. Jewish identity presented a particular set of challenges for the women activists. We see them struggling between past and future, shame and pride, fear and defiance. Because questions of Jewish identity are so enigmatic, this chapter examines specific moments in the women's youth when Jewishness confronted them. Their stories explore the women's early encounters with religious institutions, mixed messages from parents, experiences of anti-Semitism, and the impact of knowledge of the Holocaust on their consciousness. Out of these multivalent experiences and insights, the women questioned and forged many ways of being Jewish.

TALKING ABOUT JEWISH IDENTITY

It is a formidable task to characterize nonreligious meanings of *Jewish identity*, a slippery term indeed. The first step is to distinguish between Judaism as religion and as ethnicity. Ethnic identity is shaped by the interplay among a group's history, its interactions with other social groups, its relation to the dominant culture, and by the group's members. Because these interactions and relations shift continuously, ethnic definitions are a constantly moving target. The fluidity and complexity of racial and ethnic identities in today's multicultural world are leading scholars to begin to speak of "post-ethnicity."[2] Nevertheless, as late-twentieth-century wars in Africa and the former Yugoslavia suggest, we have hardly reached the post-ethnic era. The questions of Jewish ethnic identity in the post-Holocaust era is endlessly debated.

Across a history that spans more than five thousand years, Jewishness has meant many different things to many different people. Jews can derive a sense of group identity in religious, national, ethnic, or racial terms. "Jewishness" can be constructed by Jews themselves or imposed (as by the Nazi state, which defined anyone with a Jewish grandparent as Jewish). Even when decided within the extremely diverse Jewish community, the question is politically fraught. Many Orthodox Jews believe that only those with Jewish mothers or those converted according to Jewish law (*halaka*) are Jewish. On the other end of the spectrum, some liberal or secular Jews believe that anyone who wants to identify as Jewish may do so. Arthur Liebman asserts that "the Jewish label can be applied to those who are secular, cultural, assimilated, or even self-denying."[3] One could add "or all of the above." However, for the purposes of this book, "Jewishness" refers to a range of beliefs, values, experiences, analyses, and worldviews shaped by the historical and ethnocultural contexts in which young Jewish women activists came of age in mid-twentieth-century America.

Yet even within the relatively short history of the Jewish people in the United States in the twentieth century, meanings and experiences of Jewishness range far and wide. The diversity of these experiences includes tensions between earlier German and subsequent Eastern European immigrants; myriad political beliefs and practices; differing customs among Ashkenazi and Sephardic Jews; and the institutionalization of Reform, Conservative, and Orthodox Jewry, to name only a few. In the late 1960s to the mid-1970s, the alternative *havurah* movement initiated a generational effort to connect Judaism to American countercultural values.[4] Similarly, the Jewish feminist movement offers a rich array of options to link women to Jewish traditions and practices, reinterpreting and transforming them in the process.[5] An emergent Jewish gay and lesbian movement also asserts its connection to Jewish tradition. A new school of Jewish cultural studies critiques essentialist or unitary notions of Jewish identity, documenting and analyzing the diversity of Jewish expression. Influenced greatly by gender studies, this school posits "concepts of identity that emphasize process over product, multiplicity over unity, and becoming rather than being."[6] These new currents offer many opportunities to explore alternative ways of being Jewish.

However, without the luxury of these diverse choices, the women's families in the postwar era were struggling with a very basic problem of American Jewish identity: assimilation. Echoing the Jewish community's anxiety, parents sent conflicting messages about Jewish identity. A number of chroniclers of Jewish life in this period note the coexistence of increasing secularization and the growth of Jewish religious and social institutions—the rise of "religion without religiosity."[7] Specifically, although second-generation parents identified less as Jews ethnically or religiously, they often felt the need (particularly those who were more isolated in the suburbs) to join or send their children to a synagogue or other Jewish social institutions. The purpose of sending children to synagogue, Hebrew school, or Jewish camp seems to have been to give them both a sense of Jewish identity and tools for handling anti-Semitism when they encountered it.

The conflicting messages that many of the women received reflect a Jewish response to the mid-century mainstream American assault on cultural pluralism and difference. Given the era's climate of conformity, fear, and repression, it was not wise to be too different in the 1950s. Grappling with this climate, American Jews were torn between two sets of values: Jewish group survival and integration into American society.[8] Most of the women's second-generation parents opted for the latter, while retaining an often reactive and eclectic sense of Jewish identity. In the creative space opened by this variable state, their daughters fashioned passionate political identities with multiple relations to Jewish experience and traditions.

Nevertheless, several of the women interviewed initially had mixed reactions about discussing links between Jewish identity and civil rights activism. Responses included confusion over whether one "counted" as a Jew if not religious; anger at being identified as a Jew because of political, cultural, and religious disagreements with what is perceived as mainstream Jewry; and pride—ranging from tentative to fierce—in claiming Jewishness. Talking to Jewish radicals at Berkeley in the early 1960s about his planned study of connections between Jewishness and radicalism, Arthur Liebman found a similar "fervor and uneasiness" about the topic.[9]

As political radicals, the women lacked both concepts and contexts in which to discuss their Jewishness. Many Jewish civil rights workers do not recall conscious Jewish identification during their time in the movement, though they were not hiding or suppressing their Jewish identity. As Trudy Weissman Orris remarks, "If someone asked, I told them I was Jewish." Rather, the muted nature of Jewish identity in the movement is consistent with the universalist, non-nationalist ethics espoused in the early 1960s.

Like the women civil rights activists, Jewish radicals have historically had a range of responses to Jewish identity. Emma Goldman, for example, balanced the universalism of her anarchist philosophy with an appreciation for Jewish culture and a clear commitment to speaking out against anti-Semitism.[10] Revolutionary socialist leader Rosa Luxemburg, on the other hand, was hostile to any attempts to link her politics to her Jewish identity and was particularly critical of the Jewish socialist Bund.[11]

The intensity of these reactions, past and present, itself has a certain "Jewishness" about it. As Jonathan Boyarin comments, "In Jewish identity, the desire for totality [a tendency toward total commitment and total identification with various causes, groups, etc.] can lead toward attempts either to reify or dissolve Jewish distinctiveness."[12] In the case of Jewish radicals, this can lead to overstating the "Jewishness" of a radical commitment or totally denying any connection between Jewishness and progressive activism. When asked if she identified with Jewish culture or radical history, for instance, Parents of SNCC founder Gladys Blum answered no, but then proceeded to describe proudly her Jewish atheist father, who distributed radical pamphlets in the Ukraine during his time in the Russian army. Blum's response actually confirms a multi-generational tradition.[13]

Regardless of the extent to which they were aware of the history of a Jewish radical tradition, Jewish women civil rights activists formed another link in its chain. A brief history of Jewish women's activism in the Old World and in the early-twentieth-century United States provides an important context for understanding Jewish women's activism and identifications during the civil rights era.

RECLAIMING JEWISH WOMEN'S RADICAL HISTORY

Jewish women's activism in the United States has roots in older, Eastern European traditions. Until the last quarter of the nineteenth century, women in Eastern European Jewish communities traditionally managed businesses to support their families and to enable husbands to study Torah. At the same time, custom demanded that they keep a kosher home, cook all meals, make the family's clothing, and prepare the house for the Sabbath. Toward the end of the nineteenth century, urbanization and industrialization changed traditional Jewish *shtetl* (small Eastern European town) life. Inadvertently, the conditions of Eastern European Jewish life bolstered Jewish women's radicalism.

Facing economic hardship, anti-Jewish laws, and *pogroms*, a number of Jewish women became involved in nascent revolutionary movements. The Jewish Workers' Bund, founded in Russia in 1898, captured many of these women's imaginations. The Bundists, who were atheists, wanted to retain their Jewishness but within a secular, internationalist framework. It is not surprising that women formed a large part of the Bund.[14]

Jewish women's social roles also primed them to respond to revolutionary movements. "The Jewish woman had for centuries combined assertiveness and *self-abnegation* [italics added]; this made her an apt recruit for radical activities which demanded practical initiative together with an at times masochistic readiness for self-sacrifice."[15] Jewish women, who combined their private and public roles as family breadwinners, were used to stepping out of the dominant culture's gender norms in order to fight fiercely for family and cultural survival.

Revolutionary movements such as the Bund also spoke to Jewish women's yearnings for an enlarged realm in which to express their per-

sonal passions. Jewish women's "search for self-esteem through political involvement was part of a large transformation of feminine social
identity" that began in Eastern Europe and flowered in U.S. immigrant
communities.[16] Jewish women aspired to educational opportunity,
more social freedom, release from religious obligations, and the right to
a public role.

The material conditions of life in the United States further fostered
the development of women's political consciousness. Jewish women
played a significant role in the early-twentieth-century labor movement
because they came to factory and union experiences with a sense of
competence rooted in traditional recognition of their labor. Their competence enabled them to renegotiate their domestic and public roles.
Jewish immigrant women's identities were "complex and fluid," enabling them to move freely among "work, activism, and domesticity."[17]

In the United States, women negotiated the realms of work and politics by organizing locally. Jewish women organized in their own neighborhoods around three practical issues: food prices, rising rents, and
women's suffrage.[18] In addition, though distribution of birth control literature was illegal, Jewish women were well represented at the opening of Margaret Sanger's first birth control clinic in Brownsville, Brooklyn. They were involved in supporting the loyalist cause in Spain, active
in the Communist Party and other left organizations, and in the peace
movement as well. In the 1950s, June Croll Gordon founded the Emma
Lazarus Federation of Jewish Women's Clubs. The women of these
clubs wrote curricula on Jewish women, radical women, and Black
women; held interracial luncheons; and faced harassment during the
McCarthy era. In 1963, they sent a contingent to the March on Washington and also held their own gathering of fifteen hundred women at
New York's Cooper Union to celebrate interracial collaboration for civil
rights.[19] When seen against this larger backdrop, the story of Jewish
women's activism in the 1960s civil rights movement was an outgrowth
of a long-standing tradition.

ENCOUNTERING RELIGION AS GIRLS

Although the women of this study can claim a place for themselves in
a larger tradition of Jewish women's radical activism, claiming their
place in Jewish religious experience has been much more problematic. The following stories trace their early encounters with religious

practice and institutions, revealing the roots of their struggles with Jewish identity.

Jewish women activists from the more religious homes expressed strong emotions about Jewish identity. As a girl, Trudy Weissman Orris attended synagogue with her Orthodox, immigrant father. Always "very proud to be a Jew," she recalls an incident in 1927, when she was eleven, when she faced her fear of anti-Semitism in her Irish-Italian neighborhood in Greenwich Village. One of her chores was picking up the socialist-leaning newspaper, the *Jewish Daily Forward*, the most influential of the Jewish daily newspapers, with a 1920 circulation of 147,000.[20] Aware of neighborhood kids who beat up Jews,

> every time I picked up the paper, I would put it underneath my coat. But it bothered me very much, because as I said, I was proud of being a Jew. So one day I decided that I wasn't going to do that anymore. And I took the paper, and I held it in my hand, and I walked home like that. And that was the beginning of my emancipation as a Jew.

Other women from religious homes had less positive encounters, feeling a combination of revulsion at "Old World ways" and anger at being excluded from the core of Jewish religious experience because of gender. Florence Howe "lost my religious consciousness early," when she could detect her grandfather's guilt about providing access to religious texts to a girl. "I knew there was something wrong in his teaching me in that I couldn't go to *shul* with him. I'd have to sit upstairs in the smelly section with the old ladies, and I could never speak in synagogue."

Miriam Cohen Glickman grew up in a kosher home with a strong Jewish identification. Her parents sent her to Sunday school and "this horrid Hebrew school three times a week for years." Her family went to synagogue on the Sabbath and fasted on Yom Kippur. As a teenager, she could not attend high school sports events on Friday night. "To my knowledge, there was no interdating. You either dated Jewish boys, or you didn't date." When asked if she and her siblings were all *b'nai mitzvah*, Glickman replied, "Oh, that's a sore subject." Her brothers had *bar mitzvahs*, but the daughters did not have *bat mitzvahs*. Glickman recalled that she wanted to experience this Jewish rite of passage into religious adulthood "desperately, oh, so bad." It was hard not to interpret this as a valuing of boys over girls.

Harriet Tanzman's father's Hasidic family had emigrated from Russia in 1914, when her father was six. He was the only one of the five children they could afford to send to *yeshiva*. Although he did acquire discipline and a love of learning in *yeshiva*, he was not interested in living religiously. Tanzman's mother's family was very assimilated and not at all religious. Tanzman's parents celebrated Passover and Hanukah but did not raise the children with a formal religious education.

Carol Ruth Silver was brought up "as a third-generation Jewish atheist." However, when she was twelve years old,

> as often happens in Jewish families, my parents suddenly decided that it was time to get a Jewish education and they *shlepped* [dragged] me across Worcester to an Orthodox *cheder* [room or school where Hebrew is taught] for Sunday school. I went to one class in which they tried to teach me Hebrew and a version of traditional religious stories that I immediately rejected. I said I'm not going back. And being a somewhat strong-willed kid, even at that tender age, there was just no way that they could make me, so I never got any kind of Jewish education.

Dottie Miller Zellner had a similar experience:

> There was Hanukah, there was Passover. Never entered a synagogue. Never, never. My mother, when I was about twelve, was racked with some sort of guilt. I went once. She chose a primitive Orthodox synagogue in the neighborhood. It was dark. Everybody was *davening* [praying]. It was all in Hebrew. It must have been very Orthodox. I have this hideous memory of just wanting to get out of there. All the screaming that was going on.

Silver's and Zellner's experiences illustrate the phenomenon of "religion without religiosity" noted above. When their daughters reached adolescence, their parents felt a twinge of conscience about Jewish continuity, wanting both to expose them to the religion and to connect them to the culture.

In contrast to Silver and Zellner, June Finer has

> very fine and fun memories of going to the synagogue for the high holidays, where my grandfather was an honored person because he had been one of the founding fathers of the synagogue in Upper Clapton

in the East End. I have quite clear pictures in my mind of sitting upstairs with the women in the gallery and watching and listening to the
men downstairs. Of course, to a child, the interminable services went
on and on and on. And I remember at *Sukkoth* [the fall harvest festival],
we had this very beautiful little house with flowers and fruit and I remember some of the pretty aspects of it.

Finer's grandmother, who visited periodically, was *shomer Shabbos*,
which meant that she would not travel, carry money, or do any work on
the Sabbath. Finer's mother tried to be careful about observing the rules
when her own mother was visiting. Finer's mother kept a kosher home
through the war, "but afterwards, we were not very careful. . . . It became increasingly difficult because of rationing. It broke a lot of habits,
having to make do with odds and ends."

The young Finer decided she was an atheist. When she was around
ten or eleven, her mother employed a Hebrew tutor for her and her sisters. "Maybe she had some notion that we might be *bat mitzvahed*, but
we hated the man. We didn't like Hebrew. It just petered out. That was
really the extent of my Jewish education." As with Silver's and Zellner's mothers, Finer's mother's attempt to connect her daughters to Judaism failed without much of a fight.

Feminist writer Susan Brownmiller (b. 1935) says her childhood in
Brooklyn was "shaped by the Holocaust" and a strong sense of Jewish
identity. Her mother was born in the United States and her father was
born near Bialystock, Poland. Although her parents wanted her to have
a Jewish education, she recalls that they became a little nervous about
her extremism. When she got "too devout," they teased her "in that
wonderful Jewish mocking way: 'Susan's going to grow up to be a *reb-
betzin* [rabbi's wife].'"[21]

Coming from divorced homes headed by Jewish women, Faith
Holsaert and Jan Goodman did not participate formally in Jewish religious activities. Both women sensed that their mothers might have
liked to maintain a stronger Jewish identification, although Holsaert
recalls that there were also a lot of things in Judaism that made her
mother uncomfortable. Her mother felt that "a Jewish household
headed by a woman in the '40s or '50s was not really considered a
Jewish household. . . . Your entree to temple . . . and a role in the community came through the male."

In contrast to her father, Goodman's mother cared about having a
Jewish connection. She went to the Shalom Aleichem school to learn

Yiddish and listened to Jewish music. She sent Jan to Sunday school for a year and to Jewish summer camps for several years. They also, Goodman recalls, "did not work on Yom Kippur or Rosh Hashanah because we didn't want the neighbors to think we did not observe." We were "socially identified Jews," said Goodman.

Barbara Haber "was not raised religiously at all, but we kept a kosher house and lit candles on Friday night." When she asked her father, who was then in his eighties, "to explain this 'inconsistency,' he looked shocked and said, 'There was no inconsistency. To keep kosher and to light candles was cultural.'" An attempt to get the adolescent Haber to attend a Reform synagogue in the suburbs failed. When her mother died, Haber "had made a quick decision that either God was hateful or there was none. I became a passionate atheist at the age of nine because I blamed my mother's death, which was caused by an aneurysm, on this horrible Jewish God, which I had an image of as a man."

Jacqueline Levine had no formal religious training and considers herself an agnostic. Her father rebelled against his Orthodox background; her mother was the daughter of a socialist father and a "card-carrying atheist"/suffragist mother. Although her maternal grandparents and her own parents were atheist ("maybe we would say agnostic today so people's feelings aren't hurt"), Levine says,

> [I]t was a very Jewish household. Not Yiddish, certainly no one knew Hebrew, but it was permeated by an understanding of what Judaism entailed in social contract terms and what its ethics and values were. Some of the first United Jewish Appeal meetings were held in my parents' home and they were very philanthropic, not only to Jewish causes but certainly to them as well as to other liberal causes.

Levine's Jewish background is characteristic of upper-middle-class philanthropic liberalism, which historians consider emblematic of early-twentieth-century Jewish attempts to become more "American."[22]

Roberta Galler's paternal grandfather and great-grandfather were also very involved in Jewish religious and social activities. Her great-grandfather never worked except "by being a Talmudic scholar in his original *shtetl* and then here." He was a *tzaddik*, a wise and righteous man, with whom people would come to consult. His son, David Galler, was equally involved in the synagogue, albeit with a different spirit. Roberta Galler recalls visiting her grandfather in shul:

> It was very embarrassing because he was such a showoff. Everybody else would be facing forward, but his seat was facing the congregation, so if you went to visit him, you were on display. He would be *davening* [praying], but you were on display. You'd look up at the clock to see what time it was and on it, it said "David Galler."

Nevertheless, Roberta Galler was proud of her grandfather's charitable work, including support for the aged. Although she did get confirmed, she was already "in rebellion" from institutional forms of American Judaism.

Galler's maternal grandparents provided alternative perspectives on Jewish identity. Her grandfather was a socialist atheist who conducted traditional Passover *seders*, but with a degree of cynicism that undercut the ritual. Galler's grandmother, however, was genuinely "devout in a very personal way. I believed in the authenticity of her religious beliefs, which were very much more consistent with her character, so it didn't feel hypocritical nor was she imposing it on anybody else."

After the death of her grandfather, Galler's grandmother moved in with her daughter and shared a bedroom with Roberta. They lit Sabbath candles and kept kosher out of respect for her. Unusual for a widow at that time, Galler's grandmother went to synagogue on her own, made *seders*, and fasted on Yom Kippur.

Roberta Galler and Elaine DeLott Baker were both inspired by grandmothers who practiced in everyday life the values they espoused. Baker grew up in the middle of a large extended family. Her paternal grandmother, Alice, an illiterate Polish woman, lived alternately in the homes of her children. Her maternal grandmother and grandfather, Esther and Meyer, lived downstairs from her family. The contrast between her two grandmothers paralleled Baker's later struggle with Jewish identity. Baker loved both grandmothers but identified more with her maternal grandmother, who had come to the United States at age fifteen. By age twenty, her grandmother Esther had worked her way through normal school in Maine tending bar and was teaching citizenship to other immigrants. Of these grandmothers, Baker has written, "Grandma Alice was as narrow as

Grandma Esther was broad. Grandma Alice gossiped on the phone for hours, enriching her life with the details of others' misfortunes. Grandma Esther never gossiped, read a chapter of the Bible each day, and was scrupulous in her ethical conduct."[23]

Baker went through a religious period in early adolescence, attending a Jewish camp and Hebrew Teachers College after school for four years. She studied the language, literature, and sacred writings of Jewish culture with rabbis and young professors from Boston area colleges. Although she reveled in the intellectual atmosphere, she also got the message that as a Jewish woman, her job was to bear children, keep a Jewish home, and pass on Jewish tradition to her children. Yet, she still insisted on being active in Jewish communal life. She was vice president of New England Young Judea and then became a Young Zionist. She grew disgusted with the hypocrisy of her family's temple because her working-class family was relegated to second-class status. She "began to see the American Jewish community that I was raised in as a cultural anomaly combining two of the worst aspects of each society: the materialism of America and the ethnocentrism of historical Judaism."[24]

Seeking adventure and a connection to the traditions she had been exposed to through her Jewish studies and Zionist youth group activities, Baker went to Israel for a year after graduating from high school. She found the nationalism of the Israeli state too narrow and militaristic, but she experienced living in a totally Jewish society as liberating:

> The first thing you realize is that everybody's Jewish and then you realize what a burden it is to be Jewish in a non-Jewish society. It's like being Black in America until you go to a place where everybody is the same and that little war is over. I think I realized the depth to which being Jewish influenced the way I interacted with the world from the point of view of the Jews and the Christians, the *goyim*. Then I began to . . . get an understanding of the paranoia, the Jewish paranoia, about the rest of the world. That mixture of arrogance and defensiveness, arrogance and paranoia.[25]

At a young age, Baker felt both the healing aspects of being in an all-Jewish environment, as well as the shortcomings of securing such environments in political forms such as the state. Her struggle with these contradictions is typical of those who have sought alternative ways of expressing their Jewishness, often based on identification with the oppressed.

Few of the women searched for a connection to Jewishness with quite as much intensity as Baker, but almost all of them encountered at least one disturbing experience of anti-Jewish prejudice. These incidents helped them recognize that they could not take a sense of fully belonging for granted.

CONFRONTING ANTI-SEMITISM

Most of the women encountered anti-Semitism when they were young, though the degree and impact that this experience had on them varied. Nevertheless, it is clear that such experiences imparted to many a visceral sense of "otherness" that helped expand their consciousness to include an analysis of racism. The settings in which the women first encountered anti-Semitism included the neighborhood, boarding school, college, and the homes of non-Jewish relatives. In addition, tales of anti-Semitism relayed by family elders deeply affected a number of the women.

Perhaps because she belonged to a generation in which assimilation was not yet fully an option, Trudy Weissman Orris experienced the most direct encounters with anti-Semitism in her childhood. When asked how she knew it was dangerous to be Jewish in Greenwich Village when she was growing up, she replies, "[T]he Irish kids would meet us at our synagogue. My father went every Friday night and he laid *tefillin* [donning Jewish ritual objects before praying] in the morning so there would be fights with the kids, and it was known that you would get beaten up."[26]

One of two Jews in her public school class, Orris had "good friends who were Irish and very good friends who were Italian" with whom she walked to school. "I was socially accepted but always with the limit that I was a Jew." One friend liked her so much that she thought Orris should be Catholic:

> She told the sisters at her Catholic school about me—this was a very
> Catholic neighborhood—so they would meet me a couple blocks from
> my house and they told me that they would save my soul if I would
> become a Catholic. And I was amazed at that. Were they going to save

my father's soul too? No, just mine. So I said I wasn't interested. Well, that was her way of showing affection.

Harriet Tanzman has no memory of experiencing anti-Semitism herself while growing up in Rockaway, a Jewish enclave. However, her mother, who was born in 1911, once told her of an experience she and Tanzman's grandmother had while living in New York's Catskill region in the 1920s. Her mother remembered seeing crosses being burned "opposite the hill that they were on"; it was unclear whether they were meant to intimidate the few Jewish or Catholic families in the area.

During the bombing of London, June Finer and her sister experienced anti-Semitism when they were sent to the country to live with their nanny's family. Finer overheard her nanny criticizing a neighbor who made remarks about the nanny's parents' "harboring these two Jewish children": "[W]hat does she think, they have forked tails?" Finer was unsure what that meant and comments, "[T]here was nothing else really overt that I saw in the way of anti-Semitism." She does, however, recount their discomfort at having to attend church services at boarding school in the country:

> Everybody went to church on Sunday and everybody had to do certain things in a certain order which was a little awkward because we didn't know what we were supposed to do. That was always very embarrassing as a child. You took a little look at the kid next to you to see when they kneeled down and when they stood up and tried to mouth the words but that was again the only awkwardness associated with religion that I was conscious of. Going to church was a bit of a trauma.

Hearing stories from her grandmother about being Jewish in the South alerted Elaine DeLott Baker to potential anti-Semitism. Her grandmother was the daughter of Russian immigrants who owned a store in the small town of Sparta, Georgia. At seventeen, she graduated as valedictorian of her high school. Yet, despite outward social acceptance by the local white community, Baker recalls that the DeLott family felt "they never really accepted us. We were the people with horns. We were there tentatively because it wasn't our place. It was volatile. There were hidden irrationalities, so that it was superficially a genteel place. But underneath they were anti-Semitic, *goyim,* and not to be trusted"[27] Even when the family moved north, however, they still felt vulnerable to anti-Semitism. Baker grew up in a predominantly Italian and Irish Catholic neighborhood:

> The Jews were a minority and there were very strict separations. We had our parents' attitude, which is "Hold up your head high that you're Jewish," but you always thought about what the other people think of you, and is there any truth in that, and you get the feeling of being a minority. You are very clearly a minority and there was no interfaith dating: very strict, very, very strict.

Unlike Baker, Roberta Galler encountered southern anti-Semitism directly as a young polio patient at Warm Springs, Georgia, in the 1940s and 1950s. She was with many children who had never met a Jew before. In one incident, some of the kids decided she was a Jewish witch because she played with a Ouija board. These children must have been exposed to anti-Semitic stereotypes of Jews having extraordinary and destructive powers, most likely in those strands of southern Protestantism that emphasized Jews as Christ killers.[28] With her antipathy to playing the role of victim, Galler used the situation to her own advantage—wowing the children with her awesome powers.

Carol Ruth Silver was similarly taunted about her Jewish identity as a child. When some Irish Catholic kids teased Silver in school for "being a dirty Jew," Silver's mother was so upset—"much more upset than I was"—that she moved her family to the other side of Worcester. They moved to a more expensive area with a large Jewish population:

> When I was in high school there was exactly one non-Jewish person in our college prep high school of five hundred kids. Blacks were certainly not expected to ever go to college. There weren't that many of them around but there was one young woman, Felicia. I sought her out and extended the hand of friendship and tried to make her feel more comfortable being the only Black in an all-white school.

Silver points to that act as an early instance of "doing things that related to my social conscience and my parent's sense of social conscience." Silver's family's typical self-protective reflex of moving to all-Jewish environments also suggests the price American Jews paid for safety—isolation and loss of access to the rich diversity of American culture.

Faith Holsaert remembers hearing that her father's family was very upset that he had married a Jewish woman:

In fact, he had a sister, with whom my sister and I spent summers, who called my mother "the Jewess." I remember my Jewish grandmother saying that you should never call Jewish women "Jewesses" because that was very pejorative.

When I was in late elementary school and junior high school I had this really strong identification with people in concentration camps. In a way, it was a glorification of persecution but also a really deep sense that Jews were not part of mainstream America. I think that was emphasized by the fact that we lived with Charity and we lived, by then, in the northwestern section of the Village, up by 14th Street and Eighth Avenue, and most of our neighbors were Irish. Although my sister and I played on the street with the kids from those families, there was a sense that somehow we were less American than our Irish playmates. Both because we were Jewish, of course, because there was no man in our household and also because Charity was a woman of color.

If a white, Christian, male breadwinner was the exemplary American in the broader cultural imagination, a divorced Jewish woman raising two girls in partnership with an African American woman was about as far from the American ideal as one could get in the 1950s. Because Holsaert's family challenged so many cultural norms, she remembers the feeling of being less than American vividly and links it explicitly to Jews' being outside the mainstream.[29]

The climate of conformity in the 1950s would only heighten the young Holsaert's stance as a sensitive but defiant outsider. For example, Holsaert became angry at her mother for the first time in her life when she transferred Faith and her other daughter from the nontraditional, progressive Little Red Schoolhouse to St. Luke's, a parochial school in Greenwich Village. Although they made the transfer ostensibly because of her sister's learning disability, Holsaert felt her mother had some desire to be identified with the non-Jewish establishment. "I think that there was always a part of my mother that felt that things that weren't Jewish were more American or somehow better."

Miriam Cohen Glickman does not remember major incidents of anti-Semitism growing up in Indianapolis, but she does recall feeling different from her classmates. "I remember in third grade a teacher held up a spatula and asked if anybody knew what it was called. My hand went right up. Then I turned beet red and pulled my hand down because I didn't know if *spatula* was English or Yiddish." She was mortified by the idea of saying a foreign word and being laughed at by the whole class. Like Elaine DeLott Baker's realization in Israel that she did have an internal struggle with fear of anti-Semitism, Glickman's memory of this small incident more than forty years later suggests that part of the subtle cost of anti-Semitism is being ever vigilant not to reveal oneself as different.[30]

Elizabeth Slade Hirschfeld went to the same elite private girls school in Michigan that her mother had attended. Despite the fact that her father's German Jewish family was quite assimilated and her mother was not Jewish, she was always known in school as "that little Jewish girl." On her first night at Cornell University, Elizabeth was very happy to meet three Hirschfelds, who were "obviously New York Jews. Practically all my friends at Cornell were Jews in the four years I was there. I kept getting closer and closer and closer to Jewish identification."

When she attended Bryn Mawr College, Jacqueline Levine states, "the only reason I felt different was because I came from a totally Jewish community." She went directly to college from Abraham Lincoln, a large public high school "where teachers, the principal, and so on, were all Jewish. . . . Though it certainly had non-Jewish people there, you had the feeling you were enveloped in a Jewish world." She went from her high school graduating class of one thousand seniors to Bryn Mawr, which only had five hundred students. "It was quite a shock to go into such a small environment and to meet a lot of people who weren't Jewish." Levine does not recall any "pronounced anti-Semitism at all" and expresses her pride in the fact that Bryn Mawr never had a Jewish quota, unlike many other Ivy League and Seven Sister schools. "Even if I say there were many [Jews] there, maybe 20 percent, that was pretty good for schools of that kind in those years."

Nevertheless, Levine knew she was "a little different":

> I rooted for the Brooklyn Dodgers and I was very much a creature of the Brooklyn intelligentsia, I guess. I never hid it and I made quite a lot out of it, just as today, on the [Bryn Mawr] Board of Trustees, I probably say the words *Jewish* and *Israel* ten times more than I do in normal conversation because I just want people to be aware. So, even if I felt a little bit of discomfort when I entered the school, that soon faded and I did well socially as well as academically.

Taking a different approach, Miriam Cohen Glickman deliberately chose to attend Brandeis because "I wanted to go to a school with Jewish kids." Jan Goodman, on the other hand, chose the University of Michigan to experience a more diverse community. However, it was there that she first encountered overt anti-Semitism:

> I worked in the cafeteria, and coming from New York, you really sometimes think all the world is Jewish. Almost everybody I knew was Jewish. I went to Erasmus Hall [High School in Brooklyn] and certainly most of the people I hung out with at Erasmus Hall were Jewish. I didn't want to go to Brandeis because I no longer wanted to be isolated in this Jewish world. And God I wasn't even there very long—I was a counter girl in the cafeteria and I was working side by side with this local woman from the community. We were friendly with each other and we were just chatting and then she was talking about somebody over there and she said, "you know, that Jew girl over there." And I was astounded. I did nothing. I mean I was just astounded. I'd never heard anybody talk like that before. So that was the first time it really hit me that there were people that just saw the Jews as real different.

Florence Howe first experienced blatant anti-Semitism as the only Jewish graduate student at Smith College in the 1950s. She learned how her classmates felt about her and the lone Black student when she overheard a conversation in the bathroom:

> The leaders of the house I lived in were planning a party and they said, "Do we have to invite the Jew and the colored?" They didn't use our names. And I'm in the bathroom, and they don't know I'm there because I came in from the other side. And I just can't believe what I'm hearing and I'm afraid to flush the toilet or leave. So I just sit there transfixed and they discussed us. It was very ugly.

Before Barbara Haber decided to go to Brandeis, her stepmother took her to visit several schools. She particularly disliked Brown University because

> it was stuffy, and they let me know that they had a Jewish quota. They said to me in a polite way that there were many bright Jewish girls from Long Island and, therefore, my chances of getting in weren't that good because, I don't remember the words they used, but obviously they couldn't take them all in. I fell in love with Brandeis, and it

wasn't because it was Jewish per se although it's true that I have always felt very comfortable being in Jewish, not Jewish religious, but
Jewish cultural settings and I loved it because it had a left wing.

Roberta Galler went to Northwestern University on a journalism
scholarship. When she arrived, she found she had been assigned to a
third-floor dormitory room, which she could not reach because of her
disability. This precipitated a crisis that revealed the school's conser-
vatism. The first floor of the dorm was a "Christian corridor," where all
the girls were pledging Christian sororities. It was inconceivable to
have Galler share a room with a Christian student, so they had to im-
port another Jewish student to be her roommate. "From then on that
was a Jewish room, in the midst of this whole Christian corridor. That
became the Jewish room, just as there had been a Black room in one of
the other dorms."

Like Florence Howe's experience at Smith, Galler's time at Northwestern highlighted obvious links between anti-Semitism and racism.
In 1953, Galler "got involved with the small Black student group which
was very unusual for a white person, a white Jewish girl." She also
joined the student government, expressing what to her were liberal positions, which were perceived as radical. Fed up with the environment
at Northwestern, Galler transferred to the University of Chicago, where
she met others with politics similar to hers.

Family, financial, and personal crises led Galler to leave school for
a while. Fortunately, one of her teachers got her a job as an assistant in
the fact-finding department of the Anti-Defamation League (of B'nai
Brith). "The fact-finding department was really their spying department on the far right wing, mostly around anti-Semitism, although it
certainly also involved racist groups as well." Though she initially simply cut, read, and organized newspaper clippings on these groups, ADL
soon asked her to be a trainer, using her expertise to prepare people
who would go undercover to attend hate-group meetings. "Then for a
while, I became a spy and I would go to a lot of these meetings myself."
Later, when Galler became involved in the civil rights movement, she
was often featured in local newspapers. Then she "was always afraid
that some of these right-wing people would remember me from these
earlier days when I was pretending to be racist myself and had been
part of this group."

When asked how, as a young woman, she was able to handle going
undercover among rabid racists, Galler replies:

Well, in retrospect, I don't know how the hell I did it because it involved so much playacting and a certain degree of danger. I think it was part of my youthful grandiosity that I could do anything. Now I would have all kinds of complicated feelings about the fact that this was cooperative with the FBI [the ADL and the FBI exchanged information, including Galler's reports]. If they were taping meetings on the right, they must have been taping meetings on the left, but somehow I was not aware of that at all.

Galler's Anti-Defamation League experience in the late 1950s provided awareness and skills that would prove invaluable to her and to SNCC in subsequent years. Her information-gathering and report-writing skills, her practice in monitoring hate groups, her experience training others to gather information, her lack of naivete about "the enemy," and her sophisticated understanding of hate groups' organizing mechanisms—all these prepared Galler for her multifaceted roles in the movement. At the time, she did not consider her ADL work to be motivated by strong Jewish feelings. However, the recent genocide of European Jews was certainly on the mind of the Anti-Defamation League, and Galler's participation in monitoring anti-Semitism and race hatred linked the two issues in her mind.

LIVING THROUGH THE WAR AND INTUITING
THE HOLOCAUST

The historical memory of the Holocaust affected the women's consciousness in powerful ways. The majority of women in this study were born immediately prior to and during World War II. Almost all of them learned of the Holocaust at relatively young ages. Some had direct experiences of the war in Europe and others with Holocaust survivors in the United States. Some of the women grew up in families that had lost relatives; others in families that were engaged politically with the war; and still others in families in which knowledge of the persecution of Jews was present but not discussed explicitly at the time. Several of the women in the last group had strong responses when they learned about the Holocaust later.

The vividness of their stories suggests that the Holocaust had a deep impact on them. Although there was relative silence in the American Jewish and survivor community about the Holocaust until Adolf

Eichmann's 1961 trial for crimes against humanity, somehow they knew.[31] Perhaps the mostly private nature of this knowledge made it all the more powerful for young Jewish girls.

Though it is difficult to "quantify" the impact that knowledge of the war, Nazism, and the destruction of European Jews had on the consciousness of Jews involved in the civil rights movement, some of the women discuss the connection explicitly. Similarly, in her study of North American leftist Jewish feminist women, Sherry Gorelick found that all had passionate feelings about the Holocaust (whether or not they had any experiences connected with it), which engendered a range of political responses to the situation in the Middle East. Gorelick contends that these positions cannot be understood "without understanding that the holocaust is not past history. It is palpable in their lives."[32]

Françoise Lionnet contends that contemporary intellectuals' resistance "to an epistemology of the particular (the different, the contextual, the indeterminate, the hybrid)"—including women and people of color—is grounded in "the 19th century discourse of racial purity."[33] This intriguing connection between racial discourse and the academic devaluation of ways of knowing most associated with women, people of color, and others historically silenced suggests the potential analytic and political power that could come from making more connections among groups with racialized histories. Certainly for many Jewish women civil rights activists, knowledge of the Holocaust fueled and legitimated their desire to fight against racism.

During the war, the families of Jan Goodman, Miriam Cohen Glickman, Carol Ruth Silver, Florence Howe, and Faith Holsaert spoke very little in front of their children about the fighting and the persecution of European Jews. Jan Goodman believes her mother was protecting her, yet she remembers that somehow she knew. Miriam Cohen Glickman's parents did not talk about it much either, but she knew "that my Aunt Rose had lost some relatives; she had a picture of a little boy. There were lots of books around the house about it and I mostly learned about it by reading those books. It just seems like something I've known about all my life."

For Miriam Cohen Glickman, memories of the war include taking both ends off tin cans, flattening them, and putting them out to be collected. Carol Ruth Silver remembers pulling down the window shades to observe the blackout, and the celebration of V-E Day, victory in Europe. Barbara Jacobs Haber remembers ration cards, blackout curtains, blackout sirens, and her father being an air raid warden.

Haber shares a childhood memory that she only later realized was related to the Holocaust. During the war, Haber's parents, aunt, uncle, and grandmother rented a little bungalow in Rockaway, New York, for the summer. She remembers "knowing before I was five that we got it really cheap because people were afraid to rent it in case the Germans landed." As a little girl, she would sit on the beach with her pail and shovel looking out at Floyd Bennett Field, an air force base in Brooklyn, watching warplanes taking off and battleships floating in the water,

> looking, looking, looking at the cannons. I knew that the Germans were very scary. All my life I had had nightmares. Whenever I want to have a nightmare with bad people in it, then it's the Nazis. So somehow I was getting all this stuff, getting it really deep but nobody ever told me what was going on in Europe. I could tell people were very upset and disturbed but I didn't know until much later what it was about and became a little obsessed with it when I was in college.

Similarly, Nazis haunted the young Roberta Galler's dreams. Rather than more abstract fantasies derived from views of airfields and battleships, however, Galler had direct contact with survivors from her mother's side of the family. Although she did not fully comprehend who they were at the time, "there were all these people coming who had numbers tattooed on their arms. I was very aware of the war and the particular oppression of Jews. It contributed both to my sense of identification and my sense of fear about potential anti-Semitism." Galler would dream that the Nazis had taken her parents when she was away from the house. With this recurring dream, she was left with the strong feeling "that I should have been there, as if I could have been the one to have prevented it from happening."

Elizabeth Slade Hirschfeld's first memory of the war is seeing the issue of *Life* magazine that covered the opening of the concentration camps. "I would sit in my father's library in a leather chair and read it over and over. I must have worn the magazine out looking for pictures of my sister and me because there were so many pictures of children." Although her parents had witnessed signs of the rise of Nazism during their 1935 honeymoon in Berlin, they did not discuss it later with the children. "There was a total wall of silence about it." About their reactions at the time, Hirschfeld knows that "my mother was scared to death because she saw it all. . . . My dad, who has changed dramatically since then, came back with an autographed copy of *Mein Kampf* and a German flag with a swastika." Although her parents did not talk about Nazism, the images of the camps stayed with Elizabeth Slade Hirschfeld.

As a little girl in Michigan, Hirschfeld walked to and from school and home for lunch, passing through a forest. "I used to play escaping the Nazis to come home from school and that's how I entertained myself." Hirschfeld thought back on the camp images when she was being transported from Hinds County Jail to Parchman Prison in a small, crowded, wooden wagon through a forest after her arrest as a Freedom Rider in Mississippi.

Elaine DeLott Baker learned about the Holocaust from one of her mentors, a "young agnostic Jewish intellectual," Arnie Band. "He was very provocative and made me think about the Jewish community. . . . I wanted to be like Arnie." Band was the person who introduced Baker to Jewish traditions of compassion as embodied in Yiddish literature (such as the work of I. L. Peretz), and to the harsher realities of institutionalized anti-Semitism. It was Band who brought in slides of concentration camps to show his students in the mid-1950s; Baker was a teenager, and it was not that long after the war ended. "He said, 'I don't want you ever to forget.'"

Jacqueline Levine credits her father with sharing his awareness of what was going on in Europe. He had gone to Germany in the mid-1930s because his sister was married to an army doctor stationed there. Levine's family made sure she grew up with awareness of the Holocaust. "We knew what was happening in Europe and cared deeply and did whatever we could to help, which mostly meant sending money. Support for the labor movement, for the not-yet-existent state of Israel, and for the European Jews," were, according to Levine, "all part of a progressive Jewish home at that time."

At the same time, Dottie Miller Zellner's father was involved in all the same issues. He was not a Zionist, "but he was keenly aware of what the Nazis were doing. He had an unbelievable temper, my father, and he would read the newspapers and go into a sort of paroxysm of fury, screaming 'Nazi swine.' That was his favorite thing."

Zellner describes her father, with whom she identified as a precocious child, as "very, very eccentric."

> My father was so preoccupied about the war from a political point of view and also as a Jew, that in between patients, he would run into the back and turn on the radio and listen to what was happening in the

war. He would listen to wartime radio broadcaster Gabriel Heatter, one of his favorites. When my brother was born in '43, that was really bad. Things hadn't started to turn around yet and my brother, poor thing, would scream, and my father couldn't hear the radio. My father would start screaming because he couldn't hear the radio and he would turn the radio up louder. He had a map—and some people were so preoccupied they would move pushpins around and all that. I don't know if he did, but there were a lot of political people coming in and out. When the concentration camps were liberated in the spring of '45, I was seven. I remember that, and it was a nightmare. I mean my father was just screaming for days and days, just carrying on and screaming.

In 1946, we had a book in our house that I referred to as the black book. It was some kind of book of atrocities. And I looked; I will never forget seeing those pictures. I was maybe seven, and I was very protective of my sister. I threw it in the garbage because I didn't want my sister to see it. Of course they rescued it. Who would throw a book out?

Zellner also recalls, "I went to see the newsreels in the movies and I remember getting under the seat. It was all very, very, very vivid." She speaks affectionately of her parents as very old-fashioned European types who did not shield children from unpleasant realities. "So I started to grow up at a very early age with an unnatural amount [of knowledge] about the Holocaust, rebellion, the Warsaw Ghetto, and all of this in a Jewish context that was totally unreligious." These vivid images stayed with her as an adolescent.

A very romantic teenager, Zellner read "zillions of books about the war and about the Holocaust." At seventeen, she wrote letters to journalist Martha Gelhorn about her war reporting. At age twenty, she and her best friend exchanged copies of William Shirer's *The Rise and Fall of the Third Reich* as gifts. At some point she posed to herself the question asked by many American Jews, "If I had been alive in 1943 in Warsaw, what would I have done? I decided very early on that I would have had to fight. I've never felt otherwise but I think I made it into a romantic thing. Maybe I could have disguised myself as a Gentile and worn a blonde wig."

Zellner's 1957 trip to the Soviet Union to attend the World Youth Festival in Moscow reinforced her fantasy about being a resistance fighter disguised in a blonde wig. This was a daring, if not risky, thing for an American to do during the Cold War. Her sense of risk was heightened when she was immediately recognized as Jewish. This was quite a shock to her. Until then, "I don't think I realized that I looked so Jewish." She believes

> this image of the blonde wig had to do with passing and being assim- ilated and being accepted and I never was accepted. I could never pass. I couldn't pass because I came from a left-wing family. I couldn't pass because I was Jewish. So many reasons I couldn't pass. I was dif- ferent. I couldn't pass in the South. I've always been different my whole life.

Whereas Zellner, who had an indirect experience with the war, was introspective about its meaning to her as a Jew, June Finer, in contrast, spoke of her experiences in wartime England much more matter-of- factly, though they had to have been quite traumatic.

Finer remembers feeling afraid a few times during the war, partic- ularly when the bombs were falling, one of which destroyed her grand- parents' house:

> The V2s were particularly damaging because you could hear them coming over, [hear] the throbbing, and then they would cut out. You sort of held your breath waiting to hear how far away the bang was. . . . I do remember early in the war before I was sent away [evacuated to the countryside] one night when there were a lot of incendiary bombs in our neighborhood and sounds of glass breaking. I remember sort of crouching under a bed. But I was lucky. As a small child, [I was] taken away most of the time.

> We also had this horrible air-raid shelter in the garden that was a very safe one. It was ten feet deep and it was like a damp concrete cell. And I do not have very positive memories of that. I'm not really claustro- phobic but we'd shut ourselves up in this cell every night. I came back [to London] in '44 because of my illness. I was in the hospital for a while, then I came home again to convalesce. And my father would carry me down into the shelter every night. They had these iron bunk beds. That was a nasty part of it.

A direct encounter in Europe immediately after the war affected Trudy Weissman Orris deeply. During the war, Orris and her husband lived in California, where he was completing his medical internship. She became pregnant with their first child and was working from home on the progressive Henry Wallace presidential campaign. She returned to New York when her husband finished his internship and was subsequently drafted into the army. Their son Peter was born in 1945, and at the end of the war, Orris and her son were allowed to join her husband in Germany. Living in Germany profoundly affected Orris. She was unable to look at a German during those years without wondering about his or her involvement during the war.

Orris also saw American troops stealing from Germans and acting very inhumanely toward the Germans who worked for them. She was distressed to see American doctors buying things from the black market. Traveling outside Munich, she got an even more visceral sense of the war. At Dachau, she saw the ovens and the sinks with signs over them that said, "Wash your hands after you finish work."

In a displaced persons camp, she was one of the Americans who brought their rations and chocolate to give to the children. There was a commotion at the end of the long line of children, so she went to see what was happening. A Jewish man, a Hebrew teacher, was taking some of the Jewish children out of the line. When Orris questioned why, he said, "They don't go to Hebrew school and so they shouldn't be allowed." For Orris, that was a distressing encounter with one of the negative aspects of Jewish behavior in the camps. She says she could understand why Jews engaged in black market activity, "but I couldn't understand Jews being against each other. So I learned that there are good Jews and bad Jews. It took me many years to learn that. It matured me."

When asked how she handled the difficult experience of being a Jew in Germany after the war, she responds:

> Well, I had to handle it, and I had to have people work for me. I had to realize that these Germans who worked for me may have been Nazis and may not, but they were human beings. Before I went to Germany, I felt that all Germans should be killed. But when I saw these people, these people could not be killed, these people were human beings. They weren't great human beings, I don't have to be proud of them, but they have a right to live. That matured me.

Orris's compassion for the Germans was considered very peculiar by her fellow Americans, who called her a "kraut-lover." She still

resented Hitler and Germany, but "as a true communist, a true socialist," she felt she was supposed to have a more humane vision.

As it did to Vivian Leburg Rothstein, who directly attributes growing up among Holocaust survivors to her embrace of "oppositional politics," proximity to survivors affected other young women who would
go on to become civil rights activists. Upon hearing SNCC worker
Travis Britt describe the beating he endured in Mississippi in 1961,
Queens College student Nancy Cooper started to make connections between what was happening in the South and what had happened in
Germany. To Cooper, "who had grown up hearing firsthand accounts of
the Holocaust from concentration camp survivors who were her family's neighbors in the Bronx, it was an almost unbelievable revelation
that these Nazi-like atrocities could be carried out in the United
States."[34] Cooper was a friend of Andrew Goodman's at Queens College. She would soon go south and later marry Jewish SNCC staffer
Mendy Samstein.

Cooper and Rothstein were not the only Jewish women making
these connections. While training to go south at Oxford, Ohio, on the
night SNCC learned about the disappearance of Goodman, Schwerner,
and Chaney, Paul Cowan overheard a young woman calling her terri-
fied parents at home: "She yelled at her mother, 'Of course I'm still
going to go down there. If someone in Nazi Germany had done what
we're doing, your brother would still be alive today.'"[35]

Although a number of women learned about the Holocaust from
survivors in their families and in their neighborhoods, Barbara Jacobs
Haber heard an even more intimate account. Her first lover, a fellow
Brandeis student, was a survivor himself. Having escaped as a child, he
had been disguised as a girl and hidden by nuns. "His whole nuclear
family got out, but he talked to me a lot about the Holocaust. He was
very cynical and a cruel person in a lot of ways. He said, 'I've seen people sell another person for an egg so I have no illusions about people's
goodness.'" Despite exposure to this harsh firsthand knowledge, Haber
still identified with "the bravery of the people who stood up in the Warsaw Ghetto knowing they had no way of escaping and refusing to die
quietly." Later she "saw the civil rights movement as being the moral
equivalent of the Warsaw Ghetto."

When asked if she made that explicit connection back then, Haber
replies, "Yes, I did. To me what it meant to be a Jew was 'never again,'
and what *never again* meant was not never again to Jews but never again
to stand by and let things like that happen. Even talking to you I feel

very emotional talking about this because I'm not living that way now and I really want to get back to those roots."

Harriet Tanzman's parents were "enormously affected" by the destruction of European Jewry. "My father lost all his relatives who were left in Europe. A lot of people died. I don't remember how they talked to us about it." However, Tanzman recalls her mother's taking her to see *The Diary of Anne Frank* on Broadway. "The play opened when I was a teenager and we talked about that. One of the main themes was how could this happen? How could such a terrible thing take place, especially—well maybe I wouldn't say especially in Germany, but people did say that—especially in a country where people were so-called assimilated."

Tanzman likens her generation to children of Holocaust survivors: "[W]hat our parents experienced really affected us."

> We were the children of people who had gone through an absolutely devastating experience. If they were in this country, they felt that there but for complete chance . . . we all would have been dead. So what does that mean, how do you live a life, and what do you do in the face of this evil? That had a great effect on all of us, whether it was discussed a lot or not. There was a tremendous sense of injustice in the world and at the same time [parents were] raising children to think that they should lead a moral and just life, [to] be there for themselves—the whole individualism thing was very strong—but also to have some sense that you are there for other people, whether the other people are Jews or whoever they are, but to take some stand or to try to avert the injustice in the world.

After the Holocaust, American Jews suffered their own version of survivor's guilt.[36] Tanzman's eloquent testimonial to her parents' generation underscores their effort to grapple with, apply, and teach moral lessons derived from this devastating experience.

Contemplating the question of how the Holocaust could have happened, these young Jewish women intuitively knew that part of the answer was the dearth of people from every background who were willing and able to resist. They vowed to themselves to take positive action—whether by helping people in need in daily life or by fighting injustice on a larger scale.

Tanzman also points out the coexistence of parental messages about individualism and responsibility for social justice. Although parents' interpretations of individual success often had much to do with assimilation and socioeconomic achievement, young Jewish women activists strategically embraced individualism to bolster their quest to create meaningful lives by fighting injustice.

∎

The stories of Jewish women civil rights activists enrich the Jewish tradition of *tikkun olam* ("repair of the world"). This tradition connects Jewish political activism with Jewish spirituality. The link needs to be claimed more explicitly by progressive Jewish activists and recognized as a form of spiritual expression by the entire Jewish community. If, as Roger Gottlieb argues, resistance is an authentic form of spirituality,[37] then the Jewish "political diaspora" is part of the worldwide Jewish spiritual community.

More specifically, in a post-Holocaust world, resistance to racism is a legitimate way to enact Jewish spirituality. Indeed, for some Jews, antiracist activism may be their most authentic assertion of Jewish identity—whether they see it as spiritual or not. Certainly, Jewish women's stories of civil rights activism provide political, ethical, and spiritual resources for creating new models of engaged Jewish life that can enrich and expand the Jewish community worldwide.

The women's civil rights activism also represents a Jewish contribution to and resource for the ongoing movement for racial justice in this country. When understood properly—neither overstated nor ignored—Jewish women's civil rights activism becomes part of the history of social change in the United States and another chapter in the long narrative of Jewish resistance to an unjust world.

NOTES

1. Isaac Deutscher, *The Non-Jewish Jew and Other Essays* (New York: Hill and Wang, 1970), 27.

2. Biale et al., 29–31.

3. Arthur Liebman, *Jews and the Left* (New York: Wiley, 1979), 3.

4. Prell, *Prayer and Community*, 15.

5. Classics of a more spiritual nature include Plaskow; Ellen Umansky and Diane Ashton, eds., *Four Centuries of Jewish Women's Spirituality* (Boston: Beacon Press, 1992); Vanessa Ochs, *Words on Fire: One Woman's Journey into the Sacred* (San Diego: Harcourt Brace Jovanovich, 1990). For a secular Yiddishist ap-

proach, see Irena Klepfisz, *Dreams of an Insomniac: Jewish Feminist Essays, Speeches, and Diatribes* (Portland: Eighth Mountain Press, 1990).

6. Laurence J. Silberstein, "Mapping Not Tracing," in Silberstein, 12.

7. Chaim Waxman, *America's Jews in Transition* (Philadelphia: Temple University Press, 1983), 81.

8. Charles S. Liebman, *The Ambivalent American Jew* (Philadelphia: Jewish Publication Society of America, 1973).

9. This spurred the writing of Arthur Liebman; Arthur Liebman, 8.

10. Sorin, *The Prophetic Minority*, 8.

11. Shepherd, 108.

12. Boyarin, 50.

13. Of course, one may choose to make a conscious break with Judaism and Jewishness for many perfectly valid historical, ideological, or personal reasons. However, the choice not to identify as Jewish can have complex roots. Factors that come from negative forces include cultural and family pressures to downplay one's Jewishness, traumatic experiences with Jewishness, or internalized anti-Semitism (which can be linked via assimilation to a desire not to appear as "different"). Other factors may result from ignorance and disconnection, lack of opportunities to learn about Jewish history and culture, and/or the inaccessibility of secular contexts in which to identify as Jewish.

14. Charlotte Baum, Paula Hyman, and Sonya Michel, *The Jewish Woman in America* (New York: New American Library, 1975), 55–89. Sorin, *A Time for Building*, 121.

15. Shepherd, 66.

16. Glenn, 6.

17. Ibid., 242.

18. Paula Hyman, "Gender and the Immigrant Jewish Experience in the United States," in Judith R. Baskin, ed., *Jewish Women in Historical Perspective* (Detroit: Wayne State University Press, 1991), 234.

19. Joyce Antler, "Fighting Fascism: The Emma Lazarus Clubs," paper presented at In Struggle: A History Teach-In, held by Jews for Racial and Economic Justice, New York, December 1993.

20. Feingold, 69.

21. Phone conversation with Susan Brownmiller, November 1993.

22. Diner, *In the Almost Promised Land*.

23. Elaine DeLott Baker, "A Social Autobiography" (1993); used with permission of author.

24. Ibid.

25. Interview with Elaine DeLott Baker, September 23, 1994.

26. *Tefillin* are leather straps attached to a small black box worn in prayer.

27. Interview with Elaine DeLott Baker, September 23, 1994.

28. Rogoff, 202.

29. Riv-Ellen Prell's reading of memoirs by Jewish Americans who came of age in the 1950s notes their "keen consciousness of being Americans entirely, and yet not quite full participants in American life." Prell, *Fighting to Become Americans*, 164.

30. Glickman's account of the "spatula" incident bears a striking resemblance to Alexander Portnoy's memory in the classic and very popular American Jewish novel *Portnoy's Complaint,* raising questons about the impact of popular culture on memory. Philip Roth, *Portnoy's Complaint* (New York: Random House, 1967), 96.

31. Judith Miller, *One, by One, by One: The Landmark Exploration of the Holocaust and Uses of Memory* (New York: Simon & Schuster, 1990), 221. Historian Henry Feingold characterizes the American Jewish community's response to Nazism as confused because of decades of Jewish acculturation, secularization, and internal conflicts, as well as by the U.S. government's ambivalence in taking action against the Nazis. Nevertheless, like many other scholars and commentators, he contends that feelings of loss and guilt about the Holocaust continue to shape the American Jewish experience. See Feingold, 226, 234, 265.

32. Sherry Gorelick, "The Changer and the Changed: Methodological Reflections on Studying Jewish Feminists," in Alison Jaggar and Susan Bordo, eds., *Gender/Body/Knowledge: Feminist Reconstructions of Being and Knowing* (New Brunswick: Rutgers University Press, 1989), 336–358. Gorelick found a common sense of vulnerability and the need for vigilance among the Jewish leftist feminist women she studied but no consensus on a political agenda. Jewish women civil rights activists, who were making their decisions to become political prior to the politically complex 1967 Arab-Israeli war, could take the Holocaust as an unambiguous moral lesson and imperative to "fight back" against racism.

33. Lionnet, cited in Camilla Stivers, "Reflections on the Role of Personal Narrative in Social Science," *Signs* (Winter 1993): 419.

34. Cagin and Dray, 49.

35. Cowan, 51.

36. Feingold, 265.

37. Roger S. Gottlieb, *A Spirituality of Resistance* (New York: Crossroad Publishing, 1999).

6

Creating a Living Legacy

Passing It On

FACING THE LIMITS OF WHITENESS

The Jewish women activists in this book who spent significant time in the South felt that it was the best possible context in which they could resist racism. Many in SNCC disagreed, arguing that whites should organize whites and building the case for an all-Black organization. During the period when this discussion was escalating SNCC's racial tensions, some of the women in this book used a semiconscious strategy of recategorizing themselves racially. Sometimes this was an automatic physical response, as when Faith Holsaert moved into the "colored" line to get a driving permit in Albany, Georgia, in 1962. In Roberta Galler's case, she circumvented some of the difficulties other white women faced in SNCC by considering herself "exceptional." "People would say to me, 'Oh, you're not really white. You're one of us.' I was male-identified and Black-identified, so I didn't have to think of myself as a white woman."

Although Galler knew about the tensions between Black and white women, "I was the one who still had good, close friendships with Black women. I tried to distance myself or find myself to be the exception to those clashes. Certainly this was self-pretension as well. I would find ways of justifying it in my own head by remaining Black-identified."[1]

Such a strategy could only work for so long. By the fall of 1966, only "a handful" of whites remained on the SNCC staff, the most powerful of whom was research director Jack Minnis. It was Minnis who helped engineer Stokely Carmichael's rise to SNCC chairmanship, which ushered in SNCC's Black Power focus.[2] At a December 1966 retreat at Peg Leg Bates, a resort in Kerhonkson, New York, SNCC narrowly passed a resolution to exclude whites. Bob Zellner was among the small group of white staffers present for the vote; all the whites abstained. As SNCC photographer Danny Lyon said, this meeting "spelled the end of the bond of interracial brotherhood and sisterhood born in the flames of the Freedom Rides."[3] Whites were in essence told to go home and work with their own people.

But the Zellners believed that affiliation with SNCC was vital to this task. As Dottie Miller Zellner puts it, "You can't organize white people in a vacuum." So although she felt "that this was a rather big compromise on my part," she wrote a proposal that Bob presented. The proposal asked, at a May 1967 meeting of SNCC's central committee in Atlanta, that the Zellners be allowed to remain on the SNCC staff to work on a project organizing whites in New Orleans. It was a way to remain connected to SNCC, which had become their true community.

There were other pressures on the Zellners to leave SNCC. Dottie knew that white organizers were at risk—and put others at risk—when they lived in both Black and white southern communities. Being a white civil rights activist with Black activist colleagues coming in and out of your house, "you knew it was only an amount of weeks before somebody would set off a bomb and burn your house down. By then I also had a child . . . [and] the very first time that I felt Margaret was in danger, I would have left."[4]

Nevertheless, when the proposal was denied, the Zellners were devastated. Like other radical whites, they had no "home" to return to in the white community. As Dottie comments, "[T]he culture portrays white people who get involved in interracial relationships or interracialism as crazy . . . because there are so many things going against you."[5] They were considered the enemy among most southern whites.

After a brief stay with Bob Zellner's parents in Alabama, his mother told the Zellners not to settle there because it would be too dangerous. They then moved to New Orleans at the encouragement of longtime southern progressives Anne and Carl Braden, who invited them to work for the Southern Conference Educational Fund (SCEF). Dottie Zellner, who was raising her children and working part-time, credits Anne Braden with insisting that she be put on the SCEF payroll.[6]

Roberta Galler also faced the challenge of justifying her presence as a white movement worker in the South in the mid-sixties. Because she was very Black-identified and very committed to her work in Mississippi, she felt a certain righteousness and moral authority about staying, which she now attributes to "a sense of privilege."

> Even after the majority of the whites had left, I still felt that it was my position to be in the state. I wasn't being asked by anybody to leave

and I still had all my friendships with both Black and white women, except I can't say there was never any strain. There was a very painful period of time for me when some of my closest friends became Muslims. I didn't have a problem with that, until they were pretty much pulled or felt that they couldn't be friends with me.

Her friends could not speak to her simply because she was white. Then Galler "knew that I was white. It took me a long time to know that I was white. In fact, even after I left the South, I had been so separate from the white community that I think I had really in some strange ways forgotten that I was white."

In relation to Blacks, northern Jewish women civil rights veterans were indeed white at this moment in history. In their neighborhoods and movement relationships, they would also soon face Black-Jewish tensions exacerbated by the 1967 Arab-Israeli war and the Ocean Hill–Brownsville school crisis in Brooklyn. These events would only heighten their ambivalence about being Jewish.

Committed to "movement life," Jewish women civil rights activists faced their greatest challenge when they had to leave the South. As Dottie Miller Zellner puts it:

> I understood what happened, I accept what happened and I have never stopped mourning what happened. You know, for somebody like me, I had found my vocation. I was going to work for SNCC forever. . . . Literally, literally for the rest of my life. Very naive in a way. We were just assuming it would go on forever. Very childlike. Because we were very young, we didn't verbalize a lot of this stuff and then when it happened, it hit us. In certain ways it was worse than my divorce.[7]

Facing the limits of whiteness and leaving the southern movement required northern Jewish women to cross back over boundaries that they had been happy to transgress. Despite the danger and conflicts they faced, SNCC had provided a more satisfying alternative to the suburban alienation Rita Schwerner and others were desperate to avoid. A number of northern Jewish women found in SNCC the community they had not found in American Jewish communal life. Vivian Leburg Rothstein's provocative comment reflects their position: "Although the Jewish community takes credit for participation in the civil rights movement, it was Jews on the fringes who actually did the work."[8] As civil rights veterans and "Jews on the fringes," the women profiled in this book faced the daunting challenge of finding new avenues for expressing their passionately held beliefs.

Instinctually trying to ground themselves after "the divorce" from SNCC, most of the women simply tried to continue "doing what needed to be done," albeit in other contexts. As Roberta Galler insists, "We did not leave the movement; we just had to leave the South." They continued to seek ways to create meaningful lives and to find again a sense of community.

FINDING THEIR WAY

Drawing on their knowledge of racism, work ethic, and commitment to helping others, many of the women turned to New Left movements and some to teaching. Faith Holsaert raised funds for the Southern Conference Educational Fund in Detroit and then moved to New Mexico and worked with the Brown Berets, the antiwar movement, and the back-to-the-land movement. She subsequently became a community college teacher and continues to write about her experiences in the civil rights movement. Miriam Cohen Glickman worked briefly in the trade union and antiwar movements but "never with anything approaching a full-time commitment." She soon enrolled in graduate school and became a teacher.

Roberta Galler returned to Chicago and worked in various antipoverty programs. The Center for Constitutional Rights then recruited her to become its first administrator. Later she received her master's degree from New York University and did postgraduate work at a psychoanalytic institute, establishing a private practice as a psychotherapist. Back in Michigan, Elizabeth Slade Hirschfeld lobbied for the Mississippi Freedom Democratic Party's Congressional Challenge and then later struggled with the sexism of the Northern Student Movement in Detroit. She worked in the United Farmworkers Movement and for a Ralph Nader–affiliated organization, the California Citizens Action Group. After spinning off her own citizens group, she eventually worked as a fund-raising/organizational consultant for women's groups, trying to help them achieve self-sufficiency and sustainability. Subsequently, Hirschfeld became a financial planner.

Bob and Dottie Zellner worked for the Southern Conference Educational Fund in New Orleans for five years after they left SNCC. In

1974, she went to school to become a practical nurse, a job that brought the issue of her Jewishness to the forefront because "nobody had ever seen a Jewish woman working like I worked." The wealthy and politically conservative New Orleans Jewish community looked down "on a Jewish woman who was not even a registered nurse," who was caring for people's physical needs in the most intimate ways. In the hospitals, the white evangelical Christian women she worked with "just haunted me. They weren't hostile; they were in sects that believed that the Jews have to be converted." After she and Bob Zellner separated, Dottie Miller Zellner raised their daughters in New Orleans by herself, suffering through the hot, humid summers and isolated as the only politically progressive parent at the Jewish Community Center. Objecting to racist remarks made by Jewish teenagers and then speaking out against Israel's invasion of Lebanon, Zellner got a very chilly reception. "I actually had that old civil rights feeling. I said, 'I'm here and I'm an alien in the white community.'"[9]

When Zellner happily returned to New York in 1984, she became an administrator for the Center for Constitutional Rights, managing the Ella Baker Legal Internship program for students of color. In 1998, she became director of publications and development at the City University of New York Law School at Queens College.

As it did for many other volunteers, the Mississippi experience led Janice Goodman to go to law school in order to effect change through the legal system. After all, SNCC could claim that the tenacity and sacrifices of its members played a significant role in the passage of the 1964 Civil Rights Act and the 1965 Voting Rights Act. As a lawyer at the Center for Constitutional Rights, Goodman went to Attica during the prison uprisings. Although she was against Governor Nelson Rockefeller's decision to send in troops to quell the uprising, she was also appalled by the way the prisoners treated her as a woman. That experience helped push her to start one of the first feminist law firms, gearing her practice toward abortion rights and employment discrimination issues.

Carol Ruth Silver worked in a variety of progressive movements in California—"I was the only lawyer in the San Joaquin Valley who would relate to the farm workers." Later recruited to open the first legal services offices in East Oakland, under President Lyndon Johnson's War on Poverty, Silver was "one of the white lawyers who slept at the Black Panther headquarters . . . to protect them from the possibility of a police raid." Her subsequent eleven-year career in San Francisco politics included serving on the city's Board of Supervisors, where she was an ally of the first openly gay supervisor, Harvey Milk. They worked together on the first antigay discrimination ordinance in the nation, sponsored the first gay marches in the city, participated in vigils for Soviet Jewry, fought for rent control and tougher environmental controls, and advocated for better services for senior citizens and people with disabilities. "He was just like me, iconoclastic. He had a wonderful sense of humor and he was always willing to do something considered outrageous by other people but which just seemed like the right thing to do."[10]

Silver continues to work as a lawyer, as does Rita Schwerner Bender. Using her legal skills, Bender helped win the arduous fight to open the files of the Mississippi Sovereignty Commission, which spied on civil rights activists from 1956 to 1977. Created in 1956 to thwart court-ordered integration, the taxpayer-supported commission, which was allied with the Ku Klux Klan and the White Citizens Councils, used illegal tactics such as spying, intimidation, false imprisonment, and jury tampering to subvert the civil rights movement in Mississippi. The files mention the names of approximately 85,000 people and suggest the commission's complicity in the deaths of Mickey Schwerner, James Chaney, and Andrew Goodman. Fighting for justice and to preserve the memory of what actually happened in the movement, Bender persevered for twenty years. When the files were opened on March 17, 1998, she told the *New York Times*, "It's important for people to know how out of control a government can become."[11]

By the time they left the South, most of the women had completely lost faith in the government's willingness to help create social justice. However, when they turned to New Left movements as the only progressive alternative, most were frustrated by the movements' sexism. When the women's liberation movement exploded from the New Left, many Jewish women civil rights veterans embraced it immediately, while trying to maintain links to a variety of progressive issues. Barbara Jacobs Haber, who had attended the historic 1962 Port Huron conference of Students for a Democratic Society (SDS), remained in the organization for about six years, struggling with its sexism. "When I got to the SDS office, I expected to be treated as a leader because I had a history of being a leader in the civil rights movement. . . . [But] it was not okay for me to be very smart, a very good organizer and thinker. . . . When I fought to be one of the boys, I was seen as uppity and out of place and was punished, as were other women, for being uppity."[12] Subsequently, Haber lived in a commune, returned to school, worked as a hospital clerk, and developed a private practice as a psychotherapist.

Vivian Leburg Rothstein did community organizing in Chicago with SDS's JOIN (Jobs Or Income Now) program; worked with southern Appalachian whites; traveled to Vietnam with a peace delegation; and was an early proponent of women's liberation in Chicago's Westside Group and Chicago Women's Liberation. For many years, she directed a large multi-issue social service agency in California. When progressive women came to her for career advice, she would tell them, "Work first with poor people, with people who have nothing, because it puts things in perspective." More recently, she has begun working again with the labor movement.

During her time in Chicago, Florence Howe called herself "the mother of SDS in Chicago." She also worked with Clergymen Against the War and the New University Conference. Howe founded The Feminist Press in 1970 and celebrated its thirtieth birthday in April 2000. A pioneer in catalyzing the development of women's studies and publishing undiscovered women's literature worldwide, Howe is conducting a major project, Women Writing Africa. It is hard to imagine the knowledge revolution that women's studies has engendered over the past several decades without her.[13] Similarly, Jacqueline Levine has been a leader in the Jewish feminist movement, working to infuse her feminism into her local and global community—the Jewish organizational world.

Harriet Tanzman worked on a SCEF project in New Orleans and has continued to do as much movement work as possible. She is an archivist and chronicler of the movement, keeping in touch with movement workers and returning to the South often. Trudy Orris has also remained politically active, in the Women's International League for Peace and Freedom, Women for Racial and Economic Equality, and the National Alliance Against Racist and Political Repression, an organization founded in 1973 to fight for the rights of Black political prisoners. For Orris, "All this, and Cuba are also on the same line as Black freedom and Jews." A board member of the U.S.-Cuban Medical Project and the Information Cuba Project, she and her colleagues are "trying very hard to lift the embargo, which we don't understand. Why have an embargo on a little country like Cuba?"

Some of the Jewish women civil rights veterans work on international issues; many followed the movement imperative to work in local communities. When she first left SNCC, Elaine DeLott Baker worked with Black and Hispanic children in East Harlem and lower Manhattan. In the '70s, Baker moved to rural Hispanic Colorado, where she has worked in a succession of initiatives focused on education and community development.

Dr. June Finer has worked at the Women's House of Detention at Riker's Island, New York; in an abortion clinic; and with drug addicts on the Lower East Side. Working in the abortion clinic as the single mother of a small son in the early 1970s, Finer enjoyed the "incredibly enthusiastic community of women counselors," who created a positive environment for their coworkers and clients alike.

Most of the women have fulfilled their parents' dreams of their daughters' rising in opportunity through education. This, however, has not insulated all of them from significant financial struggles. Some of those struggles have come from having or choosing to support children on their own.

Motherhood was an important experience for many. The majority of them had children. Florence Howe unofficially "adopted" Alice, her Mississippi-born Black daughter, as a teenager. She sent her to high school in Baltimore and then to college. Carol Ruth Silver adopted her Chinese son when he was three and a half years old and later gave birth to another son, also as a single parent. June Finer had her two children as a single parent. Faith Holsaert and Elizabeth Slade Hirschfeld identify strongly as mothers and lesbians.

In fact, Hirschfeld credits the case of Jean Julian, a lesbian mother who lost custody of her children, with raising her consciousness and accelerating her own coming-out process in the 1970s. "I didn't think anybody could lose their children. In my life, I have never loved anyone as much as my children. . . . Still they are the major passion of my life." With a son the same age as Jean Julian's son, Hirschfeld got involved in the case. "The Gay Day parade came, and it was the era of Anita Bryant, and people were coming out all over the place, and again it was joyous because it seemed such a natural, wonderful, holy, completely spiritual thing to do, to be a lesbian . . . so I just came out." For Hirschfeld, the sense of community she felt as a lesbian in the women's movement was comparable to her experiences in the civil rights movement.[14]

If being a mother was an easy identity for many of the women to embrace, Jewish identity was much more challenging. In seeking to find a Jewish identity that resonates with their life experiences, the women continue to struggle with multiple meanings of Jewishness. In relation to one of this book's key themes—"many ways of being Jewish"—the women's lives illustrate four different approaches to progressive Jewish women's identity. By delineating the struggles and different stances adopted by the women, it becomes clear that there is no monopoly on defining Jewish identity. Despite the flowering of many alternative Jewish institutions, the women's struggles also highlight a largely untapped pool of Jewish passion—to be harnessed for building progressive Jewish community and activism.

Miriam Cohen Glickman, who was from the most observant Jewish family of the women in this book, remains strongly Jewish-identified in traditional senses. The secular women with connections to the Old Left—Trudy Weissman Orris, Harriet Tanzman, Faith Holsaert, and Dottie Miller Zellner—articulate the strongest connection between a Jewish cultural identity and their politics.

The other two groups of women have taken on the greater challenge of linking Jewishness expressly with their feminist identities. Visiting Israel enhanced Janice Goodman's pride in being Jewish. Later, when her mother died, she sought out the first contemporary Jewish woman rabbi, Sally Priesand, to conduct the funeral. "It was very comforting for me to have the religious service and that was another turning point." Goodman now attends synagogue and observes the High Holidays.

Jewish feminists Barbara Jacobs Haber, Elizabeth Slade Hirschfeld, and Jacqueline Levine belong to organizations that explicitly try to link both identities. For example, since the early 1970s, Haber has been a member of a Jewish feminist group and a Shabbat group that grew out of a workshop, Jews and the Left, conducted by Michael Goldhaber. The group has participated in the antinuclear movement and protested the Persian Gulf war.

Hirschfeld asserts that Judaism is "a major part of my life today, although part of my spirituality is linked to feminist spirituality and my challenge in life is how to put the two of them together." She embraced the challenge by starting a women's *havurah.* She also encouraged her synagogue to include feminist, gay, lesbian, bisexual, and transgender concerns and lobbied her local chapter of the American Jewish Congress to send a resolution affirming gay and lesbian relationships to the national AJC.

Jacqueline Levine has been a leader and advocate for women in the Jewish communal world. She has served as national president of the Council of Jewish Federations Women's Division and president of the American Jewish Congress Women's Division; participated in dialogues between prominent Black and Jewish women; and visited the Middle East with a Jewish and Palestinian women's delegation.

On the other hand, the women for whom feminism is their strongest identity may be seen as "feminists who are Jews." Many of them expressed a desire to be part of a Jewish spiritual community in some way but have been disappointed in their attempts to connect with existing synagogues or social organizations.

Florence Howe, who grew up in an Orthodox Jewish environment until her grandfather died when she was ten, was surprised to find herself searching for a synagogue in the mid-1980s. She tried several places and eventually found "a very nice synagogue on the Upper West Side with an extremely liberal rabbi who had just come up from Argentina." Led by the late Rabbi Marshall Meyer, Congregation B'nai Jeshurun provided community to hundreds of progressive New York Jews, including Howe's good friend Bella Abzug. "And Bella turns out to have been a lifelong member, so for awhile I sat with her. And for awhile it was quite an emotional experience. I even found that I could read the Hebrew, which was really a shock to me. I felt some connection for a short time but then I stopped because either it didn't go deep enough or I didn't feel at home enough."[15]

Others, like Elaine DeLott Baker, a practicing Buddhist, have given up the attempt to affiliate with Jewish institutions entirely, though not without sadness. According to Baker, the bond she feels with Jewish culture is rooted in the traditions of compassion that she first encountered through her grandmother Esther's code of ethics and the great Yiddish writers. However, finding a Jewish community that embraced those traditions, accepted her marriage to a Christian, and shared her political views was an unachievable goal. Although Buddhism is her spiritual practice, she remains identified with Jewish culture as the foundation of her values. She is hardly alone in this, as Rodger Kamenetz illustrates in his book about Buddhist Jews, *The Jew in the Lotus*.

Like Baker, the women profiled here found creative ways to remain true to their fundamental values. Contradicting media-hyped stereotypes of '60s activists who now denounce their involvement as naïve, Jewish women civil rights veterans continue their work modestly, quietly, on a variety of fronts. Many do so without recognition or the financial security that comes from traditional career paths.

Yet to a woman, they remain enormously grateful for their civil rights experiences, insisting as many SNCC veterans have, that they received far more than they gave. Having successfully circumvented their preordained path to Jewish suburbia, they learned how to take physi-

cal, emotional, and political risks. Fulfilling their post-Holocaust fantasies, they put their bodies on the line to resist racism. They saw that
they could handle physical danger, difficult living conditions, and most
of all, uncertainty. They taught, communicated, healed physical and
psychological scars, strategized, lobbied, registered voters, and publi-
cized the movement with almost no resources except people's spirit and
commitment. They crossed boundaries and learned to live and work
with people enormously different from themselves. They learned to see
themselves in new ways.

Finally, they also faced the limits and responsibilities of being white
in America in the second half of the twentieth century. They accepted
the need for a Black Power phase in the civil rights movement. They
contributed their organizing skills to other movements. They struggled
to discern what they should not do with their privileges and focused on
what they could do—by making contributions as lawyers, educators,
healers, administrators, and activists. Finally, they raised their children
with antiracist values and infused their communities and workplaces
with the insights born of their experiences in the movement.

Most important, the women in this book are committed to passing
on the living legacy of the civil rights movement. In a speech at Maryland's Charles County Community College, Faith Holsaert explained,

> Although I am not a historian, I think it is noteworthy that the history
> of SNCC in general, and of women in SNCC in particular is, for the
> moment, almost entirely an oral history. With our view that teaching
> is simply one form of organizing, many of us seek chances to address
> classes, assemblies, convocations, and conferences. As SNCC women,
> many of us feel a community responsibility to preserve our story. We
> have been goaded by being "recorded" by those who are unsympa-
> thetic, hostile, or, most often, ideologically in conflict with the beliefs
> which, like torches, illuminated our youths—and light our way, still.
> We are, literally, subversive after all these years.[16]

The fact that the movement for social justice continues in no way di-
minishes the transformational achievements of SNCC and the entire
southern civil rights movement from 1960 to 1967. That experience (itself part of the achievement) was made possible by the coming together
of people from disparate backgrounds united by a simple common vision of justice. Inspired by this vision, Jewish women who went south
during the civil rights movement dare us, through their efforts, then

and now, to believe in the possibility of social justice. Their sense of social justice is not as a fleeting, poignant historical moment but as a tangible, achievable goal, rooted in Jewish and other living traditions of struggle for human dignity, remembrance, and survival.

If the fight against European fascism and the history of the Black freedom struggle since slavery are among the prologues to the 1960s civil rights movement, then what activist future can we imagine using the late-twentieth-century as prologue? There are hopeful signs not yet fully appreciated or mined. The civil rights and anti-apartheid movements eroded the myth that racism is an impenetrable fortress. The New Left helped stop a war. Women's liberation, feminism, and the gay, lesbian, bisexual, and transgender movement have shaken assumptions about fixed gender roles. Revitalized labor and economic-justice movements have created new cross-class and cross-racial alliances. The antinuclear and environmental racism movements have shown that our very survival rests on recognizing our interconnectedness, part of an international movement questioning globalization. The progressive Jewish, Jewish renewal, and Jewish feminist movements affirm that there are many ways of being Jewish, including fighting for a just world.

Among the greatest legacies Jewish women and their fellow activists in the civil rights movement pass onto us is not only their daring in fighting back but their resistance to cynicism and despair. At the dawn of the twenty-first century, this may be the most critical resource for the future.

NOTES

1. Interview with Roberta Galler, New York, December 30, 1994.
2. Carson, *In Struggle*, 230, 203.
3. Lyon, 175.
4. Interview with Dorothy Miller Zellner, January 4, 1994.
5. Ibid.
6. Ibid.
7. Ibid.
8. Phone conversation with Vivian Leburg Rothstein, December 1993.
9. Interviews with Dorothy Miller Zellner, November 15, 1993, and January 4, 1994.
10. Interview with Carol Ruth Silver, February 9, 1994.
11. "Judge Opens Mississippi Segregation Files," ACLU Newswire, posted

January 13, 1998, www.aclu.org; and Ed Tant, "Cesspool Revealed in Formerly Secret Files," Online Athens, posted March 28, 1998, www.onlineathens.com.

12. Interview with Barbara Jacobs Haber, February 20, 1994.

13. An April 24, 2000, review in *Publisher's Weekly* noted, "The Feminist Press has published some astonishing material in its 30 years, some of which it can rightfully claim to have rediscovered."

14. Interview with Elizabeth Slade Hirschfeld, February 10, 1994.

15. Interview with Florence Howe, December 1, 1993.

16. Quotation from speech used with permission of Faith S. Holsaert.

Bibliography

Aaronsohn, Elizabeth. "Justice, Justice Shalt Thou Do." In Christine Clark and James O'Donnell, eds., *Becoming and Unbecoming White: Owning and Disowning a Racial Identity*. Westport, Conn.: Bergin and Garvey, 1999.

Alpert, Rebecca. *Like Bread on a Seder Plate: Jewish Lesbians and the Transformation of Tradition*. New York: Columbia University Press, 1997.

American Jewish Committee. *1964 American Jewish Year Book*. New York: American Jewish Committee, 1965.

Anthias, Floya, and Nira Yuval-Davis. *Racialized Boundaries: Race, Nation, Gender, Colour and Class, and the Anti-Racist Struggle*. London: Routledge, 1992.

Antler, Joyce. *The Journey Home: Jewish Women and the American Century*. New York: Free Press, 1997.

———. "Fighting Fascism: The Emma Lazarus Clubs." Paper presented at In Struggle: A History Teach-In, New York, 1993.

Aptheker, Herbert. *Anti-Racism in U.S. History: The First 200 Years*. Westport, Conn.: Greenwood Press, 1992.

Arendt, Hannah. *Eichmann in Jerusalem: A Report on the Banality of Evil*. New York: Penguin Books, 1977.

———. *The Origins of Totalitarianism*. San Diego: Harcourt Brace Jovanovich, 1968.

Baer, Hans A., and Yvonne Jones. *African Americans in the South: Issues of Race, Class, and Gender*. Athens: University of Georgia, 1992.

Baker, Ella. "The Bronx Slave Market." *Crisis* 42 (November 1935): 330–331, 340.

Barnett, Bernice McNair. "Black Women's Collectivist Organizations: Their Struggles During 'the Doldrums.'" In Myra Marx Ferree and Patricia Yancey Martin, eds., *Feminist Organizations: Harvest of the New Women's Movement*. Philadelphia: Temple University Press, 1993.

Baskin, Judith, ed. *Jewish Women in Historical Perspective*. Detroit: Wayne State University Press, 1991.

Baum, Charlotte, Paula Hyman, and Sonya Michel. *The Jewish Woman in America*. New York: Plume Books, 1976.

Bauman, Mark, and Berkeley Kallen, eds. *The Quiet Voices: Southern Rabbis and Black Civil Rights, 1880s to 1990s*. Tuscaloosa: University of Alabama Press, 1997.

Beck, Evelyn Torton. "The Politics of Jewish Invisibility." *NWSA Journal* (Autumn 1988).

Belfrage, Sally. *Freedom Summer*. Charlottesville: University Press of Virginia, 1990.

Bershtel, Sara, and Allen Graubard. *Saving Remnants: Feeling Jewish in America*. New York: Free Press, 1992.

Biale, David, Michael Galchinsky, and Susannah Heschel, eds. *Insider/Outsider: American Jews and Multiculturalism*. Berkeley: University of California Press, 1998.

Blumberg, Janice Rothschild. "The Bomb That Healed: A Personal Memoir of the Bombing of the Temple in Atlanta, 1958." *American Jewish History* (September 1983).

Blumberg, Rhoda Lois. *Civil Rights: The 1960s Freedom Struggle*. Boston: Twayne Publishers, 1991.

———. "White Mothers as Civil Rights Activists: The Interweave of Family and Movement Roles." In Guida West and Rhoda Lois Blumberg, eds., *Women and Social Protest*. New York: Oxford University Press, 1990.

Bond, Julian. "The Politics of Civil Rights History." In Armistead Robinson and Patricia Sullivan, eds., *New Directions in Civil Rights Studies*. Charlottesville: University of Virginia Press, 1991.

Bookman, Ann, and Sandra Morgen, eds. *Women and the Politics of Empowerment*. Philadelphia: Temple University Press, 1988.

Boyarin, Daniel, and Jonathan Boyarin, eds. *Jews and Other Differences: The New Jewish Cultural Studies*. Minneapolis: University of Minnesota Press, 1998.

Boyarin, Jonathan. *Storm from Paradise: The Politics of Jewish Memory*. Minneapolis: University of Minnesota Press, 1992.

Bracey, John, and August Meier. "Towards a Research Agenda on Blacks and Jews in United States History." *Journal of American Ethnic History* 12 (Spring 1993): 60–67.

Branch, Taylor. *Parting the Waters: America in the King Years*. New York: Simon & Schuster, 1988.

Breines, Wini. *Young, White, and Miserable: Growing Up Female in the Fifties*. Boston: Beacon Press, 1992.

Brettschneider, Marla, ed. *The Narrow Bridge: Jewish Views on Multiculturalism*. New Brunswick: Rutgers University Press, 1996.

Brodkin, Karen. *How Jews Became White Folks and What That Says about Race in America*. New Brunswick: Rutgers University Press, 1998.

Brown, Elsa Barkley. "African-American Women's Quilting: A Framework for

Conceptualizing and Teaching African-American Women's History." *Signs* 14, no. 4 (1989): 921–929.

Brownmiller, Susan. "The Summer of Our Discontent." *Village Voice* (July 19, 1994): 33–37.

Buhle, Mari Jo. *Women and American Socialism, 1870–1920.* Urbana: University of Illinois, 1983.

Bulkin, Elly, Minnie Bruce Pratt, and Barbara Smith. *Yours in Struggle: Three Feminist Perspectives on Anti-Semitism and Racism.* Brooklyn, N.Y.: Long Haul Press, 1984.

Cagin, Seth, and Philip Dray. *We Are Not Afraid: The Story of Goodman, Schwerner, and Chaney, and the Civil Rights Campaign for Mississippi.* New York: Macmillan, 1988.

Caraway, Nancie. *Segregated Sisterhood: Racism and the Politics of American Feminism.* Knoxville: University of Tennessee Press, 1991.

Carson, Clayborne. "Black-Jewish Universalism in the Era of Identity Politics." In Jack Salzman and Cornel West, eds., *Struggles in the Promised Land: Toward a History of Black-Jewish Relations in the United States.* New York: Oxford University Press, 1997.

———. "Blacks and Jews in the Civil Rights Movement: The Case of SNCC." In Jack Salzman, ed., *Bridges and Boundaries: African Americans and American Jews.* New York: Braziller, 1992.

———. *Malcolm X: The FBI File.* New York: Carroll & Graf, 1991.

———. "Blacks and Jews in the Civil Rights Movement." In Joseph R. Washington, ed., *Jews in Black Perspectives: A Dialogue.* Teaneck, N.J.: Fairleigh Dickinson University Press, 1984.

———. *In Struggle: SNCC and the Black Awakening of the 1960s.* Cambridge: Harvard University Press, 1981.

Cash, W. J. *The Mind of the South.* New York: Random House, 1941.

Chafe, William H. *Never Stop Running: Allard Lowenstein and the Struggle to Save American Liberalism.* New York: Basic Books, 1993.

———. *Civilities and Civil Rights: Greensboro, North Carolina, and the Black Struggle for Freedom.* New York: Oxford University Press, 1980.

Clark, Septima, and Cynthia Brown. *Ready from Within: A First Person Narrative.* Trenton: Africa World Press, 1990.

Clifford, James. *The Predicament of Culture: Twentieth-Century Ethnography, Literature, and Art.* Cambridge: Harvard University Press, 1988.

Clifford, James, and George E. Marcus, eds. *Writing Culture: The Poetics and Politics of Ethnography.* Berkeley: University of California Press, 1986.

Cluster, Dick, ed. *They Should Have Served That Cup of Coffee: 7 Radicals Remember the 60s.* Boston: South End Press, 1979.

Cohen, Miriam. "Integration in the Deep South: Death Goes On." *Justice* (December 17, 1963).

Collins, Patricia Hill. "Learning from the Outsider Within: The Sociological Significance of Black Feminist Thought." In Joan E. Hartman and Ellen Messer-Davidow, eds., *(En)Gendering Knowledge: Feminists in Academe*. Knoxville: University of Tennessee Press, 1991.

———. *Black Feminist Thought: Knowledge, Consciousness, and the Politics of Empowerment*. Boston: Unwin Hyman, 1990.

Cone, James H. *A Black Theology of Liberation*. Maryknoll, NY: Orbis Books, 1990.

Cook, Blanche Wiesen. "Bella Abzug." In Paula Hyman and Deborah Dash Moore, eds., *Jewish Women in America: An Historical Encyclopedia*. New York: Routledge, 1998.

Cott, Nancy F. *The Grounding of Modern Feminism*. New Haven: Yale University Press, 1987.

Cowan, Paul. *An Orphan in History*. New York: Bantam Books, 1983.

Cowett, Mark. *Birmingham's Rabbi: Morris Newfield and Alabama, 1895–1940*. Birmingham: University of Alabama Press, 1986.

Crawford, Vicki L., Jacqueline Anne Rouse, and Barbara Woods, eds. *Women in the Civil Rights Movement: Trailblazers and Torchbearers, 1941–1965*. Brooklyn, N.Y.: Carlson Publishing, 1990.

D'Emilio, John, and Estelle Freedman. *Intimate Matters: A History of Sexuality in America*. New York: Harper & Row, 1988.

Deutscher, Isaac. *The Non-Jewish Jew and Other Essays*. New York: Hill and Wang, 1970.

Diamond, Timothy. *Making Gray Gold: Narratives of Nursing Home Care*. Chicago: University of Chicago Press, 1992.

Diner, Hasia R. *A Time for Gathering: The Second Migration, 1820–1880*. The Jewish People in America Series. Baltimore: Johns Hopkins University Press, 1992.

———. *In the Almost Promised Land: American Jews and Blacks, 1915–1935*. Westport, Conn.: Greenwood Press, 1977.

Dinnerstein, Leonard, and Mary Dale Palsson, eds. *Jews in the South*. Baton Rouge: Louisiana State University Press, 1973.

Dittmer, John. *Local People: The Struggle for Civil Rights in Mississippi*. Urbana: University of Illinois Press, 1994.

Dollinger, Mark. "'Hamans' and 'Tourquemadas': Southern and Northern Jewish Responses to the Civil Rights Movement, 1945–1965." In Mark Bauman and Berkeley Kallen, eds., *The Quiet Voices: Southern Rabbis and Black Civil Rights, 1880s to 1990s*. Tuscaloosa: University of Alabama Press, 1997.

Edgcomb, Gabrielle Simon. *From Swastika to Jim Crow: Refugee Scholars at Black Colleges*. Malabar, Fla.: Krieger Publishing, 1993.

Evans, Eli. *The Provincials: An Informal History of Jews in the South*. New York: Atheneum, 1973.

Evans, Sara. *Born for Liberty: A History of Women in America*. New York: Free Press, 1989.

———. *Personal Politics: The Roots of Women's Liberation in the Civil Rights Movement and the New Left*. New York: Vintage Books, 1980.

Farganis, Sondra. "Feminism and the Reconstruction of Social Science." In Alison Jaggar and Susan Bordo, eds., *Gender/Body/Knowledge: Feminist Reconstructions of Being and Knowing*. New Brunswick: Rutgers University Press, 1990.

Feingold, Henry L. *A Time for Searching: Entering the Mainstream, 1920–1945*. The Jewish People in America Series. Baltimore: Johns Hopkins University Press, 1992.

Fine, Morris, and Milton Himmelfarb, eds. *American Jewish Yearbook 1965*. New York: American Jewish Committee and Jewish Publication Society of America, 1965.

Fleming, Cynthia Griggs. *Soon We Will Not Cry: The Liberation of Ruby Doris Smith Robinson*. Lanham, Md.: Rowman & Littlefield, 1998.

Forman, Frieda, Ethel Raicus, Sarah Silberstein Swartz, and Margie Wolfe, eds. *Found Treasures: Stories by Yiddish Women Writers*. Toronto: Second Story Press, 1994.

Forman, James. *The Making of Black Revolutionaries*. New York: Macmillan, 1972.

Fowlkes, Diane L. *White Political Women: Paths from Privilege to Empowerment*. Knoxville: University of Tennessee Press, 1992.

Frankenberg, Ruth. *White Women, Race Matters: The Social Construction of Whiteness*. Minneapolis: University of Minnesota Press, 1993.

Friedman, Murray. "Interview with Rachelle Horowitz." New York: American Jewish Committee Oral History Library, 1989.

Frisch, Michael. *A Shared Authority: Essays on the Craft and Meaning of Oral and Public History*. Albany: SUNY Press, 1990.

Fusco, Liz. "Freedom Schools in Mississippi (1964)." *Radical Teacher* 40 (Fall 1991).

Giddings, Paula. *In Search of Sisterhood: Delta Sigma Theta and the Challenge of the Black Sorority Movement*. New York: William Morrow, 1988.

———. *When and Where I Enter: The Impact of Black Women on Race and Sex in America*. New York: William Morrow, 1984.

Gilman, Sander. *The Jew's Body*. New York: Routledge, 1993.

Ginsberg, Benjamin. *The Fatal Embrace: Jews and the State*. Chicago: University of Chicago Press, 1993.

Glenn, Susan. *Daughters of the Shtetl: Life and Labor in the Immigrant Generation*. Ithaca: Cornell University Press, 1990.

Gluck, Sherna Berger, and Daphne Patai, eds. *Women's Words: The Feminist Practice of Oral History*. New York: Routledge, 1991.

Goldberg, David Theo, ed. *Anatomy of Racism*. Minneapolis: University of Minnesota Press, 1992.

Goldstein, Sidney. *Profile of American Jewry: Insights from the 1990 National Jewish Population Survey*. New York: North American Jewish Data Bank, CUNY Graduate Center.

Gorelick, Sherry. "The Changer and the Changed: Methodological Reflections on Studying Jewish Feminists." In Alison Jaggar and Susan Bordo, eds. *Gender/Body/Knowledge: Feminist Reconstructions of Being and Knowing*. New Brunswick: Rutgers University Press, 1989.

Gornick, Vivian. *Fierce Attachments: A Memoir*. New York: Touchstone, 1987.

Gottlieb, Roger S. *A Spirituality of Resistance*. New York: Crossroad Publishing, 1999.

Graham, Hugh Davis. *Civil Rights and the Presidency: Race and Gender in American Politics, 1960–1972*. New York: Oxford University Press, 1992.

Grant, Joanne. *Ella Baker: Freedom Bound*. New York: Wiley, 1998.

Greenberg, Cheryl. "Negotiating Coalition: Black and Jewish Civil Rights Agencies in the Twentieth Century." In Jack Salzman and Cornel West, eds., *Struggles in the Promised Land: Toward a History of Black-Jewish Relations in the United States*. New York: Oxford University Press, 1997.

Greene, Melissa Fay. *The Temple Bombing*. New York: Fawcett Columbine, 1996.

Grele, Ronald. *Envelopes of Sound: The Art of Oral History*. New York: Praeger, 1991.

———. "An Interview with Heather Booth." New York: Columbia University Oral History Archives, 1984.

Gwaltney, John Langston. *Drylongso: A Self-Portrait of Black America*. New York: New Press, 1993.

Hall, Jacquelyn Dowd. "'The Mind That Burns in Each Body': Women, Rape, and Racial Violence." In Ann Snitow et al., eds., *Powers of Desire: The Politics of Sexuality*. New York: Monthly Review Press, 1983.

Harding, Sandra, ed. *Feminism and Methodology*. Bloomington: Indiana University Press, 1987.

Harding, Vincent. *Hope and History: Why We Must Share the Story of the Movement*. Maryknoll, N.Y.: Orbis Books, 1990.

Hartman, Joan E., and Ellen Messer Davidow, eds. *(En)Gendering Knowledge: Feminists in Academe.* Knoxville: University of Tennessee Press, 1991.

Hartsock, Nancy. "The Feminist Standpoint: Developing the Ground for a Specifically Feminist Historical Materialism." In Sandra Harding, ed., *Feminism and Methodology.* Bloomington: Indiana University Press, 1987.

Hayden, Casey, et al. *Deep in Our Hearts: Nine White Women in the Freedom Movement.* Athens: University of Georgia Press, 2000.

Heilbrun, Carolyn G. *Writing a Woman's Life.* New York: Norton, 1988.

Heilman, Samuel. "Searching for a New Identity: Being Jewish Today Doesn't Mean What It Used To." *Jewish Week* (October 15–21, 1993).

Heinze, Andrew. *Adapting to Abundance: Jewish Immigrants, Mass Consumption, and the Search for American Identity.* New York: Columbia University Press, 1990.

Hentoff, Nat. *Black Anti-Semitism and Jewish Racism.* New York: Schocken Books, 1970.

Hertzberg, Steven. *Strangers within the Gate City: The Jews of Atlanta, 1845–1915.* Philadelphia: Jewish Publication Society of America, 1978.

Higginbotham, Evelyn Brooks. *Righteous Discontent: The Women's Movement in the Black Baptist Church, 1880–1920.* Cambridge: Harvard University Press, 1993.

Hine, Darlene Clark. "Lifting the Veil, Shattering the Silence; Black Women's History in Slavery and Freedom." In Darlene Clark Hine, ed., *Black Women's History: Theory and Practice.* Black Women in United States History. Brooklyn, N.Y.: Carlson Publishing, 1990.

Holsaert, Faith S. *While We Were Singing.* Glens Falls, N.Y.: Loft Press, 1986.

Holt, Len. *The Summer That Didn't End.* New York: William Morrow, 1965.

Howe, Florence. *Myths of Coeducation: Selected Essays, 1964–1983.* Bloomington: Indiana University Press, 1984.

Huie, William Bradford. *Three Lives for Mississippi.* New York: New American Library, 1968.

Hyman, Paula. *Gender and Assimilation in Modern Jewish History: The Roles and Representations of Women.* Seattle: University of Washington Press, 1995.

———. "Gender and the Immigrant Jewish Experience in the United States." In Judith Baskin, ed., *Jewish Women in Historical Perspective.* Detroit: Wayne State University Press, 1991.

Hyman, Paula, and Deborah Dash Moore, eds. *Jewish Women in America: An Historical Encyclopedia.* New York: Routledge, 1997.

Ignatiev, Noel. "Treason to Whiteness Is Loyalty to Humanity: An Interview with Noel Ignatiev." *Utne Reader* (November/December 1994): 82–86.

Jaggar, Alison M., and Bordo Susan R., eds. *Gender/Body/Knowledge: Feminist*

Reconstructions of Being and Knowing. New Brunswick: Rutgers University Press, 1989.

Jones, Hettie. *How I Became Hettie Jones*. New York: Penguin Books, 1990.

Jones, Jacqueline. *Labor of Love, Labor of Sorrow: Black Women, Work, and the Family from Slavery to the Present*. New York: Basic Books, 1985.

Kaganoff, Nathan, and Melvin Urofsky, eds. *Turn to the South: Essays on Southern Jewry*. Charlottesville: University of Virginia Press, 1979.

Kahn, Si. *How People Get Power*. Washington, D.C.: National Association of Social Workers Press, 1994.

———. "Multiracial Organizations: Theory and Practice." *Liberal Education* 77 (January/February 1991): 35–37.

Kamenetz, Rodger. *The Jew in the Lotus: A Poet's Rediscovery of Jewish Identity in Buddhist India*. San Francisco: HarperSanFrancisco, 1994.

Kaplan, Judy, and Linn Shapiro, eds. *Red Diapers: Growing Up in the Communist Left*. Urbana: University of Illinois Press, 1998.

Kaufman, Jonathan. "Blacks and Jews: The Struggle in the Cities." In Jack Salzman and Cornel West, eds., *Struggles in the Promised Land: Toward a History of Black-Jewish Relations in the United States*. New York: Oxford University Press, 1997.

———. *Broken Alliance: The Turbulent Times between Blacks and Jews in America*. New York: Penguin Books, 1988.

Kaye/Kantrowitz, Melanie. *The Issue Is Power: Essays on Women, Jews, Violence, and Resistance*. San Francisco: Aunt Lute Foundation Books, 1992.

Kaye/Kantrowitz, Melanie, and Irena Klepfisz, eds. *The Tribe of Dina: A Jewish Women's Anthology*. Montpelier, Vt.: Sinister Wisdom Books, 1986.

Kelley, Robin D. G. *Hammer and Hoe: Alabama Communists during the Great Depression*. Chapel Hill: University of North Carolina Press, 1990.

Keniston, Kenneth. *Young Radicals: Notes on Committed Youth*. New York: Harcourt, Brace & World, 1968.

Kessler, Lauren. *After All These Years: Sixties Ideals in a Different World*. New York: Thunder's Mouth Press, 1990.

King, Deborah. "Multiple Jeopardy, Multiple Consciousness: The Context of a Black Feminist Ideology." *Signs* 14, no. 1 (1988): 42–72.

King, Mary. *Freedom Song: A Personal Story of the 1960s Civil Rights Movement*. New York: William Morrow, 1987.

Klepfisz, Irena. *Dreams of an Insomniac: Jewish Feminist Essays, Speeches and Diatribes*. Portland, Ore.: Eighth Mountain Press, 1990.

Kolsky, Thomas A. *Jews against Zionism: The American Council for Judaism, 1942–1948*. Philadelphia: Temple University Press, 1990.

Koonz, Claudia. "Genocide and Eugenics: The Language of Power." In Peter

Hayes, ed., *Lessons and Legacies: The Meaning of the Holocaust in a Changing World*. Evanston: Northwestern University Press, 1991.

Kosmin, Barry. "The Political Economy of Gender in Jewish Federations." Paper presented at Women and Philanthropy Conference. New York, 1987.

Lawson, Steven F. *Running for Freedom: Civil Rights and Black Politics in America since 1941*. Philadelphia: Temple University Press, 1991.

———. "Freedom Then, Freedom Now: The Historiography of the Civil Rights Movement." *American Historical Review* 96 (April 1991): 456–471.

Lawson, Steven F., and Charles Payne. *Debating the Civil Rights Movement, 1945–1968*. Lanham, Md.: Rowman & Littlefield, 1998.

Lerner, Michael, and Cornel West. *Jews and Blacks: Let the Healing Begin*. New York: Putnam, 1995.

Lester, Julius. *Lovesong: Becoming a Jew*. New York: Arcade Publishing, 1988.

Levi, Jan Heller, ed. *A Muriel Rukeyser Reader*. New York: Norton, 1994.

Levine, Amy-Jill. "A Jewess, More and/or Less." In Miriam Peskowitz and Laura Levitt, eds., *Judaism since Gender*. New York: Routledge, 1997.

Levine, Jacqueline. "The Changing Role of Women in the Jewish Community." In Jacob Marcus, ed., *The American Jewish Woman: A Documentary History*. New York: Ktav Publishing, 1981.

Levitt, Laura. *Jews and Feminism: The Ambivalent Search for Home*. New York: Routledge, 1997.

Liebman, Arthur. *Jews and the Left*. New York: Wiley, 1979.

Liebman, Charles. *The Ambivalent American Jew*. Philadelphia: Jewish Publication Society of America, 1973.

Lipset, Seymour Martin, and Earl Raab. *Jews and the New American Scene*. Cambridge: Harvard University Press, 1997.

Lyon, Danny. *Memories of the Southern Civil Rights Movement*. Chapel Hill: University of North Carolina Press, 1992.

Lyotard, Jean-François. *Heidegger and "the Jews."* Minneapolis: University of Minnesota Press, 1990.

McAdam, Doug. *Freedom Summer*. New York: Oxford University Press, 1988.

———. "Gender as a Mediator of the Activist Experience: The Case of Freedom Summer." *American Journal of Sociology* 97 (March 1992): 1211–1240.

MacLean, Nancy. "The Leo Frank Case Reconsidered: Gender and Sexual Politics in the Making of Reactionary Populism." *Journal of American History* 78 (December 1991): 917–948.

Marable, Manning. *Race, Reform, and Rebellion: The Second Reconstruction in Black America, 1945–1990*. Jackson: University Press of Mississippi, 1991.

Marcus, Jacob, ed. *The American Jewish Woman: A Documentary History*. New York: Ktav Publishing, 1981.

Markowitz, Ruth Jacknow. *My Daughter the Teacher: Jewish Teachers in the New York City School System.* New Brunswick: Rutgers University Press, 1990.

Mathews, Holly F., ed. *Women in the South: An Anthropological Perspective. Southern Anthropological Society Proceedings,* no. 22. Athens: University of Georgia Press, 1989.

May, Elaine Tyler. *Homeward Bound: American Families in the Cold War Era.* New York: Basic Books, 1988.

Miller, James. *Democracy Is in the Streets: From Port Huron to the Siege of Chicago.* New York: Simon & Schuster, 1987.

Miller, Judith. *One by One by One: Facing the Holocaust.* New York: Simon & Schuster, 1990.

Mills, Kay. *This Little Light of Mine: The Life of Fannie Lou Hamer.* New York: Dutton, 1993.

Minnich, Elizabeth. *Transforming Knowledge.* Philadelphia: Temple University Press, 1990.

Mitford, Jessica. *A Fine Old Conflict.* New York: Vintage Books, 1956.

Mohanty, Chandra Talpade, Ann Russo, and Lourdes Torres, eds. *Third World Women and the Politics of Feminism.* Bloomington: University of Indiana Press, 1991.

Moore, Deborah Dash. "Separate Paths: Blacks and Jews in the Twentieth Century South." In Jack Salzman and Cornel West, *Struggles in the Promised Land: Toward a History of Black-Jewish Relations in the United States.* New York: Oxford University Press, 1997.

———. *At Home in America: Second Generation New York Jews.* New York: Columbia University Press, 1981.

Morris, Aldon D. *The Origins of the Civil Rights Movement: Black Communities Organizing for Change.* New York: Free Press, 1984.

Morrison, Toni. *Playing in the Dark: Whiteness and the Literary Imagination.* New York: Vintage Books, 1992.

———, ed. *Race-ing Justice, En-gendering Power: Essays on Anita Hill, Clarence Thomas, and the Construction of Social Reality.* New York: Pantheon Books, 1992.

Mosse, George. *Toward the Final Solution.* New York: Howard Fertig, 1978.

Murray, Pauli. *The Autobiography of a Black Activist, Feminist, Lawyer, Priest, and Poet.* Knoxville: University of Tennessee Press, 1989.

Myerhoff, Barbara. *Number Our Days: A Triumph of Continuity and Culture among Jewish Old People in an Urban Ghetto.* New York: Simon & Schuster, 1978.

Neidle, Cecyle S. *America's Immigrant Women: Their Contribution to the Development of a Nation from 1609 to the Present.* New York: Hippocrene Books, 1975.

Nelson, Jack. *Terror in the Night: The Klan's Campaign against the Jews.* New York: Simon & Schuster, 1993.

Nestle, Joan. *A Restricted Country.* Ithaca: Firebrand Books, 1987.

Neverdon-Morton, Cynthia. *Afro American Women of the South and the Advancement of the Race, 1895–1925.* Knoxville: University of Tennessee Press, 1989.

Novick, Peter. *That Noble Dream: The "Objectivity Question" and the American Historical Profession.* New York: Cambridge University Press, 1988.

Ochs, Vanessa. *Words on Fire: One Woman's Journey into the Sacred.* San Diego: Harcourt Brace Jovanovich, 1990.

Omi, Michael, and Howard Winant. *Racial Formation in the United States from the 1960s to the 1990s.* New York: Routledge, 1994.

Omolade, Barbara. "Hearts of Darkness." In Ann Snitow et al., eds., *Powers of Desire: The Politics of Sexuality.* New York: Monthly Review Press, 1983.

Oshinsky, David M. *A Conspiracy So Immense: The World of Joe McCarthy.* New York: Free Press, 1983.

Palmer, Phyllis. *Domesticity and Dirt: Housewives and Domestic Servants in the United States, 1920–1945.* Philadelphia: Temple University Press, 1989.

Payne, Charles. *I've Got the Light of Freedom: The Organizing Tradition and the Mississippi Freedom Struggle.* Berkeley: University of California Press, 1995.

———. "Men Led, but Women Organized: Movement Participation of Women in the Mississippi Delta." In Vicki L. Crawford, Jacqueline Anne Rouse, and Barbara Woods, eds., *Women in the Civil Rights Movement: Trailblazers and Torchbearers, 1941–1965.* Brooklyn, N.Y.: Carlson Publishing, 1990.

Personal Narratives Group, The, ed. *Interpreting Women's Lives: Feminist Theory and Personal Narratives.* Bloomington: Indiana University Press, 1989.

Peskowitz, Miriam, and Laura Levitt, eds. *Judaism since Gender.* New York: Routledge, 1997.

Plaskow, Judith. *Standing Again at Sinai: Judaism from a Feminist Perspective.* San Francisco: HarperSanFrancisco, 1991.

Pogrebin, Letty Cottin. *Deborah, Golda, and Me: Being Female and Jewish in America.* New York: Crown, 1991.

Powledge, Fred. *Free at Last? The Civil Rights Movement and the People Who Made It.* New York: HarperCollins, 1992.

Prell, Riv-Ellen. *Fighting to Become Americans: Jews, Gender, and the Anxiety of Assimilation.* Boston: Beacon Press, 1999.

———. "Stereotypes." In Paula Hyman and Deborah Dash Moore, eds., *Jewish Women in America: An Historical Encyclopedia.* New York: Routledge, 1997.

———. "Why Jewish Princesses Don't Sweat: Desire and Consumption in Postwar American Jewish Culture." In Howard Eilberg-Schwartz, ed., *The People of the Body: Jews and Judaism from an Embodied Perspective.* Albany: SUNY Press, 1993.

Prell, Riv-Ellen. "Rage and Representation: Jewish Gender Stereotypes in American Culture." In Faye Ginsburg and Anna Tsing, eds., *In Uncertain Terms: Negotiating Gender in American Culture.* Boston: Beacon Press, 1990.

———. *Prayer and Community: The Havurah in American Judaism.* Detroit: Wayne State University Press, 1989.

Reagon, Bernice Johnson. "Coalition Politics: Turning the Century." In Barbara Smith, ed., *Home Girls: A Black Feminist Anthology.* New York: Kitchen Table Press, 1983.

Reinharz, Shulamit. *Feminist Methods in Social Research.* New York: Oxford University Press, 1992.

Rich, Adrienne. *What Is Found There: Notebooks on Poetry and Politics.* New York: Norton, 1993.

———. *An Atlas of the Difficult World: Poems, 1988–1991.* New York: Norton, 1991.

———. "Disloyal to Civilization: Feminism, Racism, and Gynephobia." In *On Lies, Secrets, and Silences: Selected Prose, 1966–1978.* New York: Norton, 1979.

Robinson, Jo Ann Gibson. *The Montgomery Bus Boycott and the Women Who Started It.* Knoxville: University of Tennessee Press, 1987.

Roediger, David R. *The Wages of Whiteness: Race and the Making of the American Working Class.* London: Verso Books, 1991.

Rogers, Kim Lacy. *Righteous Lives: Narratives of the New Orleans Civil Rights Movement.* New York: New York University Press, 1993.

Rogin, Michael. *Blackface, White Noise: Jewish Immigrants in the Hollywood Melting Pot.* Berkeley: University of California Press, 1996.

Rogoff, Leonard. "Is the Jew White? The Racial Place of the Southern Jew." *American Jewish History Journal* 85 (September 1997): 195–230.

Rogow, Faith. *Gone to Another Meeting: A History of the National Council of Jewish Women.* University: University of Alabama Press, 1993.

Rosten, Leo. *The Joys of Yiddish.* New York: Pocket Books, 1968.

Roth, Philip. *Portnoy's Complaint.* New York: Random House, 1967.

Rothman, Stanley, and S. Robert Lichter. *Roots of Radicalism: Jews, Christians, and the New Left.* New York: Oxford University Press, 1982.

Rothschild, Mary Aickin. *A Case of Black and White: Northern Volunteers and the Southern Freedom Summers, 1964–1965.* Westport, Conn.: Greenwood Press, 1982.

———. "White Women Volunteers in the Freedom Summers." *Feminist Studies* 5 (Fall 1979): 466–495.

Rothstein, Vivian. "Reunion." *Boston Review* (December/January 1994–95): 8–11.

Rubin-Dorsky, Jeffrey, and Shelly Fisher Fishkin. *People of the Book: Thirty Scholars Reflect on Their Jewish Identity.* Madison: University of Wisconsin Press, 1996.

Rupp, Leila J., and Verta Taylor. *Survival in the Doldrums: The American Women's Rights Movement, 1945 to the 1960's.* Columbus: Ohio State University Press, 1990.

Sacks, Karen Brodkin. "What's a Life Story Got to Do with It?" In The Personal Narratives Group, ed., *Interpreting Women's Lives: Feminist Theory and Personal Narratives.* Bloomington: Indiana University Press, 1989.

Salem, Dorothy, ed. *African American Women.* New York: Garland Publishing, 1993.

Salzman, Jack, and Cornel West, eds. *Struggles in the Promised Land: Toward a History of Black-Jewish Relations in the United States.* New York: Oxford University Press, 1997.

Salzman, Jack, Adina Back, and Gretchen Sorin, eds. *Bridges and Boundaries: African Americans and American Jews.* New York: Braziller, 1992.

Schultz, Bud, and Ruth Schultz. *It Did Happen Here: Recollections of Political Repression.* Berkeley: University of California Press, 1989.

Schultz, Debra L. *We Didn't Think in Those Terms Then: Narratives of Jewish Women in the Southern Civil Rights Movement, 1960–1966* (diss.). Ann Arbor: UMI Press, 1995.

Segrest, Mab. *Memoir of a Race Traitor.* Boston: South End Press, 1994.

Seidman, Naomi. "Fag-Hags and Bu-Jews: Toward a (Jewish) Politics of Vicarious Identity." In David Biale, Michael Galchinsky, and Susannah Heschel, eds., *Insider/Outsider: American Jews and Multiculturalism.* Berkeley: University of California Press, 1998.

Shapiro, Edward S. *A Time for Healing: American Jewry since World War II.* The Jewish People in America Series. Baltimore: Johns Hopkins University Press, 1992.

Shepherd, Naomi. *A Price below Rubies: Jewish Women as Rebels and Radicals.* Cambridge: Harvard University Press, 1993.

Silberman, Charles E. *A Certain People: American Jews and Their Lives Today.* New York: Summit Books, 1985.

Silberstein, Laurence, ed. *Mapping Jewish Identities.* New York: New York University Press, 2000.

Smith, Dorothy. *The Everyday World as Problematic.* Boston: Northeastern University Press, 1987.

Smith, Lillian. *Killers of the Dream*. Garden City, N.Y.: Anchor Books, 1963.

Sorin, Gerald. *A Time for Building: The Third Migration, 1880–1920*. The Jewish People in America Series. Baltimore: Johns Hopkins University Press, 1992.

———. *The Prophetic Minority: American Jewish Immigrant Radicals, 1880–1920*. Bloomington: Indiana University Press, 1985.

Stacey, Judith. "Can There Be a Feminist Ethnography?" In Sherna Gluck and Daphne Patai, eds., *Women's Words: The Feminist Practice of Oral History*. New York: Routledge, 1991.

Stack, Carol. *All Our Kin: Strategies for Survival in a Black Community*. New York: Harper & Row, 1974.

Stivers, Camilla. "Reflections on the Role of Personal Narrative in Social Science." *Signs* (Winter 1993): 408–425.

Strom, Margot Stern, and William S. Parsons. *Facing History and Ourselves: Holocaust and Human Behavior*. Watertown, Mass.: Intentional Educations, 1982.

Swerdlow, Amy. *Women Strike for Peace: Traditional Motherhood and Radical Politics in the 1960s*. Chicago: University of Chicago Press, 1993.

Thompson, Paul. *The Voice of the Past: Oral History*. New York: Oxford University Press, 1988.

Toll, William. *The Making of an Ethnic Middle Class: Portland Jewry over Four Generations*. Albany: SUNY Press, 1982.

Tronto, Joan. "Care As a Political Concept." In Nancy Hirschmann and Christine Di Stephano, eds., *Revisioning the Political: Feminist Reconstructions of Traditional Concepts in Western Political Theory*. Boulder: Westview Press, 1996.

Tucker, Susan. *Telling Memories among Southern Women: Domestic Workers and Their Employers in the Segregated South*. New York: Schocken Books, 1988.

Umansky, Ellen, and Diane Ashton, eds. *Four Centuries of Jewish Women's Spirituality*. Boston: Beacon Press, 1992.

Vogel, Lise. *Woman Questions: Essays for a Materialist Feminism*. New York: Routledge, 1995.

———. "Telling Tales: Historians of Our Own Lives." *Journal of Women's History* 2 (Winter 1991): 89–101.

Vorspan, Albert. "The Dilemma of the Southern Jew." In Leonard Dinnerstein and Mary Dale Palsson, eds., *Jews in the South*. Baton Rouge: Louisiana State University Press, 1973.

Walker, Alice. *Meridian*. New York: Simon & Schuster, 1976.

———. *You Can't Keep a Good Woman Down*. San Diego: Harcourt Brace, 1971.

Walzer, Michael. *Exodus and Revolution*. New York: Basic Books, 1985.

Washington, Joseph R., ed. *Jews in Black Perspectives: A Dialogue*. Lanham, Md.: University Press of America, 1989.

Waxman, Chaim. *America's Jews in Transition*. Philadelphia: Temple University Press, 1983.

Webb, Clive. "Big Struggle in a Small Town: Charles Mantinband of Hattiesburg, Mississippi." In Mark Bauman and Berkeley Kallen, eds., *The Quiet Voices: Southern Rabbis and Black Civil Rights, 1880s to 1990s*. Tuscaloosa: University of Alabama Press, 1997.

West, Cornel. *Race Matters*. Boston: Beacon Press, 1993.

White, Hayden. *The Content of the Form: Narrative Discourse and Historical Representation*. Baltimore: Johns Hopkins University Press, 1987.

Winkler, Karen. "Debating the History of Blacks and Jews." *Chronicle of Higher Education* (January 19, 1994): A11, A14.

Woodward, C. Vann. *The Strange Career of Jim Crow*. New York: Oxford University Press, 1957.

Woolf, Virginia. *Three Guineas*. New York: Harcourt Brace Jovanovich, 1966.

Yerushalmi, Yosef Hayim. *Zakhor: Jewish History and Jewish Memory*. New York: Schocken Books, 1989.

Zborowski, Mark, and Elizabeth Herzog. *Life Is with the People: The Culture of the Shtetl*. New York: Schocken Books, 1962.

Zimmerman, Jonathan. "Crossing Oceans, Crossing Colors: Black Peace Corps Volunteers and Interracial Love in Africa, 1961–1971." In Martha Hodes, ed., *Sex, Love, Race: Crossing Boundaries in North American History*. New York: New York University Press, 1999.

Index

Haber, Barbara Jacobs: antiracism of, 156; anti-Semitism and, 179–80; decision to go south by, 5–6; family political culture and, 148; founding of SNCC and, 31–32; Holocaust and, 182–83, 188–89; identity issues and, 135–36, 201; Jewish racism and, 97; Jewish religious experience of, 171; post-SNCC career of, 198; relationship with parents, 143
Hall, Prathia, 48
Hamer, Fannie Lou, xvii, 24, 60, 70, 75
Haney, Charlie, 151–52
Harlem Brotherhood, 45–46, 152
Harmann, Sue, 37–38
Harris, Jesse, 71
Harris, Rutha Mae, 46
Harvey, Clarie Collins, 43, 44
Hayes, Curtis, 79
Height, Dorothy, 111–12
Hicks, Greg, 85–86
Hirschfeld, Elizabeth Slade: antiracism of, 154–55; anti-Semitism and, 178; Black-white unity and, 110–11; decision to go south by, 10; Holocaust and, 183–84; identity issues and, 131, 141, 142, 201; interracial sexual politics and, 119; jail experiences of, 39, 42; motherhood and, 200; parental reactions to, 16; post-SNCC career of, 196; radicalization of, 151–52
Holocaust, women civil rights activists and, 1, 4, 181–90. See also specific women
Holsaert, Faith, 34; Albany Movement and, 45–51; anti-Semitism and, 176–77; decision to go south by, 2; identity issues and, 130, 138–39, 201; interracial sexual politics and, 116; Jewish religious experience of, 170; legacy of civil rights movement and, 203; lesbianism and, 119; motherhood and, 200; post-SNCC career of, 196; radicalization of, 152–54; southern Black community and, 108
Holtzman, Elizabeth, 51
Howe, Florence: antiracism of, 155–56; anti-Semitism and, 179; decision to go south by, 12; encounters with Klan, 101–2; familial reactions to, 16; Freedom Schools and, 71–72; Holocaust and, 182; identity issues and, 131, 132–34, 202; interracial sexual politics and, 116; Jewish religious experience of, 168; MFDP and,

75; motherhood and, 200; post-SNCC career of, 199; relationship with parents, 144; southern Jews and, 97–98
Howe, Irving, 9

Interracial sexual politics, 32, 57–58, 93, 115–20, 124nn56,58

Jackson, Jimmie Lee, 83, 84
"Jewesses," 89n50
"Jewishness": meaning of, 3–5, 163–66, 191n131; race/ethnicity and, 19–22; Southern Jews and, 92–96, 103–10
Jewish women, as civil rights activists: Eastern European roots of, 166–67; escape from suburban constraints and, 8–9, 110; ethnicity and, 20–22; gender norm transgression and, 14; Holocaust and, 1, 4, 181–90; invisibility of, in historical accounts, 18–24; Klan encounters, 100–103; lessons learned by, 87–88, 89n50; motherhood and, 200; parental relationships with, 14–18, 26n30, 142–44; radicalization of, 149–54; rationales of, 1–13; search for meaning by, 8–11; sexual issues and, 32, 57–58, 115–20, 124nn56,58; southern Black community and, 103–10; southern Jewish community and, 96–100, 121n23; work ethic and, 11–13; working with Black women and, 110–15. See also specific women
Jewish Workers' Bund, 166
Johnson, Frank, 84
Johnson, June, xvi–xvii
Johnson, Lyndon, 65, 69, 84
Johnson, Paul, 67, 78–79

Kaplan, Judy, 146
Kaplan, Temma, 73
Katzenbach, Nicholas, 69
Kaye/Kantrowitz, Melanie, 23; interracial sexual politics and, 116–17
Kennedy, Flo, 111
Khruschev, Nikita, 7
King, Martin Luther, Jr., 46, 84, 116
King, Mary, 105–6, 115
Knight, Pauline, 39–40
Ku Klux Klan, anti-Semitism and, 92, 100–103
Kunstler, Karin, 73, 78, 146
Kunstler, William, 44, 146

About the Author

DEBRA L. SCHULTZ, a feminist historian, is Director of Programs for the Open Society Institute (Soros Foundations) Network Women's Program, which works to include women in the development of emerging democracies, primarily in Central/Eastern Europe and the former Soviet Union.

As a Visiting Scholar at the Institute for Research on Women at Rutgers University, she pursued research on Jewish women in the civil rights movement while studying gender in the transitional societies of Central/Eastern Europe. With teaching interests ranging from women's history to cross-cultural studies, she has taught courses on multicultural U.S. women's history at the New School for Social Research and the history of Black-Jewish relations at Rutgers University.

Committed to forging links among research, policy, and practice from U.S. and global perspectives, she continues to research and promote women's cross-ethnic and cross-racial alliances for social change.

CPSIA information can be obtained
at www.ICGtesting.com
Printed in the USA
LVOW08s1613160817
545245LV00015B/1536/P